LOVE AND LIBERATION

LOVE AND LIBERATION

Humanitarian Work
in Ethiopia's Somali Region

Lauren Carruth

CORNELL UNIVERSITY PRESS   ITHACA AND LONDON

First published 2021 by Cornell University Press

Library of Congress Cataloging-in-Publication Data

Names: Carruth, Lauren, 1980– author.
Title: Love and liberation : humanitarian work in Ethiopia's Somali region / Lauren Carruth.
Description: Ithaca [New York] : Cornell University Press, 2021. | Includes bibliographical references and index.
Identifiers: LCCN 2021002961 (print) | LCCN 2021002962 (ebook) | ISBN 9781501759475 (hardcover) | ISBN 9781501759666 (paperback) | ISBN 9781501759482 (pdf) | ISBN 9781501759499 (epub)
Subjects: LCSH: Humanitarian assistance—Ethiopia—Somali Region. | Humanitarianism—Political aspects—Ethiopia—Somali Region. | Humanitarian aid workers—Ethiopia—Somali Region.
Classification: LCC HV593.A35 C37 2021 (print) | LCC HV593.A35 (ebook) | DDC 361.2/609632—dc23
LC record available at https://lccn.loc.gov/2021002961
LC ebook record available at https://lccn.loc.gov/2021002962

Contents

Acknowledgments

This book would never have been possible without the time and thoughtfulness of my interlocutors—the aid workers, policy makers, and residents I have gotten to know throughout Ethiopia over the last eighteen years. The writing of this book and research travel to Ethiopia were funded and made possible by support from the National Science Foundation, the Wenner Gren Foundation for Anthropological Research, the Faculty Research Support Grant mechanism at American University, and the School of International Service at American University. Jigjiga University and Addis Ababa University in Ethiopia ensured my research continued safely.

I benefited from the engagement of scholars during what is lovingly called a "book incubator" hosted by the School of International Service at American University. I invited a set of brilliant, generous, and critical people from across different disciplines: Betsey Brada, Daniel Esser, Dorothy Hodgson, Emily Mendenhall, Susan Shepler, and Lahra Smith. Michael Barnett and Susanna Campbell were also kind enough to listen patiently as I struggled with some of the major ideas presented here and generously read and responded to early drafts.

Two groups of faculty at American University provided forums where I worked out some of my early ideas: the "Ethnographies of Empire" research cluster and writing group at the School of International Service led at different times by Malini Ranganathan, Garrett Grady-Lovelace, Jordana Matlon, Anthony Fontes, and Marcelo Bohrt, and the anthropology department, at the invitation of David Vine. I benefited from discussions at the informal "Humanitarian Salon," hosted by Refugees International in Washington, DC, led by Eric Schwartz, Elizabeth Ferris, and Michael Barnett. Several of the ethical dilemmas I examine in this book were topics debated among collections of practitioners, leaders, and scholars there.

Several individuals nourished me during my research and writing—many spoke with me at length about the dilemmas this book addresses, read and responded to passages, corrected my Somali grammar, and generally encouraged the project: Bukhari Sheik Aden, Nimco Ahmed, Mohammed Jama Ateye, Farah Mussa Hosh, Awli Mohammed, Ahmed Nassir, and Brook Tadesse. Several international aid agencies allowed me to shadow providers, interview staff members, and attend workshops, meetings, and conferences in Ethiopia: UNICEF, the UN World Food Program, the UN World Health Organization, the

UN International Organization for Migration, UN High Commission for Refugees, the Norwegian Refugee Council, Save the Children, Oxfam, Médecins Sans Frontières, Handicap International, Catholic Relief Services, the Hararge Catholic Secretariat, Samaritan's Purse, and the Ethiopian governmental office of the Somali Regional Health Bureau. Additional local and district-level governmental bureaus and clinical facilities generously allowed me to conduct research with their staff and in remote areas even sleep within their compounds.

Several academic advisers and colleagues over the years have helped me think about humanitarian ethics, praxis, policies, and problems: Alex de Waal, John Hammock, Sue Lautze, Angela Raven-Roberts, Peter Walker, Patrick Webb, Helen Young, and others at the Feinstein International Center at Tufts University; Jennifer Leaning, Annie Sparrow, Andrew Cavey, Danya Qato, and others in the Harvard Humanitarian Initiative based at Harvard University's T. H. Chan School of Public Health; João Biehl at Princeton University's Center for Health and Wellbeing; Mark Nichter, Cheryl Ritenbaugh, Ivy Pike, Laura Briggs, and Linda Green at the School of Anthropology and Department of Family and Community Medicine at the University of Arizona; Billy Hamilton at Wake Forest University; and Bjorn Ljundqvist at UNICEF.

The last stages of writing and editing this book happened during the COVID-19 pandemic, when both of my children were quarantined at home. My mother, Deb Carruth, spent many afternoons on the couch reading, fixing hair, and patiently discussing Star Wars and Minecraft, and my mother-in-law, Phyllis Machledt, spent many hours reading aloud through screens so I could have time to work. Winslow Machledt provided feedback on the stories contained here and encouraged my frequent returns to Jigjiga and Dire Dawa, Ethiopia—his favorite cities, where in the summer months large packs of boys can freely play soccer for hours. Juna Machledt won the hearts of everyone she met during my fieldwork stints, and she tried almost every dish she was served. I have never loved Ethiopia more than when its people opened their hearts and kitchens to my children, and for that, I will be eternally grateful. Finally, my gratitude and unending love go to David Machledt, for his company, critiques, and unwavering support.

Abbreviations

ALNAP	Active Learning Network for Accountability and Performance in Humanitarian Action
ARRA	Agency for Refugee and Returnee Affairs (within the government of Ethiopia)
AWD	acute watery diarrhea
DPPC	Disaster Preparedness and Prevention Commission (within the government of Ethiopia)
DSM-V	*Diagnostic and Statistical Manual of Mental Disorders.* 5th ed. Arlington, VA: American Psychiatric Association, 2013.
EPRDF	Ethiopian People's Revolutionary Democratic Front
ICRC	International Committee of the Red Cross
IDP	internally displaced person
INGO	international nongovernmental organization
IOM	United Nations International Organization for Migration
HAP	Humanitarian Accountability Partnership
HEW	health extension worker
IRIN	Integrated Regional Information Networks (now called The New Humanitarian)
MSF	Médecins Sans Frontières
NGO	nongovernmental organization
NRC	Norwegian Refugee Council
ONLF	Ogaden National Liberation Front
SPDP	Somali People's Democratic Party
STI	sexually transmitted infection
TB	tuberculosis
TPLF	Tigray People's Liberation Front
UN	United Nations
UNHCR	United Nations High Commission for Refugees
UNICEF	United Nations Children's Fund
UNOCHA	United Nations Office for the Coordination of Humanitarian Affairs
UNRISD	United Nations Research Institute for Social Development

USAID   United States Agency for International Development
UTI   urinary tract infection
WFP   United Nations World Food Program
WHO   United Nations World Health Organization

Note on Transliteration and Somali Language Pronunciation

This book uses several words in the Somali language, and consonants and vowels written in Somali are often pronounced differently than they are in American or British English. There are additional differences in dialect, pronunciation, and spelling preference and practice among Somalis living in Africa and around the world. For example, some of my interlocutors who grew up and lived in Jigjiga in the Somali Region of Ethiopia used different spellings and pronunciations of words than persons living and working in the rural districts north of Jigjiga, in Dire Dawa, and close to the borders with Somaliland and Djibouti. I have done the best I can to spell and describe the words people used, as variable as they are.

Consonant sounds in Somali:

q   A voiced uvular plosive made by pronouncing a hard "k" sound in the back of the throat.

x   Pronounced like an English "h" as in "help" but more from the back of the throat. This is called a "voiceless pharyngeal fricative." For example the Arabic word for the "hajj" is spelled "*xaj*" in Somali.

ˀ   This apostrophe signals a glottal stop.

Vowels in Somali

c   Pronunciation is similar to the "ou-" as in "ouch" or "ah" in English but voiced at the back of the throat with the mouth and throat wide open. So "Ciise" is pronounced more like "ahee'-sah" with only two syllables.

a   Pronounced like the vowel in "crop" in American English

e   Pronounced as in "red" in English

i   Pronounced as in "bit"

o   Pronounced as in "top"

u   Pronounced as in "put"

ii   Pronounced as in "reed"

uu   Pronounced as in "fool"

ay, ey   Interchangeable, and pronounced as in "hay"

aw   Pronounced as in "cow"

ow   Pronounced as in "show"

LOVE AND LIBERATION

"I CANNOT GIVE IT UP"

"Oh, let me tell you a story!" Aden said, leaning back and laughing aloud.[1] Aden is an aid worker with a large, United Nations relief organization office in the Somali regional capital of Jigjiga, in Ethiopia. We sat together on a muggy July afternoon in a peaceful hotel courtyard. He wore a faded *macawiis*, a traditional cotton wrap skirt, and an ironed dress shirt, and sipped hot tea while I reclined in a chair nearby, listening and furtively scratching out ideas in my notebook.

Aden and I have known each other for eleven years—or what seems to matter more, we have known each other through several family transformations. He is now the father of four children, I am now married and the mother of two, and both our parents are aging. Like so many Somalis, who value the art of storytelling, oral history, and poetry, Aden answered most of my persistent questions about his life and work by weaving narratives and memories together through space and time.

The last time I had seen him, we never found a chance to sit in peace. It was only ten months before, in October 2017, and the Ethiopian prime minister, Hailemariam Desalegn, had just declared another official state of emergency. Grainy videos of bloody acts of violence between ethnic Somalis and ethnic Oromos, between paramilitary police forces and protesting civilians, and between farmers and pastoralists on different sides of the regional boundaries within Ethiopia were circulating on social media, and no one knew what would happen to the country. Everything felt chaotic.

"Elzaaaaaaa!"—my nickname among many in the Somali Region of Ethiopia, and a variant on my middle name that everyone remembers—"Come here my dear! I cannot believe you are here," he had shouted then, jogging toward me. We shook hands and lightly bumped shoulders. "Elza! How are you?"—but before I could answer he grabbed my elbow—"Let us go! Here—let us just take this vehicle." I jumped into the closest Toyota Land Cruiser as three other much younger men who presumably worked with Aden, all of them at least six feet tall and dressed in ironed slacks and pastel button-ups, gingerly squeezed in around me.

The truck lurched forward in first gear and proceeded through the gated compound, surrounded by the familiar United Nations–colored light blue metal walls and rimmed with razor wire, protective shards of glass, and soft pine branches delicately holding Rüppell's weaver nests. We zoomed to the right and down a dusty road, rocking side to side, making our way through the crowded, rutted streets of Jigjiga, the Somali regional capital in eastern Ethiopia. Inside the truck, everyone laughed loudly and made jokes and small talk about the weather, politics, and the woes of construction projects that never end. We passed a soon-to-be mall and a new bank building, with floor-to-ceiling glass walls and the promise of several ATM machines and cafes at its base. But just as the conversation paused, a filthy flatbed truck piled at least fifteen feet high with eucalyptus scaffolding stalled, bringing us and all the other traffic around the circle to a sudden standstill.

I used the moment to ask where we were headed.

"Oh to see the new president of the health bureau—Dr. Abdulahi—I think you remember him. You met him before, but now he is the new president so he should hear what you are doing. You must get another letter I think, so we will do that today." He paused. "I also have other business there also. You know, things are difficult now, for our work." Shaking his head, he signed audibly.

Inside the office building, our meetings were also rushed, or at least were performed to feel that way. Everyone going and coming through the halls had at least one cell phone and took calls throughout whatever we happen to be doing, excusing themselves again and again to quickly answer and then return to the personal and official conversations at hand.

Once Aden saw I was cleared for travel and research from the governmental authorities, he left to attend his own meeting and directed me to a physician working in the regional government. He thought we should meet. I crossed the noisy courtyard, stopping to greet familiar staffers and drivers every few steps, and arrived in a small suite of offices.

Two women stood in the wood-paneled reception area, hurriedly trying to fix a document on a dusty Dell desktop computer, shaking and knocking its tired looking mouse. A plastic bouquet of roses tipped over, falling onto the maroon shag carpet below.

As they reached down to clean up the mess, they saw me and asked, "Are you looking for Doctor Ali? You can go in! Go in!" They shooed me inside the suite and into his office without waiting for my answer. He was there in the back of a room, standing over a younger man, staring at another dusty Dell screen and pointing, going through the English words slowly, fixing the awkward syntax. It was part of a report on the outbreak of vaccine-derived polio among internally displaced persons. Seven additional young men sat in dilapidated squeaky office chairs crowded around the pair, watching this painstaking process, each one in ironed slacks and well-shined pointy dress shoes, asking each other questions in Somali, trying to figure out the best English phrasing. I hated to interrupt, but when they saw me there, they all stopped at once, and insisted on introducing themselves and chatting for half an hour about everything happening in the office. Doctor Ali finally drew me away from the junior staffers, to talk in more detail about his career and health emergencies in the region.

At some point during this day, just like every time I ventured to government ministerial buildings, in all the chaos, I lost Aden. Only in moments like those in the quiet hotel courtyard did I learn not just about Aden's job, but what motivates and structures the humanitarian responses[2] he oversees.

"I want to say these things," he said quietly. "My God, what am I doing here? I love this work so much." As he sipped his tea in the courtyard, enjoying the peace, he began to tell me a story.

Aden said he grew up an "innocent boy," "born in the countryside," in one of a collection of houses just outside the bustling town of Gode, at the edge of a verdant stretch along the Shabelle River, in the heart of the Somali Region of Ethiopia and in the heart of Greater Somalia, or *Soomaaliweyn* in the Somali language, the area of the Horn of Africa populated mostly by Somalis.

Aden was the darling of his mother's eye, and as a child, she let him roam with the family's goats and sheep in the morning before the sun began to blister the landscape. "Life was beautiful then," he recalled with a smile on his face, looking heavenward. Healthy livestock like camels, cows, goats, and sheep wandered the expanses with him, peeking out from between the thorny acacias in dry, shady nooks and from behind patches of soft grasses growing by the river's edge.

Now in his forties, living in the center of urban Jigjiga, with a fast-paced job and four children of his own, Aden held on to this image in his memory delicately, like the candy for sale in the shop across the street, so delicious that he didn't want to move for making it break or dissolve too quickly. As an adult, Aden looks for excuses at work to take a trip and return to

Gode and the *haud*—the fertile valley region spanning the southern Somali Region of Ethiopia.

The Ogaden War between Ethiopia and Somalia in 1977 through 1978 drove his family away from these bucolic landscapes, forcing them to flee southward, carrying almost nothing, across the wide but shallow river, through green irrigated fields of maize and sorghum, then through the mostly empty desert, into Somalia where refugee camps had been established. Luckily for him, curious and smart and full of energy, the refugee camp run by UNHCR had a decent elementary school, and its Somali teachers spoke and taught in English. When he excelled academically, and fell in love with literature and languages, his parents enrolled him in a private school nearby. But before he could graduate, in 1989, civil war in Somalia forced his family northward again, back through the harsh desert, across jagged mountains, and back into Ethiopia, finally settling in Jigjiga.

So for Aden, and for thousands of other children like him, while violence and anxiety kept his parents awake at night, for him the war was not only a tragedy. "War was an opportunity," he said. "We had to move from rural areas, where we had nothing, really, into towns and into camps where there were schools. Good schools!"

Aden is now one of the most respected and powerful policy makers in Jigjiga. He works on United Nations–funded projects that have achieved "remarkable," even "miraculous," things, elders around the city testified. Child mortality rates have halved during his tenure, and most children in Jigjiga have now had their basic immunizations.[3] Undernutrition rates have fallen dramatically,[4] and pharmacies in cities and villages throughout the region are well stocked with essential medications. Aden says he has seen "with my very own eyes!" children come back to life from severe acute malnutrition and measles, in hospitals, feeding centers, and homes throughout the region. He has also watched families go from the gift of one goat from a relief organization to managing a herd of hundreds and putting their children all the way through university. "Humanitarian aid has saved these children's lives!" he said to me with passion, casting his hands up in the air, and inadvertently, away from himself.

"But," he said, turning away, pausing for a sip of tea, placing his cup and saucer down, and continuing again, "I cannot get an international post despite the fact I have applied many times. I have been rejected and rejected. Not because of the regional or international office, but at the country level office. They want me to stay [in Jigjiga]. They want to keep me here."

I was surprised to hear this, so I asked him to clarify, that he wants to move elsewhere and that he has unsuccessfully applied for promotions, to which he said, "Yes. I cannot advance."

"Why don't you quit?" I finally countered, knowing he would be invaluable to any number of private businesses or nonprofit organizations in Ethiopia. He responded with a smile, and for a moment I thought I saw tears shine in his eyes, before he blinked, and blinked again.

"The work," he said finally. "I cannot give it up."

Full of humility and satisfaction and at times, deep frustrations, Aden is both a protagonist and a witness to remarkable transformations in the Somali Region and in the humanitarian industry. This book takes seriously the lived experiences, politics, and challenges faced by aid workers and policy makers like Aden—the fact that they have, at some point in their lives, often several times, been both the so-called beneficiaries of relief operations and the people responsible for relief operations' repeated implementation and evaluation. Their lives have been saved or significantly improved because of the humanitarian aid industry, and yet, they offer important critiques. They have an invaluable perspective on the industry's failings, blind spots, and potentials.

Books, films, television shows, and the news are filled with tales of scandal and adventure as young and idealistic expatriates fly into war zones, disasters, and impoverished communities intending to save lives.[5] At the same time, academics, journalists, and writers have long been concerned with understanding the lives and worlds of international humanitarian responders.[6] But most of the protagonists in these different humanitarian stories hail from relatively wealthy donor countries, and intervene in places that are depicted as needy, exotic, or populated by suffering strangers.[7] Humanitarians are still mostly depicted as "white saviors" on potentially perilous, but righteous, global missions.[8]

However, very few of the staff that are part of contemporary relief operations parachute into crises from afar. In 2018, a study by a network of humanitarian organizations and experts concluded that approximately 86 percent of the personnel of United Nations relief agencies, 92 percent of the personnel of international nongovernmental organizations (NGOs), and 98 percent of the personnel of the Red Cross Movement were from the countries and communities in crisis—and these figures do not include the legions of subcontracted and informally hired locals that in every humanitarian intervention provide logistical support, data collection, language interpretation, and security.[9] Humanitarian aid workers are not typically expatriates or new to the places they serve. Most aid workers speak fluently the languages of the people who find themselves in crisis, and are familiar with the difficult political terrain they are asked to navigate. They are the neighbors, daughters, midwives, uncles, and grown-up children of people in crisis; they are caregivers, teachers, and students; they are local clinicians and educated researchers; they are polyglots and travelers; they are manual laborers and prominent engineers; they are experts on and brokers of local power relations and cultures; and according to their colleagues, patients, and beneficiary populations, they are often some of the most generous and trusted souls around. Local aid workers are the backbone and the heart of the international humanitarian industry.

Recognizing this, in the last few years, numerous think tanks and global relief agencies have advocated for a localization of aid and a devolving of power from donors and aid agencies in the Global North to organizations located in crisis-affected communities in the Global South.[10] Policy makers and practitioners within the aid industry recognize that the humanitarian system must fundamentally transform in order to do better by its workforce.[11] The local and national staffs of relief organizations are frequently now cast as the heroes and the rightful focus of humanitarian response.[12]

Consequently, while emergency assistance still involves distributions of material resources, it also now entails an effort to develop the capacity of people in crisis-affected communities, and to transform individuals there from beneficiaries into competent service providers and the leaders of humanitarian missions. Local aid workers are now both the object and the subject of global humanitarian aid. By taking on the most precarious, dangerous, and lowest-paid jobs in the relief industry, these aid workers perform a variant on what Ilana Feldman calls "ethical labor": their work proves relief agencies' righteous empowerment of locals and their attention to local contexts.[13]

Accordingly, local aid workers are far from being the cause of "dependency,"[14] or hopelessly corrupt,[15] or a product of "disaster capitalism."[16] For relief workers living and working in eastern Ethiopia, humanitarian aid is both a fulfilling vocation and an important local industry. Relief operations, local aid workers insist, present opportunities in crisis-affected places for gainful employment, professional training, and relatively lucrative side gigs implementing projects and policies, driving cars, providing language interpretation, staffing security details, and helping to organize and carry out data collection. Due in part to its embeddedness, for so many years, in so many facets of local economies, people in eastern Ethiopia see humanitarian assistance more as much more a boon than a boondoggle. Jobs in the humanitarian sector—especially work for a United Nations office or for an international NGO—are some of the best jobs around.

Beyond their economic value, professional opportunities with the humanitarian industry are the means and the ends to local aid workers' and their families' opportunities in higher education, international travel, regional politics, and increased social status. These aid workers are part of a growing middle and upper class in Jigjiga and other regional capitals in Ethiopia, and as such, aid workers are expected to donate money, share housing, provide expertise, and give of their time to family members, friends, and neighbors in need. Humanitarian assistance augments existing local traditions of charity, care, and crisis response—translated broadly into the Somali language as *samafal*.

Finally, global humanitarian responses (even as unreliable and inadequate as they so frequently are) help fund a burgeoning Somali regional government in the margins of the Ethiopian state. Aid helps pay the salaries of policy experts like Aden, it subsidizes the incomes of numerous additional bureaucrats and health workers, and it funds the purchase of ambulances, vaccinations, distributions of essential medicines, veterinary care, agricultural support, and even health education initiatives by and for Somalis. As the chapters to follow demonstrate, after years of colonial occupations, colonial partitions, marginalization from Ethiopian politics, and marginalization from global development and private investments, humanitarian relief operations have become mechanisms through which Somalis reimagine the meaning and structure of government. Humanitarian responses create spaces for Somalis to demonstrate their love for one another, demonstrate their support for Somali and pastoralist traditions and livelihoods, redistribute wealth and resources across the region, build responsive systems of government, and in so doing, liberate themselves from histories of colonization, partition, and marginalization. In the words of a prominent leader in the region said, this control over humanitarian funding and programming "really helps us to be free."[17]

However, despite the many benefits and the profound potentials of emergency aid, inequities and limitations abound. Compared to aid workers who fly into crisis zones from the capital city of Addis Ababa or from outside the country, the personnel of relief operations in places like eastern Ethiopia continue to have the lowest salaries, fewest benefits, least professional mobility, least travel mobility, and greatest job insecurity of anyone else in the global aid industry. Most Somali aid workers in eastern Ethiopia spend most of their time either unemployed or piecing together short-term gigs. Without opportunities to advance professionally, stuck in small, underfunded subnational offices in places where crises recur, and often relegated to hustling for temporary jobs or informal work to make ends meet, locals shoulder the greatest financial and personal risks. Moreover, far fewer Somali women than men can obtain the kinds of graduate degrees that qualify them for work in the aid sector; fewer still are able to secure and sustain jobs after graduation. And few regulatory or advocacy mechanisms within the global aid sector are designed to redress these disparities. The humanitarian industry's precarious and inequitable human architecture remains entrenched.

This book is an ethnography of the global humanitarian industry, focused on the cultures of aid in places where relief operations recur. It provides a window into the lives, labor, and struggles of Somali aid workers in Ethiopia as they are handed impossibly narrow relief missions, as they navigate tenuous regional politics, and as they strive to meet the high expectations of the people they serve. While their stories are sometimes inspirational and point to many positive effects of humanitarian responses, their experiences and reflections also reveal a global humanitarian industry that systematically undervalues the lives and labor that make relief operations and government possible. In other words, humanitarian response is not always humanitarian.

Anthropologists and other social scientists use the research and writing method of ethnography to tell stories that matter—stories that, through devices like narrative plots and character development, reveal what brings people joy, what unites and divides them, what drives their political engagement, and what brings their lives meaning. Beyond its many problems and inadequacies, humanitarianism, translated into Somali as *samafal*, is meaningful to people in eastern Ethiopia. It both saves and animates lives.

Introduction

HUMANITARIANISM IN THE MARGINS OF EMPIRE

The research that went into writing this book began with a series of questions I have been thinking about for more than seventeen years, as I worked in and studied humanitarian response, and as I traveled and lived on and off in Ethiopia, in places where relief organizations repeatedly intervene. Who and what is "humanitarian"? What kinds of actions and people are characterized as humanitarian in our world today? Who comes to mind when we picture an aid worker, and whose labor is not typically signified, imagined, recognized, and budgeted? Finally, what does humanitarianism mean to the people who carry it out? To answer these questions, in the following pages I examine humanitarianism as it is lived, debated, evaluated, and enacted by people like Aden—front-line aid workers, health workers, program officers, policy makers, and bureaucrats within relief organizations serving communities in the Somali Region of Ethiopia.

The English-language descriptor, *humanitarian*, is frequently invoked by the news media and Western donor governments for many reasons—it can pull at the heartstrings of the public and donors, it can sell news stories, justify wars, justify extraordinary expenses and actions, and it can even justify cooperation with abusive governments and armed groups.[1] Within the quiet halls of the headquarters of international aid organizations, in cities like Geneva and New York, far away from sites of crisis and conflict, humanitarian responses continue to be much more narrowly defined as temporary interventions focused on saving and protecting human lives.[2] These kinds of interventions are justified and structured by International Humanitarian Law and the Fundamental Principles of Humanitarian Response outlined by the Red Cross,[3] and they are designed in response to discrete, measurable, and time-bound crisis events. This limited conception presents a fundamental dilemma. As David Rieff phrased it, "Humanitarianism is an impossible enterprise. Here is a saving idea that, in the end, cannot save but can only alleviate."[4] Humanitarian response, as it is defined by the Red Cross and other relief organizations and enshrined in international law, is not designed to solve the entrenched societal injustices and inequities that cause humanitarian crises and so often worsen human suffering long after relief organizations depart.

There are, however, other ways of understanding and carrying out humanitarian work. This book centers alternative but related perspectives—ones articulated and enacted by professional aid workers and health-care providers like Aden. Humanitarianism, as discussed and enacted by Somali aid workers in eastern Ethiopia, was not primarily structured by International Humanitarian Law, principles and standards delineated by the Red Cross, or the definitions, budgets, and programmatic mandates set by foreign relief organizations. Humanitarianism was also neither neutral to nor independent of Somali and Ethiopian politics and history. Instead, *samafal*—an approximate translation of "humanitarianism" in the Somali language—signifies both the affective forms of care provided at the site of individual bodies affected by years of crises, and the collective forms of healing and liberation attempted by aid workers at the site of bodies politic.

Going East

The Somali Region, in the eastern part of Ethiopia, is located in what tipsy foreign service officers at the Hilton Hotel bar in the capital Addis Ababa laughingly called "the Wild Wild East." "Be careful over there!," a blonde twenty-something American with a buzz cut warned me before I left town once, his eyebrows raised, and his head tilted in disbelief.

"Do they have food out there?," one Ethiopian staffer, originally from Addis Ababa, asked me on a different occasion, as we shopped together for groceries. The regular characterization of the Somali Region of Ethiopia by outsiders as "wild," hungry, savage, marginal, and constantly beset by disasters and conflict is, however, largely a product of ignorance and the unwillingness of most expatriates and Ethiopians from Addis Ababa to spend any length of time getting to know people and circumstances there.

Somali Ethiopians alternatively characterized the region as a historically rich, spectacular desert landscape, a gateway from Africa to the Middle East, the northern edge of the seasonally verdant *haud* pastureland, and a place where

FIGURE 1.   Camels grazing on a mountain overlooking Jigjiga, Ethiopia, 2018. Photograph by David Machledt.

children can grow up strong and healthy thanks to an abundance of fresh live-stock milk and time outdoors grazing and herding animals. While not in continuous and unavoidable states of crisis, as it is so often portrayed in the news media and in many outsiders' popular imaginations of the place, residents did describe the Somali Region as marginalized and unsettled. Politicians have come and gone quickly in recent years, often in dramatic fashion;[5] police battalions, secret militias, and military patrols occasionally roamed the region, regularly detaining activists and contraband traders; and the future of ethnic Somalis within Ethiopia and the greater Horn of Africa was a constant source of discussion and debate.

Ethiopia's national capital, Addis Ababa, is located almost four hundred miles west of Jigjiga. Addis Ababa means "new flower" in the Amharic language, and was chosen in 1886 by Empress Taytu Betul, the powerful wife of Emperor Menelik II, to be the Ethiopian Empire's new, centralized capital city in the mountainous center of the country. Ranging from 7,200 feet above sea level at its southern tip to over 9,800 at the edge of the verdant Entoto Mountains, Addis Ababa is nestled in a densely populated and hazy high-altitude basin. Approximately 4.4 million Ethiopians reside in the fast-expanding urban area, alongside a sizable contingent of foreign diplomats, aid workers, private investors, and economic development specialists from around the world.[6]

Addis Ababa is known as the "Capital of Africa." It hosts the African Union and the Economic Commission for Africa, among hundreds of other international organizations, and it boasts the recent construction of several glassy new hotels and shopping malls near the city center. Ethiopia is a typical "developmental state."[7] From the years 2000 to 2013, the country's gross domestic product annual growth rate averaged 9.5 percent, the second highest in all sub-Saharan Africa.[8] Chinese investments have helped fund the paving of several major roadways across the country, the construction of a new railroad to the port in Djibouti City, and a new light rail crisscrossing the city.

On April 2, 2018, a charismatic leader, Abiy Ahmed Ali, assumed the office of Prime Minister of Ethiopia and chairmanship of the Ethiopian People's Revolutionary Democratic Front (EPRDF) ruling coalition party, reconceptualized in 2019 as the "Prosperity Party." Abiy's ascension, his public discourses on Ethiopian unity, and his attempted reforms represent a watershed moment for the

FIGURE 2.   Addis Ababa welcomes Prime Minister Abiy Ahmed, 2018. Photograph by Brook Tadesse Woldetsadik.

Horn of Africa. Many Ethiopians at home and in the diaspora felt he might usher in a new and hopeful era.[9] Three months after taking office, he and Eritrean president Isaias Afewerki signed a "Joint Declaration of Peace and Friendship" declaring an end to twenty years of conflict, and temporarily opening their borders for travel and communication.[10] While the border crossings have since closed, throughout the summer and fall of 2018 airports and hotels in cities throughout the country were filled with the cries and embraces of thousands of families, reunited after years of war. In 2019 Abiy was awarded the Nobel Peace Prize for brokering peace with Eritrea, and in 2018 he led efforts to promote political reforms in the Somali Region of Ethiopia.[11] As of this writing, he has continued to make several unexpected appointments within the government, including several women from various minority and underrepresented ethnic groups, and women and men whose careers have been built outside party politics.

Tensions, however, remain. Ethiopia is still widely considered an authoritarian state.[12] Even though Abiy promised to upend many power structures in the country, so far he has been unable to solve political conflicts in contested areas of the country including growing ethnonationalist movements in the Amhara region, simmering discontent in the Oromia region, conflict in the Tigray region, occasional bursts of conflict along the Oromia-Somali and Somali-Afar regional boundaries, and continuing unlawful detention and intimidation of dissidents, journalists, and activists throughout the country.

But on a clear day, looking out from atop one of the new hotels rising in the center of the Addis Ababa, you can witness in every direction recent expansions of industry and suburban housing into forested hills, verdant agricultural fields, muddy ravines, and dark eucalyptus groves. And in unkempt plots of land between modern skyscrapers, five- and ten-story Soviet-era cement structures stand empty and crumbling. These juxtapositions and these contradictions—evident in the uneven Addis skyline—in a nation at once thriving on burgeoning foreign private investments, domestic economic growth, and substantial sums of foreign aid, but also, at the same time, pockmarked by long histories of failed international and national development projects, hint at the complexity of Ethiopia's political story.

As you travel eastward, away from the city of Addis Ababa, toward the Somali Region, the terrain gradually flattens and dries out. Past suburban caches of sprawling half-built apartment buildings and condominiums, past graded fields of soybeans and corn, past greenhouses growing cut flowers for European markets, and past the end of the eight-lane limited-access highway bypass and the traffic-clogged Oromo cities of Bishoftu and Adama, the population density thins out, until the arid landscape is only dotted with small settlements and scattered livestock grazing in the distance. Hours later, after passing over a bridge crossing the Awash River gorge, at the nadir of the Rift Valley, the main road begins to climb upward, slowly at first, reaching the bustling trading town of Asebe Teferi, and then dramatically rising, twisting and turning through the verdant eastern Oromo highlands. The road peaks again at around 7,500 feet in altitude.

There, frequently through fog and thickets of pines and junipers, small crooked plots of farmland cover the hillsides. These plots are stitched onto one another with neatly arranged euphorbia fencing, and interrupted only occasionally by small towns overflowing with people and livestock, Chinese fabric samples, handmade baskets, piles of plastic sandals, and neat stacks of colorful vegetables. In the view south from the main road, green escarpments rise from steep valleys, carpeted with corn, millet, and coffee fields. Every July and every December, tens of thousands of Orthodox Christians pilgrimage through the region to Kulubi, one of the small towns on the eastbound road through East Hararge, to celebrate Saint Gabriel, Ethiopian unity, and historical victories over European colonizers.

Most days, Kulubi and each successive town along the road headed east bustle with activity. Feeling freer and more empowered since the ascension of Abiy Ahmed—whose father was ethnically Oromo—in the last few years protesters fill the streets carrying Oromia Regional State flags, chanting for land rights and economic development from their government. Truckers offload dozens of cases of Coca-Cola next to cafes and hotels, and stop to drink espressos and talk politics, before hopping back into their vehicles for another long stretch of driving. White Toyota Land Cruisers, emblazoned with fading logos from locally active international relief and development NGOs and packed with Ethiopian men and women, ply the twisted and crowded road en route to field sites and distribution points nearby.

Then, three hundred miles from its origin in Addis Ababa, the road through these verdant highlands descends again, divides, and spirals into an oasis along a dry riverbed and the city of Dire Dawa. Dire Dawa is officially the second largest city in Ethiopia. Since its founding in 1902, during construction of the Addis Ababa-to-Djibouti railroad by the French, Dire Dawa has been a hub of international travel, migration, and trade—including contraband trade, untaxed by the Ethiopian government—between Africa and the Far East, South Asia, and the Middle East. The biggest market in town is called Taiwan, and there you can find for sale everything from contraband insulin vials to plastic Christmas trees to Samsung cellular phones. From Dire Dawa, journeys east through the Somali Region toward Djibouti or Somaliland become slower and more difficult.

The main road and rail to Djibouti from Dire Dawa loosely parallel ancient camel caravan routes connecting the ancient Abyssinian capital of Axum and the Muslim pilgrimage site of Harar to Zeila, historically the second largest commercial port city on the coastal Horn, in what is now Somaliland, from the seventh until the nineteenth century. In centuries past, several towns along these routes through the desert became global centers for Islamic scholarship and trade. Yet the caravans and cosmopolitan charms of these places have largely dissipated. Portuguese traders plundered markets and communities throughout the Horn of Africa and East Africa from the fifteenth to the eighteenth century; colonial partitions of the Horn strategically divided Somalis between the Italian, French, British, and Ethiopian Empires beginning in the nineteenth century, and as a result, Somalis were essentially cut off from the trade routes and grazing lands they had long depended on.[13] Following the rise and fall of railroad commerce in the twentieth century, new economies have emerged along these same routes in response to commercial truck transit.

The Somali regional capital of Jigjiga is located just over a mountain range, southeast of Dire Dawa. Along the eastbound road approaching Jigjiga, yellow, pink, and orange lantana bushes and prickly pear cactuses peek out from around towering sandstone boulders. Giant invasive milkweeds—of evidently no use to people or livestock—now line the roadways, growing atop piles of dirt and rocks left over from recent projects to pave the roads. Jigjiga's climate, and the climate of the Fafan district to its west, are cooler than in Dire Dawa and ideal for agricultural production. Few who pass through the area can resist the enormous, sweet mangoes, always perfectly ripe, and the freshly roasted corn cobs for sale by women along the roadway. But so far, very few large or industrial farms exist. Billboards on the drive into Jigjiga advertise a future resort that is planned on the outskirts of town, but construction has not begun. Most households in the area around Jigjiga rely on commercial and petty trade, the keeping and sale of livestock, jobs in governmental bureaucracies, and jobs in the humanitarian industry.

East of Dire Dawa and Jigjiga, toward Djibouti and the mountain ranges dividing Ethiopia from Somaliland, the landscape slowly descends into drier ecological zones, eventually ending in the Gulf of Aden. Volcanoes active millions of years ago have left dramatic iron-rich outcroppings and fields of basaltic igneous rock still largely barren of greenery or soil. In the few places where indigenous grasses and trees once thrived, mostly along seasonally dry riverbeds, stunted acacia shrubs and invasive mesquites now dominate. Many of these have been either chewed by livestock or hacked into stumps for firewood.

Animals, as well as people, congregate along the roadways. Construction to flatten, straighten, and pave roads eastward from Ethiopia into Somaliland and Djibouti have left occasional roadside depressions in the flat desert floor, where rainfall collects for a few days before it evaporates. Camels, cattle, and donkeys are in the best positions to take advantage of these artificial oases as herders pass through the region. But far from the crowded cities of Dire Dawa and Jigjiga, gerenuks, gazelles, giant tortoises, warthogs, hyenas, and wild ostriches also vie for the few natural resources not consumed by roving and herded livestock. UN World Food Program (WFP) donations regularly arrive at the port in Djibouti City, and must be trucked westward to warehouses throughout Ethiopia before distribution. As these trucks, laden with corn-soy blended flour, whole wheat grains, split peas, lentils, and cans of oil, bounce along the ruts and rocks, bits of food are thrown from overstuffed sacks onto the road below. Myriad bird species and several troops of baboons gather on the road during these regular distributions to scavenge and snack on the fallen food aid.

Newly paved roads through the Somali Region dramatically shortened the time it takes to travel from the highlands of Ethiopia to cities and commercial ports on the Red Sea. These roads are now central to commercial truck traffic, as well as the transnational trade in khat (also spelled *qat* or *jaat*, scientific name *Catha edulis*). Khat is an evergreen plant picked for consumption of its mildly narcotic leaves. The highlands of eastern Ethiopia, particularly in the region around Dire Dawa and the ancient city of Harar, north and west of Jigjiga, are known for the cultivation, consumption, and export of khat. Although khat is illegal in much of Europe and North America, it is popular throughout the Arabian Peninsula and Horn of Africa. Men, mostly, throughout both regions, spend much of their afternoons and evenings lounging, chewing, and drinking sodas and tea. Ethiopia is the world's top producer of khat, and it is one of the country's most important agricultural and trade products.[14] Fresh khat is picked in the hours before before dawn, wrapped in cool grasses, packaged into sacks, loaded onto Isuzu flatbed trucks, and driven eastward, through Dire Dawa or Jigjiga, eastward toward Djibouti, Somaliland, and Somalia as quickly as possible, before the leaves wilt or dry in the heat. Isuzus piled high with khat bundles drive southeastward at speeds anywhere between sixty and one hundred miles per hour. In places where the road remains broken or unpaved, this generates dust clouds visible from miles away. To motivate themselves to maintain the highest possible speeds across these long desert expanses, truckers chew khat as they drive; and companies offer a substantial cash reward to the driver who gets to coastal ports and urban markets first.

Charred carcasses of eighteen-wheelers, dismembered axels of Isuzu flatbed trucks, flipped passenger minibuses, crushed Bajaj-brand motorized rickshaws, and even wrecked military tanks from the war between Somalia and Ethiopia in the late 1970s all litter the roadsides of the Somali Region, and serve as reminders of past and potential road disasters. For a variety of reasons including lack of infrastructure, aging vehicle fleets, little to no traffic regulation, and potentially, drivers' impairment from khat consumption, Ethiopia's roads are some of the most dangerous in the world.[15] Vehicle crashes are major threats to the lives and safety of aid workers who must frequently travel hundreds of miles for site visits, distributions, and monitoring and evaluation. I have personally known two persons killed in crashes, and one of my best friends survived being thrown from the back of an Isuzu flatbed, only to endure three weeks in a coma. He has never fully recovered. Aid work in eastern Ethiopia is a dangerous enterprise, and driving along these roads is probably the greatest threat to staffers' lives. But as stories in the chapters to follow will show, travel through difficult terrain and across mountainous and desert expanses, is something aid workers enjoy immensely, and it is key to their humanitarian work.

Somalis in the Margins of Ethiopia

Somalis in eastern Ethiopia live in the heart of Greater Somalia (or in the Somali language, *Soomaaliweyn*)—the expanse of East Africa populated and governed mostly by ethnic Somalis. Greater Somalia includes what is now defined as Somalia, Somaliland, Puntland, Djibouti, the eastern part of Ethiopia, and northeastern Kenya. At the same time, Somalis are a minority ethnic group within the Federal Democratic Republic of Ethiopia (only between an estimated 6 to 10 percent of the total Ethiopian population) and occupy the sparsely populated eastern third of the country.[16]

Somalis in the Horn of Africa have been, and remain, strategically partitioned. Greater Somalia was first divided by the Ethiopian Emperor Menelik II in the nineteenth century, and then later under Emperor Haile Selassie I in the twentieth century, as European colonial powers divided much of the rest of Africa. Military conquests and territorial expansions by imperial Ethiopia during the nineteenth and early twentieth centuries led to the dispossession and forcible resettlement of pastoralist and agropastoralist groups east of the Rift Valley, including many Somalis.[17]

Keeping northern Somali lands within the Ethiopian Empire and then later, within the Ethiopian Federal Democratic State, has presented major challenges to Ethiopian leadership and unity.[18] For example, to counter rising local support for postcolonial, independent Somalia to the south, finally more free of British, French, and Italian control, in 1956, on an official state visit to the eastern edge of his country, Ethiopian Emperor Haile Selassie said to Somalis gathered nearby,

> We remind you finally that all of you are by race, color, blood, and custom, members of the great Ethiopian family. And as to the rumors of a "Greater Somalia," we consider that all Somali peoples are economically linked with Ethiopia, and therefore, we do not believe that such a state can be viable standing alone.[19]

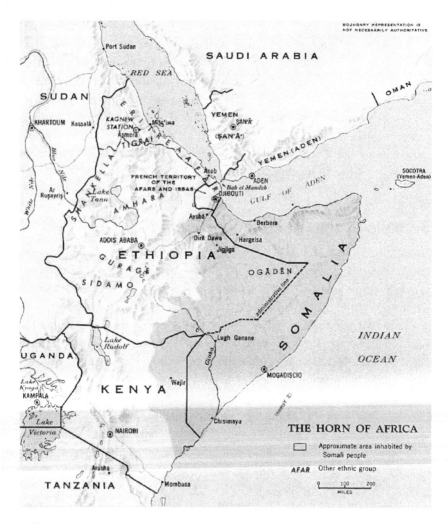

FIGURE 3. Shaded areas of the Horn of Africa indicate where there is a majority ethnic Somali population. Map created by Lauren Carruth, based on a work of a Central Intelligence Agency employee, available on Wikipedia Commons, https://commons.wikimedia.org/wiki/File:Somali_map.jpg. Outdated names for some ethnic groups were eliminated and the approximate location of Jigjiga is included.

Fearful that Somalis would defect or secede to join Somalia farther south, during the 1950s and 1960s Emperor Haile Selassie ordered repeated massacres and acts of terror in towns all along the ancient caravan routes, along the railroad, and throughout the northeastern Ethiopian borderlands (see figure 4). Efforts

FIGURE 4. Public mural painted by Mohammed Jama Ateye in the town of Aysha, in the northern Somali Region of Ethiopia, depicting the massacre of Somalis by Haile Selassie's police and military forces in 1960. Photograph by Lauren Carruth.

in years since to assimilate and forcibly incorporate Somalis and other pastoralist and minority groups into the Ethiopian state have been met with both fierce resistance and stubborn resentment.[20]

The contradictory senses of being at the margins of Ethiopia, but also purposively marginalized from Somali politics elsewhere, structure Somali Ethiopians' ambivalence about citizenship and belonging to Ethiopian and Somali states.[21] Asha, a young mother from the small and mountainous town of Biyogurgur, in the Somali Region along the Somaliland border, said to me: "People here are very poor. [We] are not Ethiopian and not from Somalia—we are neither. In between. The Ethiopian government will not do anything to help the people here, and Somalia is not our country either. There is no communication between the people here and the Ethiopian government—our people are not heard."

Despite recent political changes in Ethiopia, improvements in infrastructure, and improvements in the provision of public services, many Somali Ethiopians still feel paradoxically both forgotten and intentionally marginalized—geographically, politically, and economically—from Ethiopian sources of power and money in the gleaming capital city of Addis Ababa four hundred miles to the west. Somali political parties, nationalist political movements, Somali irredentist groups, and rebel groups farther south in Somaliland and Somalia, as well as factions within the regional government in Jigjiga, the Ogaden National Liberation Front, and others remain in active and sometimes violent resistance to Ethiopian military offensives and continuing Ethiopian diplomatic presence in Somali territories.[22]

Additionally, for decades along the borders between the Oromia, Somali, and Afar Regions in eastern Ethiopia, intermittent skirmishes between civilians, political activists, government representatives, police, military, and paramilitary groups (like the unsanctioned "Liyu" police) have flared over access to land and natural resources.[23] The existence of unmarked mass graves in public spaces, the regular and repeated quashing of political protests organized by Somali groups, the repeated arrests of dissidents and journalists, ongoing secret police and intelligence activity, and even occasional incidents of sexual abuse by military and police all reveal a violent state of affairs that live only in whispered rumors and viral social media posts.

Most Somalis residing in Ethiopia today have also at some point been either internally displaced or have sought asylum outside Ethiopia. In the wake of repeated conflicts and disasters, most people first and foremost sought assistance and hospitality from extended family members within the transnational ethnic community of Somalis residing throughout the Horn of Africa and diaspora. In addition—and in the absence of trusted and adequate Ethiopian governmental services like public health facilities, disaster preparedness and response systems, and trusted police protections—secular and religious forms of charity (in Somali, *samafal* as well as gifts of *sadaqad* for people in need and regular *zakat*, or charitable contributions mandated in the Holy Qur'an), transnational kinship networks, Somali customary law (*xeer*), extralegal economies, and the international nongovernmental aid industry all remained vital to life and livelihoods.

You might even ask upon visiting the rural Somali Region north and east of Jigjiga, a borderland almost entirely lacking fences, walls, checkpoints, or signage, where exactly are the lines demarcating one country from another? Except along the few paved roadways where manned checkpoints did exist, in the towns of Dewele and Tog Waajale for example, the precise locations of borders seemed to be of little importance to residents. Except for occasional increases in federal military and police presence during federally declared states of emergency, signs of border patrols and checkpoints were largely absent. Somalis frequently crossed the porous borders between Ethiopia, Djibouti, and Somaliland without official visas or passports.[24]

There were, furthermore, no publicly available geographic maps in existence that could accurately trace all the boundaries of the Somali National Regional

State in Ethiopia, Somaliland, or Somalia—primarily because each of these political entities is in ongoing and uneven processes of boundary making and enforcement. The Ethiopian Ministry of Maps in Addis Ababa had not updated its map of the northern Somali Region since the early 1990s even though since 1991 there have been numerous modifications to regional cartographies and administrative groupings within the Somali Region.[25] The blurry, porous, and disputed boundaries between different administrative, political, and ethnic entities all point to the long history of incomplete and contested processes of state formation throughout the Horn of Africa.

Additionally, rather than being located at the geographic edge of the state or continent, towns and remote communities east and north of Jigjiga felt more like places outsiders pass through but never stay. Every day, truckers, travelers, and livestock herders journeyed through and stopped in roadside towns for a few hours, but not longer. Isuzu flatbed trucks blazed through remote communities to deliver fresh bundles of khat leaves and offered residents affordable transport throughout the region. Health care and veterinary care providers in regional referral health centers traveled frequently between district- (or *woreda*)-level referral centers and their more remotely assigned posts. Eighteen-wheeler trucks packed with goods imported from China and the Middle East arrived from the port in Djibouti bound for points westward. Various international and Ethiopian NGOs frequently visited for a morning to deliver donated medicines or materials, but never stayed more than a few hours. And mobile teams of health workers, program monitors, and locally contracted researchers and program monitors constantly traveled from place to place in their white Toyotas, depending on the crisis or intervention at hand. The seemingly constant movement of people for work, commerce, visiting, and aid characterized the Somali Region and further obscured its political and geographic borders.

Over the last two decades within the social sciences, the margins of states have themselves become an object of study. Talal Asad famously described them as "unstable" places "where state law and order continually have to be reestablished."[26] Thus margins are not marginal, but rather emblematic of the mechanisms and limitations of contemporary forms of government and power.[27] Studying the margins of Ethiopia and also at the same time the margins of the humanitarian system—their edges and aporias, so to speak—can therefore help illuminate the relations and effects of power in Ethiopia and the Horn of Africa as well as in the halls of international NGOs and United Nations organizations headquartered in cities like Geneva and Washington, DC.

Ethnographers have also in recent years increasingly sought out subjects of analysis that defy the bounds of ethnic and territorial groupings—seeking to understand not the cultures of exotic or distant peoples, but instead how wars, migrations, disasters, and so on shape the production of borders and illusions of distance and difference between groups.[28] Ethnographic studies of politics, citizenship, and belonging are no longer usually necessarily tied to territorially bounded peoples or nation-states, but instead examine how social identities, social relationships, and social problems are shaped and revealed through people's experiences of marginalization and belonging within and across political and geographical boundaries. Whether physical, legal, or socially constructed, boundaries demarcating one group from another often divide persons who are entitled to various forms of assistance from those who are not. Boundary-making activities, mapping methodologies, and the designation of arbitrary and artificial categorizations in the humanitarian sector, such as the implementation of aid programs with limitations on who qualifies for medical care or asylum, what groups are most in need, or where displaced persons can settle or graze livestock, for example, are important methods of deploying sovereign power today.

The Humanitarian Landscape

Every year, during the long dry season in eastern Ethiopia, or the *jilaal*, from November until early March, agricultural plots wither, grasses disappear from the sandy wadis snaking through the desert expanses, and livestock herders, when possible, migrate elsewhere, often hundreds of miles south and west into the Ethiopian highlands and the greener parts of the *haud* pastureland, to find their animals food and water. The lowland desert east of Dire Dawa and Jigjiga turns ever browner, dustier, windier, and chillier, especially in the mountains and atop the arid plateau along the borders with Somaliland and Djibouti. By March every year, people across the region begin to look anxiously skyward, waiting for signs of increasing humidity, haze, the build-up of clouds, and a few sporadic downpours to begin the growing seasons. The rhythms of this seasonal anticipation, and every few years, the failure of forecasted spring rains, then the failures or delays in monsoon rains a few months later, and the predictable flooding after too many months of drought, all lead to regular, repeated upticks in humanitarian operations throughout the region.

Droughts in different parts of the Somali Region in 2003–2004, 2008–2009, 2010–2012, and again in 2015–2016 in some communities increased rates of food insecurity, outbreaks of diarrheal diseases from people having to use water from contaminated sources, and consequently, rates of severe acute malnutrition especially among young children.[29] Successive dry years have exacerbated desertification and land degradation[30] and intensified fights over access to pastureland and water along regional boundaries.[31] Prices for fresh milk, sorghum, and other staple foods increased in each of these drought periods, and prices for livestock repeatedly fell.

Repeated droughts affected the aid industry as well. These early environmental warnings of crisis repeatedly triggered the need among relief organizations for better data—on rainfall, agriculture, nutrition status, health status, food security, livestock prices, and the like—and the quick publication of donor appeals and media stories. Following indications of drought, printed advertisements in English and Somali languages suddenly papered the kiosks and bulletin boards of local universities and colleges throughout eastern Ethiopia, announcing job openings with relief organizations. Training workshops and orientation activities commenced, and occasionally, expatriate policy makers and representatives of donor organizations would arrive for a few days to inaugurate new projects and pose for photographs and media spotlights.

But then, each time, as rains fell again and drought conditions subsided, new tufts of grasses appeared along the roadsides and riverbeds, and livestock returned to the lowlands to graze and calve. Fresh camel milk flooded rural and urban markets, and people enjoyed travel, holidays, family reunions, and wedding parties. At the same time, without new reports of crisis, the pace of relief work in places like Jigjiga slowed. Fewer job announcements were posted, and the permanent, salaried staff of relief agencies settled into drafting glossy project reports and writing grant applications to donors, planning for future work. The intertwined effects of seasonal weather patterns, repeated droughts, climatic changes, and intermittent humanitarian interventions have important effects on local economies in places like the Somali Region where relief organizations regularly intervene.

However, droughts were not the only or even the most important drivers of relief work. Beginning in October 2016 through early 2018, then in 2019, intercommunal, interethnic violence occasionally erupted between ethnic Somali and Oromo pastoralists and farmers along regional boundaries in eastern Ethiopia. Roads connecting the cities of Dire Dawa, Harar, Jigjiga, Fiq, Degahabur, Gode, Dolo, and Hargeisa in Somaliland frequently closed, halting commercial transit, markets, and peoples' regular travel for work and pleasure. Protests erupted every few days along these major roads, as young people responded to political inertia or perceived neglect from their leaders in Addis Ababa. By July 2018, as I was conducting research for this book, there were over one million persons internally displaced in eastern Ethiopia, newly settled into makeshift camps and informal settlements near Jigjiga and Dire Dawa and all along the Oromia-Somali regional boundaries.

In early August 2018, an additional conflict erupted in and around Jigjiga when the prime minister ordered the arrest of the Somali Regional President

Abdi Iley. Abdi Iley's loyalists in Jigjiga protested this move and retaliated against government officials and suspected traitors. At least one hundred people were killed and nearly 150,000 people fled the immediate area.[32] By that December, there were nearly three million internally displaced persons (or IDPs) throughout Ethiopia.[33] In fact, despite the early achievements and the growing international fame of Prime Minister Abiy Ahmed, by 2019, there were more internally displaced people in Ethiopia than in any other country in the world.[34]

The Jigjiga and Dire Dawa offices of the UN World Food Program (WFP), UNICEF, and the United Nations International Organization for Migration (IOM) remained during this time the largest international nongovernmental relief offices in Ethiopia outside Addis Ababa. They coordinated and helped supply numerous relief and other related programs in eastern Ethiopia, in partnership with the governmental Somali Regional Health Bureau, the Somali Regional Agricultural Bureau, the federal office of the Disaster Preparedness and Prevention Commission, the Ethiopian governmental Agency for Refugee and Returnee Affairs (ARRA), and numerous additional local, national, and international nongovernmental organizations. Several international NGOs headquartered in Dire Dawa, Jigjiga, and the city of Gode south of Jigjiga, have staffed offices and contributed to various emergency programs throughout the region in the last two decades. These included Action Contre la Faim, CARE, CONCERN, the Ethiopian Red Cross, Handicap International, the Hararge Catholic Secretariat, Catholic Relief Services, International Medical Corps, International Rescue Committee, Islamic Relief, Merlin, Médecins Sans Frontières, Ogaden Welfare Development Assistance, Oxfam, Plan International, the Norwegian Refugee Council, Samaritan's Purse, Save the Children, World Vision, and likely more. As political insecurity and displacement repeatedly dissipated, then returned again, exacerbating the effects of droughts and outbreaks of infectious diseases and malnutrition, funding for humanitarian edifices and jobs in the humanitarian industry ebbed and flowed in parallel.

Repeated humanitarian emergencies during the last few decades have also contributed to the progressive sedentarization of many pastoralists and semi-pastoralists in eastern Ethiopia. More and more young people have abandoned careers in livestock and farming, leaving their rural, natal communities to attend high school and then university or vocational training programs in bigger towns and cities. This has produced, among other things, the availability of a young, mobile, and educated labor force now hoping to staff governmental and nongovernmental aid agencies working across the region. Young people like Aden have benefited from the movements their families have been forced to make over the years, and as adults, they, with their peers, now frequently dream of obtaining jobs in the relatively lucrative humanitarian industry.

While the relief industry has consequently grown in size over the years in the Somali Region—as measured in budgets and personnel—relief organizations have had a presence for generations, going back to the founding of colonial clinics, missionary hospitals, and foreign military outposts. During the Italian occupation of eastern Ethiopia and Somalia in the early 1930s, for example, the Italian government and affiliated Catholic organizations built a small clinical facility in the town of Aysha, approximately ten miles from the contemporary border with Djibouti and approximately twenty miles from the border with Somaliland near Hargeisa. The Italian clinic served both local Somali families—mostly traders, at the time, making a living from railroad commerce and livestock markets— and the Italian and French expatriates working on the railroad. The clinic had four rooms and a long porch, one elderly Somali man recalled, constructed with rough volcanic stones gleaned from the surrounding landscape.

This clinic in Aysha was located where French Somaliland (now Djibouti), British Somaliland (now roughly the area of Somaliland), and the Ethiopian Empire met, and separated the two Italian-controlled territories of Eritrea and Somalia. Consequently, during conflicts in Ethiopia—between Mussolini's first major attack on Ethiopia in 1935, throughout Italy's military occupation of the Ethiopian Empire, and until a peace treaty was signed with Italy in 1947—what is today demarcated as the Somali Region of Ethiopia remained caught between battling empires, along the major trade and railroad routes linking these empires to strategic coastal ports. Many Somalis who affiliate with the Issa "clan" (in Somali, *Reerka Ciise*) who lived in the northern parts of Greater Somalia (including land today in northeastern Ethiopia, southern Djibouti, and northern parts of Somaliland) were employed by Italian and French colonial administrators to help build the railroad and roadways through the region. Then, during conflicts with Ethiopia, Issas helped defend Italy's and France's territory from Ethiopia's military incursions, in opposition to Somalis living farther south. In this case, before coherent nationalist, independence movements farther south in Somalia, northern Somali groups were part of the defense of European powers, in opposition to the Ethiopian Empire's encroachments eastward.

In the end, however, with European colonial powers unable to effectively sustain their occupation of the Horn of Africa after their losses in World War II, Ethiopia gained control over territories around Aysha and farther south to the border with British Somaliland and Kenya. Italian and French Catholic organizations abandoned most of their outposts and clinics in eastern Ethiopia, leaving behind scant medical supplies. Until the early 1970s, Ethiopian police forces used the clinic in Aysha, for one, to store their equipment. The Ethiopian Empire under Haile Selassie encouraged conflict between northern Somali groups and ethnic Oromos and ethnic Afar groups living to the west and southwest, as a way to continue to undercut potential solidarities between different pastoralist groups and among Somalis living along important transit routes and controlling natural resources in that part of the country.[35]

In 1974, following a military coup d'état that deposed Haile Selassie's rule, police and military forces under command of the Provisional Military Government of Socialist Ethiopia, affiliates of a communist Marxist-Leninist military junta called "the Derg," took up residence in the little clinic in Aysha and in places all along the borders with French and British Somaliland. These security and police forces were led not by Somalis but mostly by Amharic-speaking Ethiopians from the central and western highlands of the country. They administered checkpoints all along the main road, forcibly quelled a few irredentist uprisings, and worked to ensure the safety of railroad commerce and burgeoning truck traffic.

Somalis from Aysha remember the Derg's police and military forces as brutal, obsessed with control over Somali communities, and threatened by the thriving commercial businesses and ethnic solidarity that continued across the mountainous, desert borderlands. Ethiopian governmental representatives lived in separate houses, ate at different restaurants, and lived in separate parts of town. The clinic in Aysha was used mostly, at this time, by the Ethiopian police and military, and not, almost ever, by local Somalis. A space constructed with the intention to save lives became a center for military activity and police surveillance, by forces distrustful of Somali residents.

Once the Derg lost power in another coup in 1991, the clinic in Aysha began to again house medical supplies donated by foreign relief NGOs including Oxfam and Médecins Sans Frontières (MSF). When a newer, bigger, walled public health center was constructed a few hundred feet away in 2007, the clinic returned to its former use as a residence. Graffiti painted on the outside of the old clinic, by 2008, was in the Somali language, not Amharic, and most people going in and out of its doors were local Somalis.

Remnants of numerous additional past clinical relief operations and shuttered offices of relief organizations dot the landscape. From atop a hill outside the town of Degago, fifteen miles away from Aysha and approximately thirty miles from the Djibouti and Somaliland borders, the outlines of a refugee camp's perimeter walls, irrigation ditches, and storage sheds are all visible beneath the wind-blown sand. Half-buried brick structures, now abandoned, are filled with invasive mesquite trees and tangled briars, catching wisps of plastic garbage. The Degago camp was opened during the civil war in Somalia and interclan conflicts in Somaliland in the mid-1980s. It housed, at different times, between fifteen thousand and thirty thousand displaced Somalis. One relatively large clinic was built to serve the local population and refugee camp. When it first opened, it had a fully stocked pharmacy and several examination and office rooms—several residents who still reside in Degago worked on its construction or worked inside, helping care for patients. The clinic was first built and operated by MSF, then was later administered by UNHCR and ARRA, and then was closed when refugees were repatriated back home in 2005. Most of the building was repurposed by the Somali Regional Health Bureau in 2007 as a local clinical facility, serving the remaining residential population.

Twenty miles to the east, closer to the Somaliland border, in 2002 a two-room cement clinic was erected and supplied by an international NGO for one year in the village of Elahelay, but was never staffed. Local residents threw up their hands in 2009, laughed, and joked with me about how they cannot even remember the name of the NGO. "They just left!" the town chairman cried. "Who were they? I do not know now!" The building remained mostly empty and unused until 2008, when the Somali Regional Health Bureau (the regional arm of the Ethiopian Ministry of Health, based in Jigjiga) designated the building a public "health post" staffed by a health extension worker.[36]

Another two-room building several miles farther southwest of Elahelay opened in the 1990s by another country office of MSF then closed five years later. In 2008 it reopened as another health post and is now also staffed by health extension workers. By 2018, the red and white MSF poster glued to the entrance was faded and halfway ripped off. Scales, cabinets, and posters originally purchased by the relief organization were still stored there and even still in some cases used, alongside more recent acquisitions by the extension workers deployed there from Jigjiga. Similarly, several more miles south, in bustling downtown Jigjiga, billboards and signs are erected, painted, then repainted outside houses and small office buildings, again and again, as various relief NGOs come and go from the area.

Decolonizing Humanitarianism, Decolonizing the Somali Region

Ethiopia was never colonized by Europeans. The country is widely known as the "capital of Africa," the host to the African Union, and moreover, a symbol of African independence and Pan-African potential. However, Ethiopia has achieved its political dominance and symbolic currency, in part, through military occupation and forcible incorporation of territories and communities inhabited by numerous ethnic groups including Somalis. Aden said to me during a discussion about politics in Jigjiga, "Ethiopia was never colonized, and thinks of itself as an independent nation. But at the same time, people within Ethiopia have been colonized—the Somali for one."

In the eighteenth through twentieth centuries, Somalis were strategically partitioned among four colonial powers: France fought for and claimed what is now Djibouti; the British Empire took what is now approximately the territory of Somaliland, Puntland, and the Northern Frontier District of Kenya; Italy colonized most of what is today Somalia; and Ethiopia controlled (or "colonized," as many Somalis describe it in English) much of what is now the Somali Region of Ethiopia. Historian Safia Aidid writes,

> The transformation of the Ethiopian Empire into a symbol of anticolonialism was, in fact, contradictory, given its own ongoing history of territorial conquest and slavery, which would only be abolished in 1923 as Ethiopia sought to join the League of Nations. Yet, anticolonial symbol it would become, one that was projected internationally and deployed politically as part of Ethiopia's foreign policy in the mid-20th century, obscuring the histories and self-determination claims of its subject peoples. At the center of Ethiopia's representation in Pan-Africanist thought is a fundamental paradox: how could a symbol of black freedom be complicit in the unfreedom of others?[37]

The global humanitarian industry, in parallel, also continues to reflect imperial designs and administrative structures.[38] Donini noted, "humanitarians perform functions inherited from colonial administrations and religious institutions, sometimes reproduced with similar missionary zeal."[39] Power inequities between Somalis and Amharic-speaking Ethiopians, and between Somalis and European and North American expatriates within the contemporary global and local humanitarian industry echo long histories of violence and imperialism. Money and power in the global humanitarian aid industry, for the most part, still exist mostly in countries in European and North American institutions (although the Gulf States, Turkey, China, and India are challenging this historic pattern, at least in East Africa), while relief operations mostly target populations in countries that have frequently been at some point colonized or militarily occupied by what are now the major Western donor countries.

Several of my European friends and colleagues at United Nations and NGO relief offices headquartered in Addis Ababa were the children of diplomats, missionaries, and aid workers, temporarily stationed for a time in Ethiopia or elsewhere in Africa. Many spent their childhoods in Addis Ababa or other African capitals, attending parties at embassies and enrolling in classrooms filled mostly with other expatriates. While these (mostly white, mostly elite) aid workers climbed professional ladders, earned generous salaries, and traveled the world for work and vacation, their Ethiopian and Somali Ethiopian coworkers mostly remained in low-to-mid-level positions in national and subnational offices.[40]

At the same time, what is unique about the Somali Region of Ethiopia—especially in the northern stretches of the region around Jigjiga and Dire Dawa and east from there to the borders of Djibouti and Somaliland—is that through Somalis' relative neglect and marginalization from development aid in Ethiopia, through a lack of private industrial and infrastructural investments compared to other parts of the country, through political processes of federalism and decentralization, and because of its geographic and cultural distance from Addis Ababa, humanitarian assistance in the Somali Region presents a tool of innovation and decolonization.[41] This is a prescient moment in the Horn of Africa. Prime Minister Abiy's ascension and the recent tenuous successes stabilizing the Somali regional government mean there is space for creating meaningful change. Institutions within the Somali regional government, with significant funding from international relief organizations, are rising in autonomy and authority, often in opposition to policies developed and promoted in Addis Ababa.[42]

My own perspective on humanitarian response and the industry that structures it, as well as my own desire to question knowledge production about humanitarianism, are both informed by my training and work as an anthropologist. The academic discipline of anthropology in the United States has been struggling for decades to "decolonize" itself and meaningfully modify its structures of labor so that universities and research institutions value and are more representative of the peoples who are the subject of anthropological study.[43] Many anthropologists live in and research contested imperial, postcolonial, and politically insecure spaces. Anthropologists' examinations of power are often not just about other cultures far away, but also, reflexively, about the academy itself, and our own complicity in maintaining exclusive modes of academic (and also political and economic) power. For anthropology to be a tool and a lens of liberation, as anthropologist Faye Harrison urges, it should center subaltern power and knowledge.[44]

Decolonizing humanitarianism analogously entails more than espousing worthy but abstract objectives like "localization" by people already in power.[45] It instead entails a recognition of how humanitarian modes of power and knowledge remain exclusionary and harmful even through contemporary efforts to "localize aid." For example, as this book illustrates in the chapters to follow, while the global humanitarian industry hires more and more "locals" like Aden from communities and countries in crisis to implement relief operations, these staffers remain exploitable and relatively undercompensated, even as their work is heroized.[46] Additionally, the idea of humanitarianism is still something most people perceive as embodied by mostly white Europeans and North Americans currently leading global nongovernmental organizations and UN agencies, and not by the vast majority of aid workers in the world—who are mostly from the countries and communities where interventions happen, who often lack equal access to educational and professional opportunities, who lack the ability to travel and obtain visas outside their home countries, and who, like Aden, are often themselves affected by humanitarian crises past and present. Numerous scholars and practitioners have called for systemic changes to how local and national workers are treated.[47] But a true transformation of the industry, and an atonement for imperialism and inequity, they acknowledge, cannot simply entail salary raises, new invitations to conferences or meetings, or images and stories of front-line workers on websites and brochures.

Instead, what is happening in the Somali Region, through humanitarian interventions and continuing generous funding for emergency responses there, is an expansion and a reconfiguration of global humanitarianism as *samafal*. For the legions of people like Aden, *samafal* means more than the provision of food, water, medicine, training opportunities, or even jobs in the relief industry. *Samafal* provides the mechanisms through which Somalis care for each other, repair their corporeal and collective political bodies, and organize basic governmental services in the margins of the Ethiopian state. In other words, humanitarian assistance is being strategically instrumentalized by the regional Somali government, Somali individuals, and local Somali aid workers in an attempt not just to save lives, but to recalibrate inequitable systems of governance and crisis response in Ethiopia.[48] As such, *samafal* is a tool of reparation and liberation from Somalis' histories of colonial partition, military intervention, political marginalization, and interethnic and interclan violence—histories that continue to provide the pretenses and the infrastructures for contemporary humanitarian responses. Somalis are using global aid to decolonize Ethiopia and the larger Horn of Africa, and therein, to reclaim a modicum of power over Somali lives, economies, politics, and institutions of government.

Centering *Samafal*

I began this chapter by asking a broad empirical question: who and what is signified and valued as humanitarian? But any answer to this question still invokes its same referent, *humanitarian*, repeating and accepting this dominant English vernacular, with roots in European languages and law. This is problematic for several reasons.

In foreign policy circles, the word humanitarian typically indexes a formal, narrow set of interventions to save and secure lives during and after disasters and conflicts. Humanitarian relief is guided by the body of International Humanitarian Law, and it is enforced and enacted mostly by signatory countries to these laws and statutes, United Nations organizations, and global nongovernmental relief organizations headquartered in Europe and North America.[49] Humanitarian emergencies and responses are treated as exceptional occurrences or ad hoc responses, and not intrinsic to state governance and foreign policies. The act of signifying crises and interventions as humanitarian therefore serves as a linguistic mechanism with which aid agencies and governments disclaim and distance themselves from responsibility for the problems at hand.

Likewise, in the Somali Region, humanitarian crises are perceived as exceptions to the Ethiopian success story, not an indication of its failure. Relief operations are perceived as marginal to development projects elsewhere in the country and separate from government politics, and not essential to these processes. Humanitarian crises are furthermore assumed to emerge suddenly and unexpectedly, and neither as a consequence of long histories of colonialism, partition, military occupation, violence, and inequity in the Horn of Africa, nor a product of the contemporary Ethiopian state now led by Prime Minister Abiy Ahmed.

Alternative vernaculars and understandings of humanitarianism do exist.[50] For example, in downtown Jigjiga, the word *samafal* headlines relief organizations' marquees, features on Somali radio news programs, and in conversation, describes the accomplishments of aid workers. *Samafal* pervades people's everyday conversations and common practices of care, religious charity, kinship, and communality both within and outside the walls of humanitarian organizations and clinical spaces. Relief operations designed and evaluated by exogenous European and American aid agencies are, by contrast, typically signified as *gargaarka bani'aadamnimada* (literally translated as humanitarian assistance). Thus *bani'aadamnimada* is only incidental to more expansive systems of *samafal*. Exogenous forms of global humanitarianism shape and constrain individuals' enactments of *samafal*, but do not define it. The social obligations, expectations, and exchanges that structure how people support each other during crises are more fundamental and enduring than any single foreign relief operation. Sometimes *samafal* involves opportunities or resources from international aid agencies, but on most occasions, it does not. For persons employed or subcontracted by relief agencies, this means much of the *samafal* important to them takes place outside the office or clinic, and further, what happens inside the office and clinic is contingent upon socially, economically, and politically embedded systems of *samafal*.

However, *samafal* and other local and Somali actions are not altogether different in language or in form from Ethiopian or global forms of humanitarian aid. These are false distinctions. *Samafal* represents an appropriation and actualization of occasional relief operations by Somalis. But even if they do not use the word, expatriate and non-Somali Ethiopian aid workers also enact *samafal*: they too do more than dispassionately distribute material goods, and they too expand upon and tailor the narrow dictates and material bequests provided during relief operations. *Samafal*, I have found, as a concept, beyond its Somali signification— is in fact central to global humanitarian practice, not the other way around.

In the pages that follow I place *samafal* at the front and center of my analysis of what it means to be humanitarian and do humanitarian work. *Samafal* presents an alternative humanitarian epistemology, or an alternative way of considering and learning about humanitarianism. My own perspective on this, and my articulation of *samafal* is of course subjective, and surely incomplete, but at least it is an alternative starting point. By suggesting the potential centrality and necessity of *samafal* to global humanitarian action as well as the interdependence and overlap of these different ideas, I highlight diverse forms of labor, affect, and politics that exist outside more narrow considerations and evaluations of foreign humanitarian interventions.

Researching *Samafal*

Writing this book involved trying to put myself into the shoes of the people who work in the humanitarian sector in eastern Ethiopia. I tried to see what they see in their work; I spent time during fieldwork accompanying local aid workers and clinical providers, walking through their workdays with them, chatting informally during and between their official duties, and organizing moments in which we had the opportunity to reflect on work and life. I traveled around with them and negotiated the arid landscapes, fragmentary infrastructure, and crowded urban streets with them; I shared pots of espresso and thermoses of sweet hot tea; I lived in the repurposed army barracks, sandy clinical spaces, and crowded government compounds where they live or sleep while on assignment; I attended monotonous meetings and workshops in uncomfortable desks alongside them; and I celebrated family reunions and the slaughter of valuable camels. I have gotten to know the people who experience humanitarian relief by spending time in professional spaces as well as in the communities where relief operations recur.

Ethnography is a way of knowing and a way of representing the world through written work.[51] The method of ethnography gives anthropologists and other researchers a way of understanding and communicating about where people are coming from, first through long-term participant-observation and other data collection methods, then through the process of writing out and rethinking and rewriting stories from the field. Years of living in communities of our own choosing and for our own research purposes, of literally breathing in and embodying the environments of others, of sharing with people both mundane activities and ceremonial rites, and of awkwardly reaching out to people to help us understand often the most basic things about their worlds and their words, offer anthropologists the possibility of an analytics of and through intimacy and imagination. Ethnography—as a method, methodology, and epistemology within the discipline of anthropology—is both creative and generative, and it can bring meaning to the stories we and others tell.

In the course of over a decade of on-and-off multisited ethnographic fieldwork in the Somali Region, I spoke with, shadowed, and observed hundreds of local aid workers and health-care providers who work for various emergency relief departments within the government of Ethiopia, United Nations offices, and nongovernmental organizations in zonal, regional, and district-level offices in the eastern part of the country. On separate occasions, and since 2003, I have also been part of several research initiatives to study food security, child survival, and the success of the mobile team projects in Ethiopia with colleagues at the UN World Food Programme, UNICEF, and the Feinstein International Center at Tufts University.[52]

Over the course of six trips to Ethiopia between 2007 and 2018, totaling twenty-four months of fieldwork, I have been trying to better understand the humanitarian enterprise. For this, I have organized repeated private interviews with and observed at work thirty-six Somali Ethiopian aid workers, at various levels within the humanitarian industry in eastern Ethiopia—from temporarily hired researchers and medical assistants in communities where interventions unfolded, to the heads of regional headquarters in Jigjiga. All of these individuals were based in the Somali Region or Dire Dawa, and except for one who had taken a temporary job elsewhere in the country, had worked in eastern Ethiopia for their entire career. I interviewed and spent additional time with sixteen non-Somali Ethiopian aid workers and clinical providers in relief agencies headquartered in Addis Ababa, Dire Dawa, and Jigjiga, but many of these persons had been deployed to several different regions throughout the country during their careers. I also conducted thirty semistructured, private interviews about humanitarian work with a sample of twenty non-Ethiopian expatriates who have worked in the humanitarian industry in eastern Ethiopia, or have specific expertise in human resources and the staffing of relief operations there. During all these research activities, with most of the people I interviewed formally, I attempted to speak with them several times, in different circumstances and places, such as at work and at home, during professional meetings and in informal spaces afterward, during structured interview sessions and over afternoon tea or macchiatos, and with our children or our colleagues present, and then later with some degree of privacy. In addition to planned data collection opportunities, I engaged in participant-observation and informal conversations about the ideas presented here with numerous additional persons within aid agencies and research institutions.

During my trips to the Horn of Africa, I also conducted research on other topics that have affected the course and findings of the work I present here. My dissertation fieldwork over a decade ago in 2007–2009 examined the lasting effects of recurrent relief operations on popular health cultures in the Somali Region.[53] During two mixed-method, collaborative studies of zoonotic disease risk and zoonotic tuberculosis, I studied pastoralists' health, diets, and exposures to livestock in rural towns north of Jigjiga;[54] and in a 2018 collaborative study of diabetes among Somalis, I examined the relationship between medical insecurity, food insecurity, and health outcomes among type 2 diabetes patients in the same area.[55] Finally, since 2017, I have been studying the migration of Ethiopian women from the Oromia Region through Djibouti to the Gulf States.

Lisa Smirl writes that white Toyota Land Cruiser SUVs—ubiquitous in every global humanitarian response—are literal and figurative vehicles of segregation between foreign aid workers and the populations they serve.[56] They provide distinction, distance, and potential escape for those inside. This could just as easily be applied to foreign researchers like me, traveling throughout the country, making conversation and hustling for data. But the numerous SUVs zooming across newly paved highways and bumping along rutted dusty roads in eastern Ethiopia only rarely carry expatriates. White SUVs owned by humanitarian agencies symbolize something different when they drive local hires to field sites and distribution points within a region they may already know and love. And for me, as an expatriate researcher trying to accompany these aid workers, Land Cruisers offered opportunities not just for exclusion (for I surely could never have escaped this segregation entirely) but also, it provided a vehicle for exploration. My exploration was, however, mostly focused on people's life trajectories, jobs, and social relationships.

I heard many stories while riding in vehicles—and SUVs have long been my favorite location for conversations and interviews. Trips across town and across long desert expanses provided exceptional, liminal spaces: places and moments neither part of the communities we traveled between nor officially part of the workday or workspace per se. The vehicle literally elevated each of us, in a way, to the same level: the student, the professor, the politician, the entry-level aid worker, the senior project manager, the translator, and the driver. It undermined gender, age, racialized, and status differentiations so common in workspaces and everyday life, and instead, for a time, placed us within a private, intimate space, side-by-side. The few women who traveled with me traveled without children in tow, and consequently, they were freer to spend time in reflective conversation. Men in vehicles had to grapple with being in unusually close physical proximity to me, a white woman. Clocking hundreds of desert kilometers crammed into vehicles with all sorts of folks allowed me to broach subject matters more freely and broadly than in perhaps any other place, even in people's bustling homes. Vehicles were my mobile social science laboratories. Writing while riding proved difficult but worth the trouble; my most thoughtful conversations and much of the data collected for this book happened as I bumped along roadways en route to meetings, aid distribution points, clinics, and other destinations.

But these spaces were also filled mostly by men like Aden and his colleagues debating and discussing decisions about aid throughout the region. Although more women are trained and hired every year in the humanitarian industry in the Horn of Africa, far fewer Somali women than men have jobs as project officers or managers with assigned vehicles. Aid work at all levels requires significant travel and time spent far from home, and at least in the Somali Region, employment with aid agencies typically also requires graduate university degrees—opportunities women and their families struggle to access and manage. I ventured elsewhere to get to know many of the women profiled in this book. The intimate spaces within vehicles, to some extent, mirrored the relaxed nature of time I spent inside crowded kitchens with women cooking and feeding children, sometimes women who are aid workers, but also women who received aid, the wives of aid workers, and participants in research about particular interventions.

Mobility is central to pastoralism, trade, religion, medical care, education, and kinship relations in eastern Ethiopia, and it is central to the lives of those tasked with implementing and evaluating humanitarian operations there. Consequently, this ethnography attends to the rhythms, chronicity, and travel of people, aid commodities, aid workers, data, and ideas about aid, all the way from the capital Addis Ababa to the eastern cities of Dire Dawa and Jigjiga, to the roadways, railways, and footpaths connecting small municipalities and remote encampments of pastoralists, to the edges of the region along the borders of Somaliland and Djibouti.

Thus this analysis attends to the sociality of humanitarianism as it moves and is lived, interpreted, and critiqued by many different folks. My invocation of the word *sociality* blends the notion of a tangible, structured society, a term commonly invoked in sociology, with the emotional intimacy of the social relationships a society contains. It is "a dynamic and interactive relational matrix through which human beings come to know the world they live in and to find their purpose and meaning within it."[57] Because humanitarian assistance, for local aid workers, so often involves caring for individuals and families during crisis and at the site of their physical bodies, and is so often focused on providing for people's basic biological and medical needs, I draw on theoretical debates within medical anthropology to help me decipher the significance of these humanitarian subjectivities.[58] Local aid workers find meaning, demonstrate love for one another, fulfill their social and religious obligations, and even engage in politics through their humanitarian work. And likewise, I found purpose and meaning through the intimacy of collaborative ethnography with them.

Ethnographic writing about humanitarianism requires a historical perspective as well. The lives and labor of professional humanitarians exemplify how crises and relief operations are never one-time phenomena, and how the memories and the half-lives of past interventions profoundly shape people's experiences, narrations, and evaluations of future interventions.[59] Exploring local histories of intervention, the biographies of specific aid programs, and the biographies of people involved in the aid industry all illustrate the long-standing embeddedness of humanitarian responses within aid agencies, governmental bureaus that receive humanitarian funding, and the communities where interventions recur.

Finally, the conceptions and enactments of *samafal* represented in this book are a product of time spent talking, writing, and imagining with a diverse collection of interlocutors, colleagues, and friends. We came from different places, and had different vocabularies and ideas about what it means to be humanitarian and do humanitarian work. To do justice to the diversity and the iterative nature of our discussions, thoughts, and actions, I draw on a dialectical approach to ethnography. By *dialectics*, I mean that this book represents a collaborative way of experiencing and writing about the world with others, exploring differences, taking stock of entangled histories, and in doing so, also imagining other possible futures.[60] In conversations and interviews, most people were ambivalent about the value and effects of humanitarian response. Many expressed genuine gratitude for life-saving aid and job opportunities during humanitarian emergencies, but also struggled to understand this exotic and exclusionary industry, to improve how it translated into local relief operations, and to enhance their own power to make more systemic changes.

What I did not expect years ago, at first meeting and getting to know the personnel of relief agencies in eastern Ethiopia, was how ethnographic research and participant observation with aid workers would so fundamentally alter my perception of humanitarianism and the global humanitarian industry. Anthropologists often talk about their "lenses," or their practice of using different theoretical lenses to attempt to see and understand phenomena and other ways of being in and knowing the world. But the process of attempting this level of understanding has involved greater perceptive and cognitive shifts than I initially imagined. My own altered states of thinking and sensing the world around me while studying humanitarianism in eastern Ethiopia—during, for example, the mourning, the awkwardness, and the confusion I often felt when sharing spaces with families, the boredom I experienced while mired in bureaucracies and unending workshops and long drives through the region, and also the love I've felt for people I've gotten to know—have not been comparable to placing temporarily on my nose a new pair of glasses, or peering through some sort of magical telescope that can provide apparitions of others' realities.

Instead I feel as if I have new eyes. I cannot take off these lenses, and I cannot move away from any specialized eyepiece. My lenses, so to speak, are part of me. Ethnographic research and writing have entailed a partial reforming of my vision itself and my situated perspective on the rest of the world. This is of course not to say that I have become a front-line health-care provider or a local aid worker, or ever even once truly spent a day in the shoes of someone like Aden—this would erase all the other parts of me, my own eyes, my education, my research questions, my personal and professional experiences, my privilege, my whiteness and gender, and all the vast distances and differences between myself and the interlocutors I've chosen to work with.

Over time I have intentionally—and maybe sometimes to their annoyance or confusion—entangled myself with a set of professional humanitarians, and from that vantage point, through writing and questioning and texting on cell phones and visiting repeatedly with and without my family, I have considered anew the subjects this book takes on: humanitarian forms of labor, humanitarian principles, Ethiopian and Somali politics, and the politics of relief operations. As a result, this book reflects my own perspective from within the global humanitarian landscape rather than providing an objective vision of what happens "over there" and for "others." Through ethnographic writing with and about humanitarianism in relation to others, this book has become a site of collaborative speculation with these local experts, on what humanitarianism offers, what it means to people, where it fails, and what it might alternatively entail.[61]

This book provides an ethnography of *samafal*: the heart and, I believe, the future of the humanitarian industry. Long-term ethnographic engagement with aid workers, policy makers, and beneficiaries of aid in the Somali Region re-centers the study of global humanitarianism away from North American and European histories and headquarters, to reveal its power, expertise, practice, and political effects in places like eastern Ethiopia where humanitarian interventions recur. By examining *samafal*, I also provide an ethnographic portrait of Somali life and politics in the margins of the Ethiopian state. Rather than an ethnolinguistic group known for their violence and manipulation of global humanitarian interventions, Somalis emerge in this story as powerful but also imperfect and often frustrated actors, working to transform mercurial injections of foreign humanitarian assistance into tools of love and liberation.

Chapter 1, titled "Humanitarianism Is Local," argues that decentralization in Ethiopia and in parallel, the trend to promote localization within the global aid industry, have together resulted in more funding and autonomy to subnational governmental affiliates in places like the Somali Region, giving increasing power to aid workers there. However, at the same time, the Somali Region remains marginal to the Ethiopian political project and broader economic development initiatives in Africa. Ethiopia's Somali Region (like other crisis-affected localities around the world) remains a site of presumed danger and disaster, and therefore receives only limited and temporary humanitarian interventions.

Chapter 2, "Humanitarianism Is *Samafal*," examines the meaning of *samafal* in greater detail. *Samafal* is not just a local or contextualized version of global aid mandates. Instead, it presents a subaltern humanitarian epistemology and an alternative way of enacting care at the site of individual bodies and bodies politic. In chapter 3, "Humanitarian Work," I outline the inequitable hierarchy of global humanitarian labor on which the aid industry depends. The industry is characterized by steep and exclusive gradations in wealth, whiteness, international mobility, job security, and power to produce relief operations.

"Crisis Work," in chapter 4, describes the artificial production of humanitarian crisis required to ensure flows of funding continue. Much of the labor local aid workers performed in the Somali Region entailed measuring, narrating, and marketing news of an urgent crisis afoot, to which aid agencies can and should respond. Aid workers and clinical medical providers recognized, however, that much of their work required the amelioration of chronic forms of suffering, entrenched poverty, and marginalization from reforms happening elsewhere in the country. Crisis work required local aid workers' modification and expansion of metaphorical Band-Aids to provide lasting basic services and care to people in need.

The fifth chapter, "Humanitarianism Is Anti-Politics," critically examines the mythopoesis of global humanitarian aid, beginning with the origin story of the Red Cross in the nineteenth century and the emergence of an ideal form of politically neutral aid carried out by compassionate strangers from Western donor countries. Instead, relief work builds local political power, builds intraethnic and interethnic solidarities, and can even promote peace. Humanitarian response is neither neutral nor apolitical, but rather, it is an "anti-politics" industry that depends on the ability to outwardly deny political strategy and political effects in order to achieve political aims.

In the final chapter, "From Crisis to Liberation," I concede that while the global humanitarian industry remains an artifact of the imperialist world in which it began, it has also funded and structured mechanisms of decolonization in Ethiopia. With material support from global and Ethiopian relief organizations, Somalis have leveraged relief operations to gain a modicum of power over their careers and government. Marginalized from the Ethiopian political project and largely neglected by global development and private investments, Somalis have transformed sporadic international humanitarian responses into mechanisms of solidarity and liberation.

HUMANITARIANISM IS LOCAL

In her landmark book on refugees in Africa, the anthropologist Liisa Malkki says:

> When these black citizens of Burundi and Rwanda exercise their exit option, most of them will do so on foot. And as they cross the international border, they will undergo a transformation: they will emerge knowable again, on the other side, to international wire services and international relief organizations and developmental agencies and scholars as "African refugees." . . . They will become not only a "problem," they will also become an object of humanitarian relief . . . In becoming objects of the philanthropic mode of power, the political, historical, and biographical specificity of their life worlds vanishes.[1]

Malkki's book, and this passage in particular, still fascinate me. Her observations inspired my first journeys for ethnographic fieldwork in eastern Ethiopia— inundated as it was with long histories of families fleeing across borders, episodic international relief operations, and the displacement and sedentarization of livestock herders and traders.[2] But, as Malkki acknowledges, her characterization of refugees, as invisible to the gaze of the international community before their official request for asylum, also represents *her* gaze, like my own, a gaze of an expatriate, and not the perspective of the more typical, average aid worker there, who, most likely, was also Burundian or Rwandan.

The "philanthropic mode of power" Malkki identifies in these relief operations is a product of the global humanitarian aid industry and the adjacent academic, development, and international business communities, made up mostly of Europeans and North Americans, who for generations have often rendered the Burundian and the Rwandan exotic, mysterious objects of concern, and the sites for colonization, exploration, resource extraction, labor exploitation, and intervention. So from the vantage point of the African refugee and African aid workers helping meet the needs of these refugees, this "philanthropic mode of power" may very well have been an exotic artifact of a largely mysterious and distant global humanitarian industry, and not something inherently accessible to most aid workers. Global humanitarian intervention, or *bani'aadamnimada* in Somali, likewise, is "an ideology, a movement and a profession structurally, economically and culturally 'of the North,'" Antonio Donini writes.[3] Relief operations like this are produced through a dominant "white gaze" that views persons and political systems in the Global South as deviant and underdeveloped, therefore in need of intervention and salvation.[4]

I am part of this industry. My academic and policy research have allowed my international travel and interpolations into relief operations, and given me a privileged (while partial) perspective on the lives and communities of persons who appropriate and affect these "philanthropic modes of power." I have worked for and with UN agencies carrying out relief work. I have worked as a visiting scholar and graduate student at various universities in Ethiopia and the United States conducting research in different parts of the country. And now I am a professor, still regularly traveling to Ethiopia for research and advocacy work.

However, spending extended time with relief workers and policy makers in eastern Ethiopia—both participating in policy making and response processes as well as observing people at their work—has made me aware of additional humanitarian epistemologies and alternative ways of defining and being humanitarian. In other words, there are other modes of power afoot within relief operations, outside the actions and perspectives of expatriates. Emic forms of humanitarianism— in Somali, *samafal*—and the labor of locals are what make humanitarian interventions actually work. Expatriates like me, only staying in the Somali Region for short periods of time, remain peripheral to these subaltern modes of power and these alternative ways of understanding and responding to crises.

Somali aid workers, by contrast, have transformed global humanitarian modes of power to render themselves vital to the everyday functioning of relief agencies. Somali Ethiopians implemented and evaluated almost all the relief operations unfolding in eastern Ethiopia. Somali Ethiopians authored most donor appeals to garner funding for programs in the Somali Region, wrote or helped produce many of the news media stories, negotiated with Ethiopian political figures, oriented outsiders newly deployed to the area, cared for crisis-affected persons both within and outside the structures of relief operations, and even shaped public perceptions of crisis and humanitarian response through their posts and photographs of crisis on social media platforms. Even the recipients of aid were part of humanitarian modes of power. In large numbers they volunteered to participate in focus groups and interviews designed to evaluate crisis and various forms of aid, and they allowed themselves and their children to be counted, measured, logged, vaccinated, diagnosed, and treated. The operations of power within humanitarian programs involved the vernacular, ideas, and activity of all these "locals"—people who represent the heart and the workforce of contemporary global humanitarian aid. Their articulations and enactments of *samafal* were therefore central to the global humanitarian industry and what it means to be a humanitarian today, and not merely local or uniquely Somali interpretations of humanitarian response.[5]

Decentralization in Ethiopia: Making Global Humanitarianism More Local

"Decentralization" refers to the strategic devolution of power, decision-making authority, and accountability to regional and other smaller, more local, administrative catchment areas and away from centralized federal governmental offices.[6] In the Ethiopia context, the idea of decentralizing power and governmental authority out from offices in Addis Ababa to regional governments in places like Jigjiga represents an effort to offer, in return for Ethiopian unity, a modicum of autonomy to regions throughout the country, populated by various minority ethnolinguistic groups.[7] Acknowledging Somali regional power and autonomy within Ethiopia counterbalances powerful Pan-Somali nationalist movements and forms of economic cooperation across the Horn of Africa.

Decentralization in Ethiopia additionally provides an antidote to histories of colonization and violent, centralized power during past Ethiopian governments—including, most palpably, the Marxist-Leninist military junta called "the Derg." In 1991 the Tigray People's Liberation Front (TPLF), with assistance from other ethnicity-based militia groups, toppled the Derg.[8] In the wake of the revolution, an alliance of groups from across the country formed the Ethiopian People's Revolutionary Democratic Front (EPRDF), led by the Tigrayan military commander, Meles Zenawi.[9] In 1995 the Transitional Government of Ethiopia ratified a new constitution that established the Federal Democratic Republic of Ethiopia and divided the country into mostly ethnic-based regional states. Ethnic-based regions—like the Somali Region—were based loosely on ethnolinguistic groups that were able to form coherent political parties and align with the EPRDF.[10] Memories of famine, forced resettlement, abuse from police and military forces, and the previous stifling of political dissent during Haile Selassie's rule and during the Derg's rule led many Somalis in Ethiopia, years later, to embrace the TPLF, then the EPRDF, and most recently the Prosperity Party, as more peaceful and promising alternatives to imperialism and tyranny.

Federalism in Ethiopia was accordingly a postcolonial political project, and promises of regional autonomy and power sharing were central to its implementation and popularity. The Ethiopian Constitution asserts that:

1. Every nation, Nationality and People in Ethiopia has an unconditional right to self-determination, including the right to secession.
2. Every Nation, Nationality and People in Ethiopia has the right to speak, to write and to develop its own language; to express, to develop, and to promote its culture; and to preserve its history.
3. Every Nation, Nationality and People in Ethiopia has the right to a full measure of self-government which includes the right to establish institutions of government in the territory that it inhabits and to equitable representation in state and Federal governments.

   "Nation, Nationality or People" for the purpose of this Constitution, is a group of people who have or share a large measure of a common culture or similar customs, mutual intelligibility of language, belief in a common or related identities, a common psychological make-up, and who inhabit an identifiable, predominantly contiguous territory.[11]

The constitution thus guarantees democratic representation and equitable resource allocation to a set of politicians representing ethnolinguistic groups—a term Alemseged Abbay calls, "consociationalism" or power sharing between elites at the federal level.[12] These elites optimally governed in parallel and as a complement to the leadership of existing secular *ugaas* (sultans or chiefs within kinship groups or "clans," in accordance with *xeer*, or customary Somali law), and Islamic religious leaders (sheikhs and mullahs). Decentralized ethnic federalism in Ethiopia was originally conceived (by Meles Zenawi and others in power within the EPRDF alliance) in order to end domination of Ethiopian politics by the Amhara ethnic group, and to dissuade revolt and secession among other ethnic groups by allowing them to manage their own economic and political affairs.[13]

The Somali National Regional State was included in the first national conference of representatives in Addis Ababa in 1991, and in the two years following this, hundreds of thousands of Somalis either fleeing crises farther south or returning to their homes in Ethiopia, crossed back into the region.[14] After ensuing conflicts between different political parties and kinship groups, the

Ethiopian Somali People's Democratic Party (SPDP) formed in 1995, and has represented the Somali Region in the national parliament since 1998. In every election since 2000, the SPDP has officially allied with the EPRDF and most of its elected Members of Parliament have supported the EPRDF. After the Somali regional president Abdi Mohamoud Omar (known as "Abdi Iley") was arrested by police forces from Addis Ababa in 2018, he resigned, and Prime Minister Abiy Ahmed and the EPRDF working with SPDP leaders, nominated Mustafa Muhummed Omer, a relative outsider to party politics, to fill the vacancy and stabilize the region. As of 2020, Abdi Iley remained imprisoned in Addis Ababa, and has been charged with inciting violence, allowing a secretive police force to operate extralegally and with impunity (the Liyu), running a covert and abusive penal system (the infamous "Jail Ogaden"), and attempting to undermine constitutional order.[15] Despite recent changes and conflict since 2018, both within the Somali Region and within the federal government in Addis Ababa, President Mustafa promised to continue with reforms of the region's political and penal systems.[16]

Since the Somali Region's inclusion into the Ethiopian federal state system and constitution, Somalis have been variably integrated into multiple, fluid, and often antagonistic political organizations: on one hand, the Somali Region is incorporated as one administrative unit within the Ethiopian federalist state. On the other hand, Somali residents continue to regularly interact, travel, and trade with other Somalis living in Djibouti, Somaliland, Puntland, Somalia, Kenya, and the swelling diasporas abroad. Somali Ethiopians' bifurcated and dynamic practices of citizenship—at once officially belonging to the legal entity of the Ethiopian state while also belonging to transnational communities of Somalis— challenge various projects of Ethiopian unity and the governmental provision of humanitarian services.

Historians and social scientists find that, long before the Derg rose to power, lineage-based "clan" affiliations and other kinship structures (such as the *qabiil* or *reer*, translated in English as the clan, tribe, or family group) in Somali societies surpassed or superseded formal state, colonial, or international authorities.[17] Tobias Hagmann and Mohamud Hussein Khalif call the Somali Region a "frontier space," where repeated attempts to centralize political power have clashed with traditional, more egalitarian, systems of governance.[18] Centralized political projects were, according to Virginia Luling, "suspended above a society which would never have produced and did not demand" such centralization.[19] Likewise, Jon Abbink argues that before colonization and partition by British, Italian, French, and Ethiopian empires, Somalis in the Horn of Africa were not united by a single culture or any one particular nationalist project, but instead, remained only loosely associated through their common religion and language, and only infrequently connected through trade and intermarriage.[20] David Laitin and Said Samatar find that even modern Somali social organizations were "acephalous."[21]

Others disagree. Lee Cassanelli described largely coherent and powerful "clan" hierarchies and wars for domination of land and natural resources between groups throughout much of the last thousand years.[22] The powerful Ajuraan dynasty during the fifteenth through seventeenth centuries, for example, produced a highly cohesive and long-lasting Somali polity replete with administrative stratification, theocratic ideologies, suppression of local conflicts over water and grazing rights, and unified opposition to other ethnolinguistic groups in the Horn of Africa. Peter Little, similarly, finds a "radical localization" of politics that overshadowed various nation-state authorities through time, characterized by an array of residual customary social structures, such as the hierarchical structures for traditional leadership and Somali customary law.[23]

Following a series of failed nationalist and unification projects, continuing civil strife, and intermittent humanitarian crises and interventions throughout the latter half of the twentieth century and in the twenty-first century, many Somalis I spoke to professed a lingering distrust of both formal state institutions as well as international interventions.[24] As Hagmann and Khalif argue, "both the imperial government [under Haile Selassie] and the Derg had, in typical centralist manner, regularly indulged in micromanaging politics in the Ogaden."[25] Indeed, local governmental bureaus and governance structures (such as police forces and the judiciary) in the Somali Region remained, during this research, largely detached and less active in everyday life than kinship support and customary law (*xeer*). Elders (*oday*), including sheikhs and mullahs (*wadaaddo*) and chosen leaders (*ugaas*) frequently organized conflict resolution through mediation, individual dispute resolution, and their own interpretation and enforcement of laws and contracts. Religious leaders maintained positions of authority outside their "clan" (*qabiil* or *reer*) affiliation and apart from formal Ethiopian systems of governance, drawing instead upon their scholarship, experiences with pilgrimages, and talents for Qur'anic healing, divination, and mentorship.

In addition, Somali nationalist and secessionist movements within Ethiopia and the greater Horn of Africa repeatedly attempted to undermine divisions based on kinship or "clan" in order to unite Somalis through the invocation of remembered oppression and partition during the colonial period, the involuntary and exploitative conscription of Somalis into wars between Ethiopia and Somalia, human rights abuses at the hands of various Ethiopian police and military forces, the continuing dispossession of nomadic pastoralists throughout the Horn of Africa, generalized economic and social inequality between Somalis and other ethnolinguistic groups in Ethiopia, and marginalization from the current Ethiopian democratic system.[26] The Somali concept of *samafal*, discussed in detail in the chapter to follow, frequently operated outside formal state apparatuses as well, but, even so, often supported work by officials within the Somali regional government and in so doing, indirectly engendered ethnic unity, regional cohesion, and the government's effectiveness.

Thus while many Somali individuals distrusted Amharic-speaking Ethiopian political elites in Addis Ababa, they were far from united on this and other political matters. Hagmann says of the region in general: "Variegated political devices by the Somali Region's political groups illustrates plural, contradictory, and differentiated relationships between the centre and periphery, state and society."[27] He calls governance in the Somali Region "hybrid political domination," where power is based simultaneously but variably on patrimonial kinship-based and legal state-based forms of legitimacy. The politicization of kinship and ethnicity through the construction of fictively cohesive and homogeneous minority ethnic-based regions, outside the customary *ugaas* structure, has been a major engine of instability. At the same time, since the ratification of the Ethiopian Constitution and the organization of the SPDP in the mid-1990s, *qabiil* and *reer* divisions and hostilities (such as Issa versus Ogaden) have progressively lessened, while tensions between Somalis and both the Ethiopian government in Addis Ababa and oppositional ethnicity-based political and military organizations like the Oromo Liberation Front have continued. In the years between 2016 and 2018, in particular, fights over land, mobility, and regional power ended in violence and forced displacements along the Somali-Oromia and Somali-Afar regional boundaries.[28]

Somalis' reactions to governmental relief programs during the years of this research (such as clinics opened, vaccines distributed, or roads rebuilt after floods) were ambivalent and diverse. On one hand, a majority of people had long been aligned with the EPRDF and supportive of programs first from Meles Zenawi and later Abiy Ahmed. On the other hand, they also distrusted the Ethiopian government in Addis Ababa and the EPRDF due to their continuing marginalization from many beneficial federal programs, their anger over Ethiopians' perceived abusive politics vis-à-vis other Somalis, ethnic Oromos, and other ethnolinguistic minority groups in the southern part of Ethiopia, and their apprehensions about contemporary ethnonationalist movements in the Amhara and Tigray Regions of Ethiopia farther west and north.

Decentralization complicated this picture. Most Somali regional governmental programs were not directed by bureaucrats or politicians located in Addis Ababa, but rather, by Somalis living and working in Jigjiga or in rural *woreda* (district) capitals. Popular relief programs like the Mobile Health and Nutrition Teams, or deliveries of potable water by tanker truck, while funded in part or entirely by foreign humanitarian grants, were carried out by regional and local government affiliates. Trucks and SUVs were purchased with NGO or UN money, but ultimately given to and owned by the government. Drivers and users of these vehicles were Somali Ethiopian governmental employees or subcontractors, and the delivery of various aid commodities was carried out explicitly in support of existing governmental programs. Injections of external aid thus enhanced the regional government's efforts to organize and control relief programs for Somalis. Foreign humanitarian aid, essentially, buttressed and expanded regional, Somali state functions.

In subsequent chapters I further demonstrate that even as decentralization has meant Somalis have greater control over resources and administration of the regional and local government offices, decentralization has not significantly improved either the terms of Somalis' citizenship within Ethiopia or their marginality from power in Addis Ababa. Somalis may staff the bureaus and drive the government-owned vehicles but they remain marginal to the Ethiopian political project. Somalis in Ethiopia also remain largely alienated from positions within the aid industry that produce the policies and design the projects they ultimately implement and evaluate. Decentralization has been an uneven political process through which local Somali agents and agencies have gained limited power within Ethiopia.

Localization in the Aid Industry: Producing the Objects and the Subjects of Aid

The decentralization of humanitarian assistance in Ethiopia has been affected by broader changes and calls for reform within global development and humanitarian aid. Beginning in the latter half of the twentieth century, international development organizations working in low-income countries began calling for greater "local participation" to improve the effectiveness and ethics of aid. Increased participation was envisioned as a way to improve both the skills and the work ethic of the poor, and prevent their "dependency" on foreign aid distributions.[29] By the 1980s, local participation was seen as a mechanism of potential empowerment as well.[30] New methodologies for designing international interventions, like "participatory rural appraisals," or PRAs, for example, were designed to meaningfully engage beneficiaries in producing and evaluating the aid projects that unfolded in their communities, and in so doing, to ensure local ownership and improve the effectiveness and sustainability of aid. Thus participation was potentially "transformative," at times upending tyrannical and undemocratic regimes.[31] And beyond economic growth, many participatory development projects modeled and indirectly encouraged democratic participation in government as well.[32] Ground-up transparency and accountability mechanisms, at times, became sites of local resistance and effective democratic reform.[33] "Participation" had positive political—not just economic—effects.

But, others countered, the power of locals involved in PRAs and other participatory research and development initiatives frequently dwarfed the power of governments and international nongovernmental organizations (INGOs) that ultimately delimited the aid people hoped to qualify for.[34] Often, despite assertions that interventions were participatory and therefore were designed to empower their target populations, international development schemes actually depoliticized aid, allowing for its manipulation by undemocratic governments and foreign aid organizations in power.[35] Participation worked best in democracies where officials were held accountable for their actions through voting and the media.

Attention to the needs of the local residents and beneficiaries of aid is therefore not new—even in places where conflicts remain unresolved and aid agencies struggle to maintain access to communities in crisis.[36] The 1991 United Nations General Assembly Resolution 46/182 that institutionalized the United Nations humanitarian system,[37] the Code of Conduct for the International Red Cross and Red Crescent Movement and NGOs in Disaster Relief,[38] the new and revised Core Humanitarian Standard on Quality and Accountability,[39] and the Sphere principles and minimum humanitarian standards[40] all underscore the importance of engaging local residents and local organizations. In 2013, the Overseas Development Institute called on the humanitarian industry to "let go" and progressively work to hand over resources and power to organizations and people in crisis-affected communities.[41] Workshops and publications by relief organizations now frequently portray locals and local organizations as the heroes and the rightful focus of global assistance.[42]

Localization was also designed to increase "local ownership," or "the degree of control that domestic actors wield over domestic political processes."[43] In other words, scholars argue, for development and peace to last, it cannot be imposed, enforced, or organized exclusively from the outside, by actors with interests outside those of people affected by crises and conflicts at hand. However, because so many humanitarian emergencies happen in places like eastern Ethiopia affected by combinations of civil conflict and long histories of colonization and the marginalization of minority groups, effective decentralization and localization both require the further devolution of power and authority to subnational actors and offices. Locals can ideally adjust the demands of global agencies to expectations and needs on the ground, and in so doing, inspire better organizational performance, enhanced organizational learning, and policy change, including at the federal level.[44]

But making aid more local requires substantial work and expertise, especially on the part of national and subnational staff. Aid programs like popular food-for-work and cash-for-work programs in the Somali Region of Ethiopia, for example, required time and resources to organize and train participants, distribute materials, enforce compliance, and monitor and evaluate projects.[45] Clinical medical operations required the training and formal supervision of new hires and community health workers, in addition to the provision of medical care and distribution of medical supplies. Local aid workers frequently had to mediate frictions between the NGOs and UN agencies partnered with governmental relief agencies and the local leaders in communities where aid agencies intervened. And local aid workers frequently had to deal with people's demands for more or different services or their aggressive challenges to aid workers' authority. Finally, aid workers expressed fear of being blamed or shunned when projects failed to meet their own communities' expectations.

While aid programs very often hinged on local aid workers' skills at mediation and negotiation, these were not explicitly valued, acknowledged, regulated by, or integrated into human resource departments. Experience and expertise in these matters often did not lead to promotions or raises for the local staffers who shouldered the most risk and responsibility. Further, as Susanna Campbell points out, because local staffers' work often remains informal and outside accountability mechanisms set up by aid agencies, their responses and adjustments to local expectations risk being perceived within headquarters as corrupt, examples of "bad behavior," or examples of "rule-breaking."[46] Even so, despite these potentials and challenges, enhancing local participation and ownership remained one important way aid agencies in Ethiopia worked to foster positive economic and political change.

Powerful global relief organizations like UNICEF, Save the Children, Oxfam, and Médecins Sans Frontières, have progressively funneled more money to regional and district-level (*woreda*) governmental offices and programs in eastern Ethiopia. These organizations have hired progressively more locals and fewer Amharic-speaking Ethiopians from the capital Addis Ababa, as well as fewer expatriates, to staff field offices in the Somali Region. These trends paralleled and even augmented the government of Ethiopia's efforts to decentralize aid. Like decentralization within Ethiopian politics, localization was therefore a political movement within the humanitarian industry (an industry that in some corners still idealistically casts itself as apolitical or at least neutral to partisan politics).[47] Localization and decentralization, in the humanitarian sector and in Ethiopia, have had profound and cumulative political effects.

Moreover, interventions and people that are perceived to be "local" are also assumed to be somehow better, more attuned to local realities and cultures, and more accountable to beneficiary populations. While aid still involves material distributions of resources, it also now entails an effort to develop the capacity of organizations and people in crisis-affected communities, and to transform individuals there from beneficiaries or victims of crisis into competent service providers and the leaders of humanitarian missions. Local aid workers are therefore both the object and the subject of global humanitarianism. They are trained and employed by aid agencies—often to perform the most difficult and dangerous jobs within the relief industry—and yet at the same time, their work is also a variant on what Feldman calls "ethical labor": it proves global relief agencies' and the government of Ethiopia's righteous empowerment of locals and their careful attention to local contexts.[48]

For example, a man I call Doctor Hamza, a physician and a former leader in the Somali regional government within Ethiopia said, "Today the [governmental] Health Bureau here is 100% Somali. . . . Most INGOs are headed by Somalis now too, and . . . five years [ago] the heads of office were mostly either white or highlander. This is a big change for us now, and it really helps us to be free."

However, while Doctor Hamza and others recite the various positive effects of these changes in terms of training and hiring more Somalis to serve the Somali Region, these changes also problematically reinforce the legitimacy of segregated ethnonational groups that hinder reconciliation processes so necessary for an end to violence in Ethiopia. Further, designing policies and funding programs based on supposedly discrete ethnicity-based regions belies the blurry and contested nature of ethnicity throughout the Horn of Africa, and regional political borders transecting mobile and diverse communities within each country and region.

There is not a monolithic or neat representation of what local is or fails to be in the Somali Region or among Somalis. It is not possible to clearly distinguish what is "local" from what is "Somali" or "Ethiopian," and it would be nonsensical and impossible to identify or implement an intervention that is somehow authentically Somali. Likewise, local participation cannot meaningfully only equal the training and hiring of Somali, much less Ethiopian workers. And hiring "100 percent Somalis" to serve the Somali Region, as Doctor Hamza suggests, cannot end interethnic turmoil or undo histories of ethnicity-based discrimination in Ethiopia. Focusing on artificial distinctions between ethnic or other politicized or racialized groups serves in fact to amplify narratives of cultural difference and exceptionalism that already undermine so many policies and political movements in the region. Accordingly, demonstrating local engagement or local accountability alone cannot solve the ethical, programmatic, and logistical challenges humanitarian interventions present.

By contrast, conceptions and enactments of humanitarianism among aid workers in eastern Ethiopia, ideas and actions detailed in future chapters of this book, contain within them not expressions of nationalism, tribalism, prejudicial bias, or partiality to one's own group, but rather, salient and popular ideas about religious charity, kinship, care, mobility, hospitality, and political unity that complicate typical renderings of clan, ethnic, religious, and partisan divides. Multivalent discourses about what it means to be humanitarian flourish within informal, interpersonal, and community spaces. And ways that aid workers there imagine the future of humanitarian response frequently undercut the potentially divisive nature of global aid, focused as it so often is on identifying and funding "local" causes and predicated on demonstrations of adequate "local" empowerment and participation.

Furthermore, in Ethiopia, efforts to empower locals and to localize aid are not isolated, but parallel and are shaped by the government's continuing efforts to decentralize federal emergency preparedness and response from the capital of Addis Ababa to regional capitals like Jigjiga. The formation of a constitutionally autonomous Somali Region within the federalist Ethiopian state decades ago has guaranteed the Somali Region a degree of independence over the hiring and implementation of relief projects. But the fact the regional government has to use monies earmarked for crisis response to fund day-to-day operations also contributes to the economic and political marginalization of Somalis vis-à-vis the federal government in Addis Ababa.

Marginalization through Relief

Despite the challenges of unity, equity, and ongoing political violence within Ethiopia, the country is frequently portrayed as a global model: a model of economic progress in Africa, a model of public health provision in a low-income country, and a model of political stability, at least within the Horn of Africa. Its governmental health extension worker program, for example, managed to deploy thousands of health-care providers to rural parts of the country and helped to improve many Ethiopians' access to basic primary health care and vaccinations.[49] In 2017, the former Minister of Health during the development of the health extension worker program, Dr. Tedros Adhanom Ghebreyesus, was appointed to a five-year term as the director general of the UN World Health Organization.

Ethiopia is also a model "developmental" state. It has achieved remarkably high and consistent economic growth rates over the last fifteen years.[50] Economies in Addis Ababa and other Ethiopian cities, from the perspective of many middle-class and upper-middle-class Ethiopians, are thriving, and infrastructural improvements to roads, internet connections, and banking continue. So despite continuing political insecurity and economic volatility in several of its regions, despite its use of authoritarianism and one-party dominance to enforce stability and silence police dissidents, Ethiopia's development remains a success story told among international elites. Ethiopia remains a top recipient of foreign aid and foreign economic investment.[51]

However, disparities between the Somali Region and the rest of Ethiopia also persist. Infant and maternal mortality rates in the Somali Region are higher than almost anywhere else in the country; people's access to and use of regulated primary health-care facilities is lower in the Somali Region than in other regions; and major investments in technology, industry, and agriculture are few and far between.[52] Although the Somali Region has been given the constitutional right to organize its own systems of governance, according to politicians and bureaucrats within the regional government, it garners little federal support to do so. And despite reforms since the ascensions of Prime Minister Abiy Ahmed and the Somali Regional State President Mustafa Muhummed Omer to power, political insecurity, population displacement, human rights abuses, and outbreaks of violence in eastern Ethiopia continue.

The Somali Region is also an artifact of what happens both within and outside its borders. "What the state means to people," Akhil Gupta and Aradhana Sharma write, and therein essentially what government *is*, and how it is constructed and bounded and given meaning, "is profoundly shaped through the routine and repetitive procedures of bureaucracies."[53] Citizens within political boundaries, as within the borders of the Somali Region, construct the state through their claims on and engagements with governmental services, according to Lahra Smith.[54] Basic health, protection, water, food, and education services for many Somalis in Ethiopia are funded in large part by global aid organizations, but then implemented through mechanisms of the regional government or in partnership with governmental agencies and politicians. In this way, citizenship and state power are realized, in part, through humanitarian response.

The Somali Region is, therefore, not just a piece of land but an idea shaped by politics and society within and outside its borders. In conversations with expatriate and non-Somali Ethiopian aid workers about Somali regional politics, during this research from 2007 until 2018, the roots of continuing violence and insecurity were described as primarily located at the sites of both ethnic and political boundaries. These were discussed as the "margins," the "borderlands," and the "dangerous," transgressive, and volatile edges of the country. But interethnic and regional conflicts and disputes were not marginal to Ethiopian politics at all. They festered in these locations and were discussed with this language, as discussed in previous chapters, because of past negotiations between the Italian, British, French, and Ethiopian empires as well as more recent postcolonial and nationalist political movements throughout the Horn of Africa. Conflicts and disputes along regional and international borders have long symbolized the strategic and violent partition of Somalis and other pastoralist groups in the Horn of Africa. As the presumed site of continuing contestation and threats of secession, these margins remain threats to the narrative of Ethiopia's successes. They are indicative of the continuing challenges of power sharing and unity at the core of the Ethiopian federalist political project.

For example, expatriate writers and foreign relief organizations reinforce divisiveness and marginalization by continuing to call the whole Somali Region "the Ogaden"—named after the largest kinship group south of Jigjiga, the *Ogaadeen*.[55] This name for the region obscures the existence of numerous and diverse ethnolinguistic, kinship, and livelihood groups residing in eastern Ethiopia, including the many Issa Somalis living north of Jigjiga, and ignores long histories of contestations between self-described Ogadeni individuals and other minority Somali groups. Calling the region "the Ogaden" also ignores the regional government's contemporary, explicit effort to unite Somalis across these clan divides— especially across the contested Issa-Ogaden divide. Signifying the whole region as "the Ogaden," erases Somali diversity and even more problematically, reinforces the idea that the region continues to be governed primarily through undemocratic, potentially nepotistic and corrupt, clan affiliations. Characterizations of clans as static, cohesive, and naturally xenophobic also presume that political boundaries and governments can neatly and legitimately determine and divide social groups and landscapes. These characterizations oversimply conflicts in the region that frequently complicate and defy kinship- and ethnic-based divisions.

The same happens with Somalis as an ethnicity-based contingent. Problems in the Somali Region of Ethiopia tend to be mapped onto Somalis' inherent character and culture, despite the flexible and complex nature of geographic, political, and ethnic divisions in the Horn of Africa. Expatriates and Ethiopians repeatedly argued to me that "the Somali People," meaning a sort of discernable and homogeneous Somali culture, as well as the territories they inhabit, are both dangerous and marginal to politics and economic investments within and to the rest of the country. Non-Somali Amharic-speaking Ethiopian relief workers repeatedly expressed their anxieties about my safety during upcoming travel or work in the Somali Region.[56] I was told of crime, violence, and starvation outside major Ethiopian cities. Hagmann and Khalif locate one source of these animosities in the 1977–1978 Ogaden war between Ethiopia and Somalia, saying, "The Ogaden war is vividly remembered and Somalis are often portrayed as Ethiopia's enemies. The Somali civil war and state collapse have enforced popular clichés of Somalis being an 'anarchic,' 'dangerous,' and essentially 'unreliable' people."[57]

My family and I were told several times we were oddities. The only people from the United States most Somalis said they had ever seen had been either

US military troops or NGO or United Nations staffers, only visiting, and always accompanied by military escorts. A Somali man in a small town near the Djibouti border once told me, laughing, "You are like a French person, not an American. Americans are always too afraid to sit here at our houses and enjoy the day." Indeed, days before, an Amharic-speaking Ethiopian employee of an NGO in Dire Dawa warned me about the rural Somali Region by saying, "You don't want to stay there. It is dangerous for foreigners"—including, presumably, himself. Another Amharic-speaking Ethiopian, a nineteen-year-old nurse from Addis Ababa who had been deployed to work at a Health Center in the Somali Region, once said about the local Somali population: "Somalis are very racist. They are a very racist people. . . . We are foreigners to them."

Several expatriates, at universities, aid organizations, and in social settings also urged me to reconsider the location of my research, asking, "Why don't you just work here with us in Addis?" "Why would you want to work there? Will you have to stay long?" They told me they worried about my safety among "fundamentalist" and "sexist" Muslim Somali men. Part of their experiences and fears of Somalis and the Somali Region were reinforced by their employers' attitudes toward work there. Everyone bemoaned the battery of security protocols, road closures, and curfews inherent to work east of the Rift Valley, and instead expressed a preference for spending time in urban, central areas of the country where they could freely walk, drive, and visit nightclubs after hours. Fears reinforced racist tropes and stereotypes about Somalis as a threatening contingent.

These concerns had real consequences. Outsiders' reluctance to spend time in the Somali Region contributed to the increasing trend of progressively hiring more Somalis and fewer other Ethiopians or expatriates for work there. One-time or short-term distributions of material goods and services continued to be commonplace, despite the need for lasting assistance and country-wide partnerships to solve health, agricultural, and economic problems. Somalis living in the rural stretches of the region critiqued the Hararge Catholic Secretariat (the eastern Ethiopian arm of Catholic Relief Services) and Oxfam–Great Britain, for example, for repeatedly driving up to small villages and dropping off bags of pharmaceuticals or unassembled wheelbarrow parts, and then quickly driving away.

The regional government was relegated to obtaining funding for many of its *basic* services—like primary health care, provision of potable water, community-based veterinary care and the like—from sporadic bursts of foreign humanitarian funding. Bureaucracies within the government that carried out these tasks were therefore shaped by the chronicity of aid work and the priorities and reporting requirements of exogenous relief organizations. The budgets and architectures of the Somali regional government remained lopsided: bureaus that could garner global humanitarian assistance and could partner with big international relief NGOs, such as the health and agricultural bureaus, were disproportionately inflated, while other governmental offices, such as the Somali Regional Education Bureau, atrophied and struggled to attract funding and human resources. Less money in the region was earmarked for disease surveillance, adult-onset chronic diseases, scientific research, or infrastructural improvements, while there continued to be ample funding for the control of infectious disease outbreaks, vaccination campaigns, and specialized therapeutic foods for the treatment of children's severe acute malnutrition.

In the last few years a handful of nongovernmental organizations—UNICEF, Save the Children, and the Norwegian Refugee Council, among a few others—have been working with Somali governmental entities to try to translate emergency funding into sustainable improvements in basic governmental services. However, these efforts were undermined by the enduring structures and limitations of foreign humanitarian aid. Case in point: during June 2018, dozens of local aid workers at several major international NGOs and UN organizations lost their jobs. Their temporary contracts were not renewed, because the droughts and political crises of the last few years had ended, at least according to outside assessments. Then following Abiy Ahmed's ouster of Abdi Iley, the former president of the Somali Region, political insecurity increased, the numbers of internally displaced persons rose dramatically, and to compound the crisis, rainfalls and agricultural harvests in parts of the region failed.[58] With their offices in Jigjiga relatively empty, aid agencies struggled to find trained staffers to manage the needs assessments and write the donor appeals required to mount a response.

The challenges of using emergency projects to fund basic social and public health services highlight not a technical failure or a failure caused by neglect, but a fundamental problem with the humanitarian system as it is currently configured. The Somali Region of Ethiopia is frequently a focus of police and military intervention, but there is little funding for public hospitals, the public university, or major infrastructural improvements like piped water. Eastern Ethiopia continues to get sporadic emergency funding from relief organizations, but lacks steady and long-term investments in the health systems, technologies, industries, and research, that might redress its vulnerability to humanitarian crises. Ethiopia remains a presumed model of development and a progressive partner for international organizations, so the recurrence of humanitarian emergencies in the margins of the country are seen to represent only exceptions, and are not indicative of or threats to the country's overall development or stability.

In sum, while Malkki's "philanthropic modes of power" produce Somali aid workers and Somali beneficiaries as both visible and knowable subjects and objects of intervention to global audiences, these modes of power also produce

Somalis and the government they run as marginal to trends happening elsewhere in Ethiopia and Africa, and undeserving of investments or credit for progress made. Somali Ethiopians are profiled as aberrations to the Ethiopia success story, once again somehow different from and less deserving than other Ethiopians, and therefore in need of external intervention. However, at the same time, Somali aid workers and institutions are powerful, and provide an important case study in the potentials of localization and decentralization. Plus, as shown in the next chapter, local staff transform relief operations, when possible, into mechanisms to save lives, minister to suffering neighbors and loved ones, generate additional local employment opportunities, rebuild governmental bureaucracies, rebuild the reputation of the government, and even begin to repair histories of violent regional politics. Somali aid workers, essentially, make being "local" and being "Somali" work.

HUMANITARIANISM IS *SAMAFAL*

Mussa, a young Somali Ethiopian man from Jigjiga who had worked for a year as a program officer at a European relief organization, described humanitarianism in the following way:

> Allah will help the one who gives. If I have even one *Birr* [Ethiopian currency], I try to give it to him, the man in need. Most people do this. It is our culture. We share what we have. That is who we are. We are the same people, all of us, the same blood. And when you do this, the people will know. People would see if I was doing this work at [the relief NGO] professionally and not living it. What you are doing and saying in the community, it has to be what you are. If I am not practicing, they will know. . . . You should not go to a hotel, but you should sleep there with them [recipients of aid], and then they will know you are serious. . . . I love to think broadly, to help all the people, not just our clan or our region. All the people. That is humanitarian aid.

Mussa is both a humanitarian aid worker and a humanitarian person. For him, these subjectivities are mutually constitutive. Humanitarianism is something, for him, realized both through the projects he implements with the aid organizations that employ him, and through his prayerfulness, religious pilgrimages, care for family, and financial contributions to neighbors in need. This chapter unpacks the pluralistic forms of humanitarianism like the ones Mussa articulates, as these shape and are shaped by the prominent trend within relief organizations to localize aid, or to deploy more and more locals to do relief work for global aid organizations, as well as the popular mandate to "decentralize" emergency response promoted by the government of Ethiopia.[1] Rather than assume that emergency responses are innately humanitarian, as the word is understood and used in English, here I examine how humanitarianism is variably socially and subjectively constructed and discussed in different spaces and moments.

Perhaps the best way to complicate and expand the meanings of the English word *humanitarianism* is to translate it into the Somali language. Humanitarianism is similar to the Somali concept of *samafal*. *Samafal* may be translated directly as "humanitarianism," but it encompasses far more than official humanitarian polices and projects. *Samafal* can mean help, charity, philanthropy, and even crisis response. *Samafal* signifies loving, reciprocal, and expected ways of responding to others' needs. Like the common English-language invocation of humanitarianism, *samafal* is both sentimental and political.

This chapter reflects the part of my work that attempts to better understand global humanitarianism through an understanding of *samafal*—as an industry, a concept, and a way of relating to others. To complicate the humanitarian studies disciplinary canon and the production of knowledge about humanitarianism within universities and aid organizations based mostly in Europe and North America, I use ethnography and the Somali language to ask again a series of basic questions: what is humanitarianism, and similarly, what is *samafal*, according to professionals employed within the aid industry? How do beneficiaries also variably perceive and shape humanitarian action and humanitarian organizations—and not just passively receive distributions of relief commodities? Additionally, how might the English term humanitarianism expand to incorporate these other ways of knowing and enacting assistance to persons facing crisis? After generations of their engagements with the global humanitarian system, Somalis have much to share about what humanitarianism is and means in the world today—within and beyond the Horn of Africa.

Samafal is a prevalent but dynamic cultural feature in Somali communities, and as such, it exists both within and outside the bounds of international relief operations. Dynamic and hybrid enactments of *samafal* have long existed in communities where foreign interventions recur, and are continually enacted through the personnel and projects supported by global aid agencies. *Samafal* happens and is discussed in relation to the financial and political structures imposed by relief organizations, but it is also distinct. Consequently, Somali policy makers and aid workers continually try to satisfy local expectations of *samafal* with limited forms of international and federal humanitarian assistance.

Multiple Humanitarianisms

Somali Ethiopian aid workers, project and policy analysts, researchers, and medical providers during and after humanitarian crises worked largely unconcerned with trends and controversies discussed at professional conferences and within the academic discipline of humanitarian response in Europe and North America.[2] Reforms within the humanitarian sector—for example, the admonition that aid organizations should "localize" and "devolve" their operations, discussed in the previous chapter of this book—had not been discussed with aid workers I met in subnational or local offices and bureaus in Jigjiga or Dire Dawa. Aid workers from the top to the bottom of the humanitarian professional ladder within eastern Ethiopia reported they received no orientations to the laws, histories, or ethical mandates their organizations adhere to and espouse on their websites, in publications, and at meetings. Conversely, no one reported any attempts by expatriate or Ethiopian leaders within locally active relief organizations to understand the expectations of humanitarian assistance or the notion of *samafal* that Somalis enacted—beyond the administration of needs assessments and surveys to describe and quantify the crises at hand.

As many scholars have pointed out, what it means for a person, organization, or intervention to be humanitarian can vary.[3] "Humanitarianism is contingent," Betsey Brada argues, it "depends on circumstance and varies from one context to another."[4] Many Somali aid workers in Ethiopia are required to speak and write in English for work, but their use of the word *humanitarian* remains limited; the words *emergencies, disasters, assistance,* and simply, *organizations* predominate instead.[5] When *humanitarian* is invoked, it does not index morality, sentiment, or international law, but rather it repeats official designations or distinct funding mechanisms within the headquarters of international relief organizations like Médecins Sans Frontières, the Norwegian Refugee Council, or UNICEF. In the Somali language used in Ethiopia, the variably and broadly defined English word *humanitarian*—or aid to someone in a crisis—most closely translates as *samafal*. Humanitarian interventions funded or organized by outside relief organizations, by contrast, are called *gargaarka bani'aadamnimada*. *Samafal* is a culturally resonant, generative, and dynamic concept among Somalis in Ethiopia. And so its linguistic, social, and political uses and effects transcend the narrow English-language usage of *humanitarian* in the region.

Humanitarianism in English and *samafal* and *bani'aadamnimada* in Somali are not unambiguous or immutable labels, but rather represent unstable social categories that must be discursively and strategically negotiated as they variably apply to individuals, organizations, policies, and interventions. These terms exist in what Barchiesi calls a "contested field of signification"[6] as, on the one hand donors, governments, politicians, NGOs, and expatriate aid workers promote and implement aid projects, but on the other, as beneficiaries and local aid workers also enact and express their own expectations of what makes assistance humanitarian. In other words, what it means to do humanitarian work and to be the subject of humanitarian intervention are socially and discursively constructed and contested in particular places and situations. Signs adorning relief NGOs in Jigjiga city often say *xafiiska samafal* or the humanitarian bureau, rather than the more formal *xafiiska bani'aadamnimada*, which would refer more narrowly to the international relief organizations distributing aid. Billboards and websites for local organizations advertise that relief agencies do *samafal* and are not only edifices or material instantiations of *bani'aadamnimada*.

Furthermore, ideas and principles fundamental to global humanitarian action founded and governed predominantly through the International Committee of the Red Cross and other large global relief organizations are not necessarily helpful or appropriate to people on the ground. As Mussa articulated at the beginning of this chapter, "being the one who gives" means the aid worker, the health-care provider, should be present with people, or in his words, "should sleep there with them, and then they will know you are serious." "That is humanitarian aid," he said to me emphatically, clapping his hands together, as if beginning to pray. Another relief worker from a different organization in Jigjiga said similarly, "Sometimes the people won't trust you until you spend time with them. You have to go to the field and see them."

A midcareer staffer named Fatimah at a European relief organization based in Jigjiga said, "When we [at the international NGO] say 'human rights' etcetera I have my own way of understanding what this means and the community needs this understanding the most. We [at the NGO] say 'right to life,' 'right to health' but you see a person drinking filthy water out of a puddle or out of ruts in the road where vehicles drive. For example at [the NGO] I help deliver soap to people because there is a 'right to soap.' That is in our reports. But here people are drinking filthy water every day, so in a way, what can just soap do to help them? This seems a bit crazy."

On the other hand, later in the same conversation Fatimah said, in answer to a question I posed about the difference between the work her relief NGO does and the work her family does to help people during crises in her hometown, "NGO work is the same as community humanitarian action really. It's to save a life . . . [it] should not be opposite or different from our religion and culture." She continued a few minutes later, "Rich people help the poor. They evacuate them, give them food, money, shelter, whatever they need. People help their relatives and neighbors first. And religion says you must help the poor. When your life is safe, so you can give to others since you are safe. Helping each other is how we are." Diverse forms and simultaneous enactments of *samafal* as humanitarianism are not identical, but also not incommensurate.

Islamic Charity (*Sadaqad*)

It is not righteousness
That ye turn your faces
Towards East or West;
But it is righteousness—
To believe in God
And the Last Day,
And the Angels,
And the Book,
And the Messengers;
To spend of your substance,
Out of love for Him,
For your kin,
For orphans,
For the needy,
For the wayfarer,
For those who ask,
And for the ransom of slaves;
To be steadfast in prayer,
And practice regular charity;
To fulfill the contracts
Which ye have made;
And to be firm and patient,
In pain (or suffering)
And adversity,
And throughout
All periods of panic.
Such are the people of truth, the God-fearing.[7]

One of the five pillars of Islam, as described in the Qur'anic verse above (Part 2, Section 22, Verse 177), is the *zakat* (sometimes alternatively spelled *zakah*). The *zakat* is an obligatory contribution to benefit persons in greatest need of help, mandated by God. The vast majority of Somalis in eastern Ethiopia share a Sunni Shafi'ite Islamic tradition, and central to most of their religious tradition includes regular charitable gifts to people in need.

"Charity begins at home," Asha, a project officer at a relief NGO in Jigjiga, said in English, clasping her hands neatly in her lap and smiling at me as we spoke. She continued, "A drought came a couple of years ago, and cattle and other livestock, everything died. People then had to move to the big towns and search for their relatives. They would go to the towns that were less affected by the drought, where people had more money, and where they knew they had relatives who could assist them. That is charity, *sadaqad*," she said. "That is how we do it here."

Aden, at the UN relief agency headquartered in Jigjiga, introduced in the early pages of this book, has worked for fifteen years to connect various religious leaders concerned with health care to the clinicians and policy makers who organize health interventions. Religious leaders, he argued, want to be part of humanitarian assistance—they see it as their "collective duty." From about 2000 to 2005, as the global Polio Eradication Initiative redoubled its efforts to quell the sudden rise in polio incidence across the continent from Northern Nigeria all the way eastward to the Somali Region of Ethiopia, Somalia, and Somaliland, Aden helped international NGOs wanting to vaccinate children meet with religious leaders who could help increase the public's understanding and participation. But once these networks of leaders were engaged for polio, he continued to organize and deploy them to address additional health concerns like measles and even the more contentious cause of improving women's access to family planning services.

"People really love it," he said, smiling at me broadly, and clarified he meant that beneficiary communities appreciated the UN's investment in their local religious leaders, but also, expatriate leaders at the UN office in Addis Ababa appreciated Somalis' help translating and adapting the organization's policies to meet local expectations.

Aden was adamant there was even more that could be done to integrate Islamic notions and practices of *sadaqad* with externally funded and organized forms of humanitarianism (*bani'aadamnimada*)—it is something he has discussed many times with colleagues from work. "*Zakat* is money that comes directly out of people's income, based on their income level, as well as money that should be given as charity from every single person or Muslim, no matter their level of income. For example, even after eating, you should give a portion of your food as a ration to the poor." He continued, "Local *zakats* that used to exist in the old time helped take care of the most vulnerable people." The ideas of the *zakat, sadaqad, samafal,* and *gargaarka bani'aadamnimada,* among Somali aid workers and health-care providers in Ethiopia, he opined, are essentially "the same": united by the tenet to provide aid to those in greatest need, and to do so in what he called, a "spirit of volunteerism" and "with love." Rather than a tax enforced by the state, Aden noted the affective and personal nature of this kind of *samafal.*

The *zakat* in particular contrasts with implicit relations of giving within many global humanitarian responses in which, typically, resources are transferred unilaterally from wealthy donors to beneficiaries in need. Instead, the *zakat* models an act of giving that more broadly redistributes resources within communities, effectively evening out natural and economic resources from God among all persons—ensuring those in greatest need receive the most, rather than a portion equal to others. The *zakat* also simultaneously represents a gift from God, a gift to God, and a duty in service to God. Thus it complicates the binaries and unequal power relations inherent to conceptions of donors versus beneficiaries.[8]

More generally, what Aden and others called in English "need-based aid" pervaded discussions about how best to enact *samafal* and the *sadaqad* within homes, social gatherings, and even informal banter within the offices and vehicles of governmental and nongovernmental aid organizations. What Somali aid workers in Ethiopia signified in English as "need-based aid" differed from what they called "per capita aid" or equal distributions of aid. The former reflected for them the structure of Qur'anic teachings and Islamic ethics, but the latter, by comparison, guided most of the federal government's efforts to promote the decentralization of funding to regional and local bureaus. Per capita aid was seen as unfair, because needs were never distributed equally among people. People's approvals of need-based humanitarian aid and critiques of decentralization thus reflected two things: first, the desire for *bani'aadamnimada* to redistribute resources from those with wealth or steady incomes to those who are in crisis or are in the greatest need of resources in the immediate term; and second, the use of *bani'aadamnimada* to augment the common and communal sharing of knowledge, resources, and money within extended families and residential neighborhoods.[9]

Aid workers like Aden, Asha, and Mussa proffered a bifurcated, pluralistic enactment of *samafal* through on the one hand their religious practices and *sadaqad,* but also concurrently through their secular work in the humanitarian sector and their creative imaginations with me of a better, more expansive form of the *zakat* religious charity through *gargaarka bani'aadamnimada.* For Mussa, quoted at the beginning of this chapter, his professional work was not separate from his mandate from God to be charitable and generous, but rather animated and motivated by it. Thus discourses encouraging the localization of humanitarian assistance and efforts to localize, devolve, and decentralize power from the highest echelons of the aid industry out to beneficiary countries and communities augment local patterns and practices of religious charity. Aid workers' appropriations of humanitarian responses to fulfill collective and individual obligations to provide religious charity shaped their ongoing humanitarian work as well as their religious practice, care, sharing, and hospitality outside work.

Samafal Is Metaphysical

Samafal represents a pluralistic response to the wide range of intertwined crises people in the Somali Region face—individual, corporeal, collective, and spiritual. In addition, disease, conflict, forced displacement, and marginalization also have metaphysical effects and expressions.[10] Somalis' notion of health (*caafimaad*), for example, was seen as ultimately dependent on the will of God, but also manifested in perceived vulnerabilities to possession by malevolent, invisible demons (or jinns). Most people I knew in eastern Ethiopia, at some point in their life, experienced possession or attack by jinns (in Somali *jin, jinni*, or the plural, *jinniyo*), and spirit possession had serious emotional and corporeal effects.[11] Spiritual afflictions like demonic possession were typically diagnosed and treated by religious leaders who are able to discern the etiology of a given presentation, then dominate and dispel the jinn through invocation of the Holy Qur'an and words of the Prophet Mohammad.[12] Somali aid workers were also regularly consulted about spiritual afflictions. Persons presenting to health-care providers during relief operations complained of jinns causing acute paralysis, seizure disorders, psychological disturbances, hallucinations, infertility, nonspecific joint or bone pain, edema (or swelling of the extremities), or recurrent and otherwise inexplicable headaches.

Jinns lived under houses and underground—they could become angry and attack humans when boiling water is spilled, someone stands on top of them, or heavy objects are dropped. They also lived in the giant termite mounds and anthills that dotted landscapes throughout the Horn of Africa, and could escape at night and attack humans if they walk too close. Jinns also hid in dark, dank latrines, so numerous rituals exist to protect people or conceal their presence as they urinate, defecate, and bathe inside. Women, consequently, often tried to avoid using latrines altogether, especially in remote areas when they can find privacy out of doors.

Jinns entered human bodies primarily through their orifices and were attracted to people's stress, jealousy, bodily fluids (as with menstrual blood or *caado*), khat highs (*mirqaan*), and disobedience to God. Jinns could enter and wreak havoc in women's wombs and kill fetuses, so protection from malevolent jinns was crucial for women's health and fertility. Anxieties about the activities of jinns increased during ceremonial rites like genital cutting, during romantic dating, marriage, childbirth and postpartum recovery, career or educational advancements, and during women's struggles to conceive a child. Jinn possession was also associated with moments of social anxiety.[13] Political upheavals, stressful migrations, droughts, floods, losses of livestock, and other humanitarian crises weakened people's abilities to resist or dispel the jinns in their environment. In general, individual bodily possession was seen as both a consequence and expression of distress and crisis outside the physical body.

Mullahs and sheikhs—the local leaders of mosques—performed most Qur'anic healing rituals. Qur'anic healing required someone to either exorcise or pacify the demon, usually through incantation of the words of the Prophet Mohammad or specified verses of the Holy Qur'an, and then provide a modicum of protection like an amulet as the person recovered. Qur'anic healers were typically holy and trusted men; they drew on their relationship with God and their ability to comfort and minister to individuals. Sometimes, these religious healers realized a person's illness was not due to a spiritual affliction or jinn possession, but should instead be treated through the application of various herbal remedies or through consultation with a biomedical doctor. Despite common recognition of ultimate divine causality, mullahs frequently recommended consultations with different practitioners, including aid workers and licensed health-care workers, for the treatment of problems that might potentially fall outside their purview.

Thus consultations with religious leaders and Qur'anic healing rituals offered more than just treatment of singular pathologies or dysfunctions to individual bodies, and were tailored to the individual's and family's circumstances, rather than being an offering of prayers for unidirectional divine intervention. In ceremonies I witnessed and discussed with people, health problems were diagnosed and treated according to complex but specific formulas outlined in various hadiths (*kitab* or *xadiis*), or small Qur'anic manuals, as well as the characteristics, symptoms, and conversations between the healer, other healers or clinicians, the patient, and the patient's loved ones. Healing required understanding the symptoms at hand, and also required understanding the person, their particular situation, and their physical, social, and emotional needs and verbal expressions of distress. Relationships of trust and care between healers, patients, and families were vital.

Sara's story provides a case in point. When I met her, Sara was a young mother of four children and wife of the local mullah in a small town northeast of Jigjiga.

For several years she had suffered from a seizure disorder. At first she feared her seizures were the fault of a jinn, but after several healing ceremonies and consultations with multiple healers and two nurses on a UNICEF-funded mobile team temporarily deployed to her home community, she became convinced her sickness was from epilepsy (*suuxdin*), a disease of the brain, ultimately in the hands of God.

> I know that [I have] epilepsy. When God brings something, we human beings call it various names, but God does not call it such names. I have been going to [biomedical] doctors and religious healers have checked the book [the Holy Qur'an]. They all have said the signs and symptoms say that this epilepsy disease comes from heaven. . . . The book [a hadith] recommended many medicines, and the Qur'an was recited over me, many things were written for me [scriptures and prayers] from the holy book.
>
> Surely to God it was as recently as three or four months ago when I also went somewhere called Midda. An Oromo Mullah has done many things for me there, this Mullah from Midda. For our people there is no other treatment for epilepsy but the Mullah's treatment. Surely to God the real experts in epilepsy do not stay around here, except those that read the Holy Qur'an over me, there is no other alternative than what these Mullahs do.

A few months before Sara visited the Mullah of Midda with her husband, and a few months before the UNICEF mobile team arrived, she visited a public hospital in Dire Dawa on the advice of several religious leaders and family members. She continued,

> So the doctor in [the hospital] said to me, "Here are pills for epilepsy." And I took them and felt better. But when it [the medicine] goes out of my body, [the seizures] start back like before. . . . And I now have a shortage of pills. . . . The shortages of pills are because I am coming from a distant place and my house is here.
>
> When you are ordered to take these [pills] for a number of months, the doctor examines you, then he says to you, "Take for two months or three months." When you finish that amount, you know, you are not always near to the doctor. But if he was nearby, every time you could you go to him because you would be near. But when you are here, you are responsible for taking care of your home, you cannot be outside it. That has caused the problem with me . . . and the hospital is far from me. The doctor gives me pills only for a limited period of time.

While Sara's description of her epilepsy revealed a pluralistic understanding of medicine and healing, at the same time she also highlighted her lack of adequate health services.[14] Sara's problems were simultaneously metaphysical, biomedical, and structural. They were long-lasting, and not solvable through six-month relief operations or distributions of limited supplies of medications. The mobile team encouraged her to visit a hospital, and could provide a paper referral, but otherwise, given the narrow scope and short timeline of the UNICEF program, they could not help.

To provide another example, many Somali women I knew struggled with infertility—and many times, they felt strongly that attacks or possessions by a jinn were to blame. Many sought Qur'anic healing to restore their womb to health. Still, several of these same women also suspected they had some sort of physical malady caused by past infections in their reproductive organs, injuries, overexertion after delivering a child, or a miscarriage. Yet women were reluctant to tell all this to traveling mobile teams of male nurses or young, inexperienced health extension workers in rural health posts nearby. Local mullahs, instead, were sometimes seen as the closest, easiest, and most trusted resource on matters of reproductive health.

Awli—a well-respected local mullah and Qur'anic healing practitioner living in another community northeast of Jigjiga—explained that exorcising and dispelling jinns, plus occasional regimens of antibiotic medications, were the most effective treatments for women's infertility. He provided both. During an explanation of diagnostic procedures using various hadiths, he said, "For infertility, I sometimes also prescribe pills (*kiniini*)."

Which pills?' I asked, surprised at first that he said this.

"Ampicillin (*ambasaliinka*). One times three," he stated plainly, meaning, one pill three times per day "for seven days, with the five hundred milligrams of ampicillin capsule means twenty-one pieces," he calculated quickly on his fingers.

Although Awli was not trained or certified in biomedicine or pharmacology, he regularly purchased medications from unlicensed pharmacies and small shops nearby. He did so, he said, because he wanted "to help women" when mobile team nurses were not around, or when women demurred travel or treatment in local clinics. He tried to ensure that he both rid women's reproductive organs of jinns and when possible, rid their bodies of what he called "harmful germs." But Awli's practice was, according to other women in the same town, inadequate. Two of them whispered to me, not wanting to impugn his reputation on matters of spiritual afflictions, that they do not trust his ability to correctly diagnose and treat their bodily infections. These women preferred to seek care from "doctors" (*dhakhaatiirta*)—especially expatriate clinicians with relief organizations headquartered outside Ethiopia, staffing clinics in refugee camps or mobile teams.

These women's uncertainties about Awli's medicine and Sara's struggle for relief from her seizures both demonstrate the pluralistic ways in which suffering was understood and ameliorated, but also highlight a desperate need in many remote communities for reliable and continuing health care, instead of one-time distributions of materials or short-term provision of clinical care. Illnesses existed and were treated both within and outside the metaphysical realm; prayers or pills alone, in both of these cases, were inadequate. In general, illnesses persons presented with during relief operations—everything from epilepsy to infertility—were treated through multiple and pluralistic treatment strategies.[15] With only limited supplies and scopes of work, relief workers worked within these ambiguous and pluralistic popular health cultures to try to ease suffering and at least temporarily fill enormous gaps in basic health care.

Samafal Means Treating People like Family

Don't say the man was closer in blood relation to me, but say that he was good to me—people will not forget that.

popular Somali proverb

The global news media, Hollywood movies, politicians in the region, and even some social scientists portray Somalis as stubbornly loyal to their own clan (*qabiil* or *reer*)—even to the point of xenophobia.[16] Others have long objected to this framing and define Somali kinship structures through other means.[17] Abdi Ismail Samatar for one, derides the way "clan" has been linguistically and broadly appropriated, calling it instead "an anthropological fossil." "Somali identity and tradition" he claims, "were always a living and ongoing process resulting from multiple interactive forces."[18]

At the same time, socially constructed and politically contingent definitions of *qabiil* and *reer* in the Somali Region of Ethiopia continued to shape the local targeting and distribution of international aid as well as people's migrations for and control over natural resources and trade.[19] Family networks of support were realized or strengthened through mechanisms of assistance and the redistribution of wealth in times of crisis.[20] Doctor Hamza, a senior leader at an international NGO office in Jigjiga and former head of a Somali Regional Bureau, explained it this way in English: "*Jilibka* [the subclan], the family, they are always helping each other. If there is a drought many pastoralists will lose animals so the traditional sharing and coping mechanisms are weakened, but they do still exist and are important to support and regain. Family helps family," he said in English.

Doctor Hamza lived in a modest but sprawling compound in Jigjiga, and at the time of our first interview, he was housing six people in addition to his wife, some of his children, and several grandchildren. People like him, who have been successful in their career and have worked for NGOs or UN organizations that pay relatively high salaries, typically support numerous family members and the children of their closest friends, especially subclan members from their natal communities, sometimes by giving cash amounts or sponsorships for students in high school or at a university. Doctor Hamza has purchased cows and goats as milking animals for several family members outside the city. And that "helps to provide for our whole family." He has five brothers who communally own and manage a large herd of cattle, send cash to each other at different times, and share bank accounts, vehicles, and houses. "We put all the children in the family through school," he explained.

A much younger program officer at another NGO similarly said to me once in conversation, as we watched a distribution of vaccinations at a rural field site near Jigjiga: "The people are connected to each other. If one family loses livestock, the rest of the family will gather livestock to donate to that person. If someone dies, it is common for people to collect money for the mother, and then also give her social and psychological support. They will tell her stories about this happening before. People also share food items in drought times. INGOs try to help local people to enhance these coping strategies, but the INGOs really have their own approach, their own specific focus, like [providing] medicine at the health facility level."

According to relief agencies and beneficiaries in the Somali Region, among the most successful and notable humanitarian relief programs are the aforementioned Mobile Health and Nutrition Teams—organized through the Somali Regional Health Bureau and funded with donations from several relief organizations. Mobile teams have been active in the Somali Region since 2005 during a measles and polio outbreak. Most mobile teams are designed to provide vaccinations, a few essential medications, water treatment equipment, referrals to higher medical facilities, supplies of ready-to-eat fortified BP-5 biscuits, and therapeutic PlumpyNut peanut paste.[21] A majority of mobile teams in the Somali Region in the last ten years have been funded by UNICEF, which prioritizes programs to save the lives and improve the health of infants, children under five years of age, and their pregnant and lactating mothers. Typically, communities qualify for mobile team visits based on local rates of acute malnutrition in children under five years or reported outbreaks of infectious disease in the local population—but even so, most humanitarian relief targeted the lives and health of young children and their mothers and not the entire community. To many persons accustomed to traditions of *samafal* focused on providing aid to persons in greatest need, these demographic restrictions seemed nonsensical. Nurses and health extension workers on the mobile teams, consequently, had to repeatedly negotiate and explain the rationale behind such limited beneficiary groups and limited material donations to the numerous sick and impoverished men and older women lined up to receive care—people who otherwise lacked access to medical care and medicines.

One afternoon in the final weeks of that year's *jilaal*, or its longest dry season, I traveled again with one of these UNICEF-funded mobile teams to visit the small town of Elahelay near the eastern edge of the Somali Region where I have spent time on and off since 2008. There had been an outbreak of diarrheal disease in the last three months, and the team was in the middle of a six-month rotation visiting once per week. On this particular day, everyone knew the mobile team was coming ahead of time, and so several families had lined up outside in a court-yard near the small, two-room health post.

A mother, placing her children in the care of another woman nearby, quietly approached the intake desk and estimated her age was something like forty years. She reported she had been coughing for a very long time, down in her chest, and she was having night sweats. The two mobile team nurses whispered discretely to each other in English and then in Somali ordered her to get better diagnostic tests at a hospital in Hargeisa, Somaliland or Dire Dawa. They signed a slip of paper to ensure the referral was official, and recorded the interaction in their notebook.

Next, a man who looked a bit older, maybe fifty years old, leaning on a cane, pushed his way past three mothers and their children at the entrance to the clinic, shouting, and letting everyone around know he needed to be seen by the doctors, but that too many women and children were in line. The two nurses, taken aback for a moment, nodded in his direction, and said firmly that they would check him out next. After a few more minutes, one of the nurses led the man into the back room, presumably gave him a brief exam, and then, a few minutes later, walked back through the clinic with him, arm in arm, moving him through the now mumbling crowd of women and children. As he again passed by the busy intake table, the man paused and said directly to me: "*Ma jirto dawo oday ah*," or there is no medicine for old men.

At three o'clock in the afternoon, as I helped the two nurses clean the clinic space, I asked about this man's comment—what the two nurses thought of it. One said, "He only had arthritis! We gave him some ibuprofen but I do not think he was happy."

Then, putting aside their exasperation with this older man, the two nurses did what I had already seen them do on three previous trips to this town. They unearthed a box of BP-5 biscuits from the back of their truck, located a few packets of PlumpyNut, and headed by vehicle to the other side of the community, to a compound with four small structures: a kitchen, an open shade, and two living spaces. As they gingerly hopped out of the truck, with their stethoscopes still around their necks and their arms packed with boxes, they quietly entered the compound. A woman about thirty years old rested in the shade, unable to rise to greet us, because her legs did not work. She dragged herself forward a bit, kissed all of our hands, and asked us to sit. The two nurses proceeded to ask her questions about her health, and about her appeal for help from the district governmental office. They listened to her lungs, looked at her feet, covered as they were in sores, and asked if they could leave with her some extra bandages. Finally, before leaving, they quietly handed over boxes of BP-5 biscuits and PlumpyNut, and promised to return soon.

There were at least sixty individual clinical and interpersonal encounters on this particular day in Elahelay. It was a day like just about every other working day for the mobile team. But notably, the distribution of material goods and medical services did not exactly follow the contours of the agency funding humanitarian aid in the area. The donations and encounters with the older man and the woman struggling with a debilitating disability fell outside the purview of UNICEF's work in Elahelay. These patients were not suffering from the diarrheal disease that inspired the intervention, nor were they young mothers or children. However, the nurses on the mobile team bent the official criteria for inclusion in the mobile team intervention, and made sure these patients also felt cared for.

In addition, the mobile teams often worked late into the afternoon and slept overnight in the local health posts wherever they happen to be working. Before dinner, they typically shared evening khat and attended evening prayers with community members. When I visited five years later, I learned one of the mobile team members—originally from over two hundred miles farther south in the region—had married a women from Elahelay, and now the couple has three children. Even very literally, kinship developed from interventions to provide medical care.

Beyond this, the recipients of this mobile team project and others I witnessed throughout the region appreciated explicit efforts to forge meaningful social relationships during the teams' brief stints deployed in remote locations. In the words of a beneficiary of the same mobile team intervention from a nearby town, "People loved the mobile team. And they [people here] believed in those pills, during the six months they were serving here. The people all of them they focused on the mobile team, they liked them personally, they took the [medical] services from them and they believed that their medicine was high quality medicine. The people even said that these pills were not sent by Ethiopia, they were surely sent by Allah! If I was the chairman of this *kebele* or the *woreda* I would recommend this mobile team to serve the community as much and as long as possible."

Humanitarian responders like UNICEF's mobile team of nurses and health extension workers, despite being far from their homes, despite the requirement that they incessantly travel between community sites and never spend much time in one community, and despite the fact they are typically deployed only for a few months at a time in any one area, acted intentionally to create relationships of care that extended beyond the walls of clinical spaces. Their relationships of trust in this community and others were neither accidental nor products of a shared language or shared ethnic heritage alone. Mobile teams, across the Somali Region, are interpolated into communities and families. They share food, khat, prayers, and even intermarry. And the mobile teams are, consequent of this, remarkably popular and beloved by Somalis in just about every place they work. In other words, one important way in which these aid workers make inroads with patient populations is through *samafal* and not just *bani'aadamnimada*—the many ways they care for others in need, above and beyond the limitations of particular projects.

"Moving Out Widens the Heart"

A young and ambitious man I call Bashiir, who works for a European relief agency headquartered in Jigjiga, replied to my question about if the incessant travel required by his job bothered him, "No. Not at all." He continued, "We are pastoralists. We were born to move, movement, migrations. You see," and with this, using his hands and showing movement across the table between us, "the camel tender moves from here to here regardless of the territories and boundaries. Moving is learning. You're exposed to culture. Indigenous knowledges. Moving out widens the heart."

Somalis are known for incessant travel and seasonal migrations for herding, religious practice, trade, and work.[22] And contingent and geographically dispersed kinship structures are vital to nomadic and seminomadic livelihoods in the Horn of Africa.[23] Like the mobile team of nurses deployed for six months in an emergency, there are additional nomads in the Somali Region—the legions of local aid workers and health-care providers funded by relief organizations.[24]

The chronicity, rhythms, and seasonality of these nomadic workers' frequent travel back and forth between rural and urban locations resonate among many Somalis who have been raised among nomadic pastoralists and traders always on the move.

Everywhere I traveled in the Somali Region I encountered a burgeoning cohort of young aid workers—men as well as women—moving around the region for education, training, and employment opportunities. Wherever they traveled, they slept in the homes of extended family members or the close friends of their parents and uncles and aunts. Even when they stayed in small hotels, they spent most of their time eating and praying with relatives and old friends living nearby. Mohammed, a program officer at another relief agency recounted: "There is high population mobility here, there are mobile phones, there is social media, and the like. People move around a lot and they are familiar with many different people. Traveling is good. Trying new things is good. . . . I like to pass through different zones [in Ethiopia] and it's good. For example if you are on a field trip passing through kebeles you should stop and spend five or ten minutes in a place. And you can ask them if there is anything they need."

Somalis' dependence on and love for mobility did not just enable the kinds of job opportunities provided by the relief industry. Mobility "widens the heart." It was a moral experience to travel, meet new people, experience new ways of life, and provide assistance wherever and however you can. Mohammed, from Jigjiga, continued, "One day . . . they said 'you are passing through and providing for another community—but don't pass us. We have needs too!' At that time we [the relief NGO] were only targeting one side [of the district boundary] and didn't realize others' needs. Then we could come back, get all the information we needed, and prepare for future projects."

Women, in my experience, loved to travel too. Nimo, a female project officer in a European relief agency, told me once that "there is a perception of Somali women that they are conservative and do not want to travel and work outside the home." Another woman named Mona nodded nearby, saying, "Yes! Indeed there is a perception but it is not the culture that is constraining." It is not cultural, they both insisted, but rather in Nimo's words, "practically how can you work there when there is so much hardship? Where can a woman use the toilet? Where can you sleep?" Nimo explained, "We are not divided from men. We have even been left with a situation in the field where we had only one room to share with other male staffers!" Both women were laughing at this, Mona encouraging her to keep talking, "We were willing to share the one open room, but the men decided to sleep outside the building, and let us sleep inside." This helped Nimo carry on with a modicum of decorum, and she said again how glad she was to have the opportunity to work in humanitarian relief. "I love to work here. Even there in the field." When I asked specifically what motivates them to do this kind of work Mona chimed in with enthusiasm, "Number one, I get more money. Two, I am building my own experience and education, and three, I have the potential to travel to different places, different countries even maybe. In the government you stay in one office, one clinic, one duty, but with NGOs you can get different experiences."

Many relief operations require front-line workers travel across contested regional boundaries, in and out of conflict zones, and to camps and settlements of displaced persons from all over the Horn of Africa. Being able to travel, to meet new people across these boundaries, and also to then advocate for people in need, were all vital and potentially transformative for local aid workers there. Mobility instantiated a world—articulated and enacted by so many in eastern Ethiopia, inside the aid industry and outside it—free of borders, camps, and geographic enclosures. "Moving out widens the heart," and in so doing, it contains the potential to emancipate individuals from being trapped inside or limited by artificial, political enclosures.

Samafal Means Interdependence

Doctor Hamza defined *samafal* for me through the following story: "When I was a child in the bush, some families were broke—they had no camels, no money. Nothing at all. At that time, early in the morning, our family would milk a camel, and then we would bring a container of that milk to the person's house. And the container would stay there at their house, in the front of their house [he gestured, demonstrating a container shape]. Many people would contribute milk to the same container, filling it up. That family would then have more than enough milk, you see, it would be totally full, and then they would be able to share the milk from the full container with others. We share. That is how we have enough."

On another occasion, during a conversation about his extended family's move from a rural village to the bustling city of Jigjiga, Farah, a program officer at a UN relief agency said, "If you have five camels for example, you will distribute each of the five camels to your family members or other people who need them. People share and redistribute resources during crises to make sure everyone has enough to survive." Being "blessed," he said later, "means being able to give."

Most of the local aid workers I spoke to for this research had themselves survived multiple crises, and most of their families had at some point, often repeatedly, received humanitarian assistance—a food ration, supplies of clean water, schooling in a refugee camp, and so on. Many spoke of being inspired by the professionalism and competence of Somali, Ethiopian, and expatriate clinical providers during relief operations and inside refugee camps. Of course, aid was also widely critiqued by locals for its late arrival, its inadequacy, and the way it was manipulated by politicians. But even so, the life stories of these staffers very often involved the phrases, "when my parents fled with me to . . ." and "I was a refugee once, too" and "my God we had nothing then." Most Somali aid workers in Ethiopia have witnessed, time and again, the miracles of lives saved through various forms of humanitarian engagement—children recovered from cholera in a UNICEF-funded hospital or childbirth attended by a woman trained and supplied by Médecins Sans Frontières. These life experiences have changed them; these are neither trite nor insignificant observations.

A man I call Jira, the head of a regional UN relief office, with white and grey spots in his beard said, "When I was a child I knew so many children who were so malnourished. Children who died. Child deaths." He grew up in the 1970s and 1980s, as most of the country suffered repeated conflicts, forced displacements, and famines. "But now child deaths are rare," he said, hands raised to heaven. Then he wove together his own personal and professional trajectory, continuing, "Of course, this is the contribution of donors, government partners, and so on, but we [as aid workers]," he placed his hands on his own chest, "we also contributed to this. Regardless of the salary I'm getting, this is important work. . . . I was born in a rural area, and I knew many children who died, including my friends. . . . Families used to share relief food, and this is what kept me alive back when I was in high school. It was two years we were depending on that food." Jira loves the fact he can, as he put it, "give back" and "continue to give" through his work in humanitarian assistance.

People like Jira enjoyed talking about past personal inspirations for their work, but they also loved to talk about the remarkable benefits work in the humanitarian industry offered them and their families. One thing aid workers rarely shied away from was matter-of-factly discussing the relatively high salaries they made, especially compared to government bureaucrats and their peers working in local commerce, health care, and nomadic pastoralism. But everyone who mentioned to me the high salaries said, without prompting, that the value of high salaries is it means you can give more to others. For example, Farah said, "I love the salary, with which you can help yourself and help others." Similarly, Asha said she loved making a "good salary" because she could contribute so much to her family at home, and pay her parents and extended family members back for helping her get through school. "When you're rich," she clarified later in English, that she meant when you are making a "good salary," "your life is safe, so you can give to others since you are safe."

Generous hospitality is a core Somali value, and my family and I have been the lucky recipients of numerous people's graciousness.[25] In every home we

FIGURE 5. Inside a typical Somali home in the Somali Region of Ethiopia. Photograph by David Machledt.

entered, whether for research or just socializing, my children, husband, and I were showered with drinks and food and drawn into enjoyable conversations. And we were no exception. I have witnessed all sorts of people hosted like this: Somali family members returning home from the diaspora, impoverished herders who have unexpectedly met with trouble, elders on pilgrimages traveling through town on foot, and families merely traveling through the area for visiting and pleasure.

Expectations and acts of hospitality help Somalis bridge the vast distances between trading centers and towns in the harsh arid environment of the Horn of Africa. And land sharing and flexible restrictions on access to natural resources like grazing land and water help people survive a changing climate, desertifying landscapes, and volatile agricultural economies. "Rejecting or ignoring a visitor," a refugee, a stranger, or any person in need risks being "cursed," Yoonis, a local community leader explained to me, "and potentially, if the violation is serious, the family will have to pay blood money (*diya*) or livestock to the other person in compensation," just as they would have to do for violent crimes. Being inhospitable, Yoonis went on, "is a total insult; it is . . . like violating a law. *Ugaas* [traditional leaders outside government administrators] set standards for hospitality and enforce these traditions. Hospitality is the fundamental, core ethic here."

This ethical system affects the humanitarian industry as well. The localization and decentralization of relief work with its focus on training and hiring ever more local staffs and deploying them throughout the region—often on mobile, dynamic projects—requires hospitality on the part of hosting family members, friends, and recipient communities. Hospitality is therefore necessary to accomplish the logistics and travel humanitarian interventions require, but it is also an expected and sentimental aspect of *samafal*.

Samafal as Care

In addition to the generosity and hospitality of aid workers, the humanitarian industry in eastern Ethiopia is populated with countless affable characters. For example, Abshir is one of Aden's best friends and colleagues. He is joyful, insatiably curious, and when not at his desk, can usually be found with arms around his friends' and colleagues' shoulders, teasing them, making small talk around the office, and talking about his children's latest achievements. Abshir is a program officer and for the last fourteen years, with Aden, he has helped organize and staff dozens of mobile teams—including the one to Elahelay.

In 2012 and 2013, reports of rising rates of severe acute malnutrition in children and outbreaks of diarrheal disease increased, especially in areas southeast of Jigjiga populated mostly by members of the Marehan *qabiil.* Abshir described these places to me in 2014 as "perhaps the most marginal and remote in the country," due in part to the fact that Siad Barre, the former dictatorial leader of Somalia who went to war with Ethiopia in 1977, was born and raised there. Early on, during the implementation of a mobile team operation, Abshir expressed frustration at the reluctance among his Ogadeni colleagues to travel and stay overnight in Marehan-dominated territory. Like most of the mobile team nurses, Abshir is Ogadeni, and he told me, "I understand how they feel about us Ogaden people coming down from all the way here in Jigjiga." His staffers were afraid to stay the night, and begged him to let them drive until after curfew and sleep in the Ogaden city of Gode instead. But there had been no outbursts of violence and no threats against the nurses, so Abshir required them to stay. Then, gradually, over time, he said, first following a successful polio vaccination campaign, and then after another clinical response to measles along the border, misgivings between the aid workers and the patient population noticeably relaxed.

Abshir concluded his story, saying, "People"—meaning aid workers and health-care providers—"need to go. Just go! Be present there." With his index finger pointing to his eye, he repeated to me insistently, "They must look the other people in the eye. . . . It makes a difference. It makes a big difference." In other words, being "present" with people can facilitate successful interventions. It can help build new relationships of trust, and in so doing, undercut fears, animosities, histories of violence, and political insecurity.[26]

Samafal, likewise, saves individual lives and attends to suffering bodies, and yet it does so by building reciprocal relationships of care across generations, geographic expanses, and even political and social divides. Annemarie Mol states, "In practice, after all, the activities categorized as 'care' and 'cure' overlap."[27] Both the treatment of a disease, for example, and the care required to comfort and heal the afflicted, encompass multiple ways of attending to suffering. Mol and her colleagues further suggest that the most challenging aspect of centering practices of care might not be in, "*which* words to use, but dealing with the limits of using *words* at all. Care, after all, is not necessarily verbal."[28] It is enacted and felt. The verb "to care" in English and *daryeel* in Somali both index care *for* and care *about* someone.[29] Health care, for example, in Somali, may be translated as, *daryeel caafimaadka* and to provide caregiving services to a patient is *daryeelka bukaanka.* To provide care to someone and to care for their well-being are both articulated as *si loo daryeelo.* Both parts of caring are rooted in the same word. Caring for individuals, bodies, and pathologies cannot be excised from caring *about* those bodies and the histories, lives, families, communities, environments, and futures those bodies inhabit.

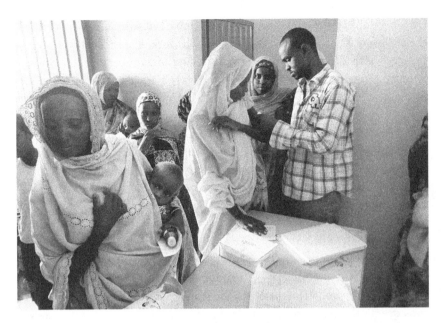

FIGURE 6. A Mobile Health and Nutrition team of nurses in the Somali Region of Ethiopia screening a mother for malnutrition. Photograph by Lauren Carruth.

Acts of caring, comforting, and assisting people beyond the narrow mandates of relief operations, are not integrated into official scopes of work or valued as billable services. Because the meaning of the verb "to care" is realized only through mutuality, affect, and sociality, the recognition of its centrality to aid work challenges the ways in which humanitarian responses are typically defined and designed—as temporary, focused on basic needs, and structured by an assumption there should be a one-way transfer of goods, services, and expertise from a "donor" to a "recipient." Recognizing and centering *samafal* instead highlights the necessity of intimate and compassionate care as central to humanitarian work.

Arthur Kleinman, not long after his wife's death, and not long after his caregiving for her concluded, wrote, "Theorists of caregiving have also identified 'presence'—being there, existentially, even when nothing practical can be done and hope itself is eclipsed. . . . What is at stake is doing good, for others and for oneself, if need be, despite the emotional and material cost. Indeed, the rewards—unvoiced or explicit—can be transformative, going to the heart of who we are and what we can offer, or endure."[30] To repeat Abshir's words, being *present*, as during the provision of medical care and during the implementation of programs to ensure people's basic needs are met can be personally and morally transformative, in that these actions can change or make real what it means and what it requires to be human and to have dignity. Individuals' instrumentaliza-tion of compassion and their professional aid work, like Mussa's described at the start of this chapter, are co-constitutive and interdependent. It is through affective and reciprocal relationships of care, inside and outside the boundaries of the relief operations, in people's roles as aid workers, clinicians, supportive family members, hospitable neighbors, and charitable and devout Muslims, that *samafal* and the humanitarian mission are both realized.

Being "present" with people, as Abshir phrased it, "looking them in the eye," listening to their stories, caring for them, advocating for them, and as Mussa states, staying with them even in austere settings, requires far more than affabil-ity and ethnic and linguistic affinities. This kind of care requires time and labor beyond merely the one-time distribution of material goods. Aid workers there-fore do not only distribute things, but are also tasked with providing comfort, emotional support, and care.[31]

The labor of these aid workers is therefore one form of "care work."[32] Their jobs very often center around intimate, emotionally taxing acts of caring for people, and consequently the management and distribution of emotions figure prominently in what they do. Feminist political theorists point to how the naturalization of many informal forms of care like this as "women's work," like elder care, raising children, and so on, has meant related forms of employment like professional nursing are frequently taken for granted or undervalued.[33] As the next chapter of this book will demonstrate, local humanitarian aid workers, like other caregivers, are also vulnerable to exploitation. In addition, incorporating care work into capitalist economies and rigid state bureaucracies threatens to kill the elements of affect, or "warmth and love," in Annemarie Mol and her colleagues' words, that make this kind of work so meaningful to the people involved.[34] Recognizing and valuing the provision of affect and love, therefore, necessarily require fundamental transforma-tions in the way labor and caregiving are valued by the local, national, and global political and economic systems of which the humanitarian industry is part.

In sum, *samafal* is a defining moral practice and meaningful form of work where relief operations recur, and it exists both within and outside the formal architecture and legal structures of global humanitarian relief operations. *Samafal* pervades everyday life, professional vernacular, and fundamentally, aid workers' interpolation into inclusive, expansive, reciprocal, and lasting kinship, community, religious, and political and caregiving networks. Thus *samafal* as a concept has the linguistic potential, at least, to re-center notions of humanitarianism originally conceived so long ago and so far from the places where humanitarian interventions mostly happen today. To understand global humanitarianism, one must understand *samafal*, and how *samafal* shapes aid workers' participation in and evaluations of more narrowly defined humanitarian interventions.

Furthermore, recognizing the multivalent and generative humanitarianisms at work within aid agencies—staffed, as they are, mostly by persons like Aden, Abshir, Doctor Hamza, Asha, Mona, and Nimo—undermines popular imaginaries of humanitarian action as something mostly carried out by white expatriates on rescue missions, or corrupt or dispassionate Somalis distributing material goods, and highlights instead the dynamic and socially and politically embedded actions of people caring for each other where foreign interventions recur. Enactments of *samafal* reveal our interdependence across contested political divides, across vast distances, across generations, and even in the absence of adequate humanitarian interventions.

Samafal Is a Gift

Somalis enjoyed the work they did so much, I had to wonder sometimes, were these aid workers actually self-interested and more than anything else focused on their own salaries, prestige, moral accolades, or personal salvation, or were they truly altruistic and selfless?[35] Why did aid workers get into this business, if for more than the money? Does humanitarianism or the provision of assistance to people in need entail either selfish or selfless motives, or both? In a more general sense, why do people give? The French sociologist Marcel Mauss wrote a book called *The Gift: The Form and Reason for Exchange in Archaic Societies*, to tackle related questions. He set about to compare the nature, rationale, and effects of various kinds of traditional gift exchanges in different places around the world. He said,

> Exchanges and contracts take place in the form of presents; in theory these are voluntary, in reality they are given and reciprocated obligatorily. . . . We seek here to study only one characteristic—one that goes deep but is isolated: the so to speak voluntary character of these total services, apparently free and disinterested but nevertheless constrained and self-interested. Almost always such services have taken the form of the gift, the present generously given even when, in the gesture accompanying the transaction, there is only a polite fiction, formalism, and social deceit, and when really there is obligation and economic self-interest.[36]

In other words, Mauss argued, there is no such thing as a "free gift."[37] Giving is not ever a neutral, impartial, impersonal, or isolated act born only of self-interest, but instead, the act of giving necessarily draws the giver and receiver into reciprocal and enduring relationships of obligation and exchange.

The humanitarian industry embodied by organizations like the Red Cross, by contrast, does not envision itself as involved in obligatory, enduring gift exchanges but instead casts itself as providing unidirectional, temporary, and free gifts.[38] In other words, global humanitarian responses or *bani'aadamnimada* are mostly still conceived as separate from acts of reciprocity and mutual relation. For example, one of the fundamental principles of the Red Cross Movement is "independence," or the ability to maintain autonomy from governments and other organizations. Another principle is that of "voluntary service," defined as "not prompted in any manner by desire for gain."[39] Voluntarism and independence help deny and disclaim the fact that donors or aid workers may well benefit and act strategically in their own interest through humanitarian acts. Specifically, the "polite fiction" or the "formalism," in Mauss's language, is that humanitarian assistance is provided by governments and nongovernmental organizations without political and self-interested aims.

Monika Krause complicates this picture by demanding a recognition of the fact that, in general, gift exchanges during humanitarian relief operations are not one-way donations of goods and services, but instead "are mediated by a market and involve labor."[40] She explains further, "In Mauss's analysis we have individuals exchanging gifts *with each other* in a community. In the case of humanitarian relief, we have a set of specialized producers, who have a professional interest in encouraging gift giving and gift taking." Therefore, "This way of distributing relief allows donors to accumulate status, and NGOs to accumulate money and status. Populations in need—whether they really are beneficiaries or are simply evoked as beneficiaries or potential beneficiaries— lend authority to agencies and donors under circumstances over which they have very little control."[41]

In the Somali Region, however, while donor organizations (like the United States government) may fund narrow relief missions (like distributions of food, water, medical services, and the like), and governmental and international nongovernmental aid agencies may capture a significant portion of the money and power from the aid industry, local and regional organizations and actors are left to transform *bani'aadamnimada* into *samafal*. Their burgeoning power and their activity derive from the exchange of humanitarian goods and services within the communities where they also reside and stay.

Additionally, the subject positions of "beneficiary," "aid worker," and "donor" Krause identifies were, on the ground, dynamic, multivalent, and indistinct categories.[42] Most aid workers in the Somali Region had at one time also received humanitarian assistance; many helped fund aid projects and distribute donations in their hometowns where their friends and family members benefited; and many aid workers donated funds and cared for crisis-affected family members outside their jobs at aid agencies. While the value of *bani'aadamnimada* may be in its potential to accumulate or display power, status, and wealth at the highest echelons of the aid industry, *samafal* is different. It represents a reciprocal, complex system of exchange and a mechanism of restoring balance across Somali communities in eastern Ethiopia, sometimes augmented by relief operations and sometimes not, involving alternative expectations, actions, and materials (like redistributions of wealth across kinship groups, shared and transferred livestock herds, shared food, and shared housing arrangements). Somalis were agents in negotiating, building, and expanding these systems of exchange. They worked to ensure *samafal* existed beyond the time and material limitations donors and foreign aid agencies placed on *bani'aadamnimada*, and whenever possible, they used *bani'aadamnimada* to augment *samafal*.

In contrast to *bani'aadamnimada, samafal* therefore represents a true Maussian gift: it is reciprocal, symbolically rich, potent with meaning for those involved, and an integral part of enduring local social, economic, and political systems.[43] *Samafal* is explicitly reciprocal and presumes and creates obligatory reciprocal social relationships over time; it does not entail one-way, one-time donations or transfers, made voluntarily and autonomously, without expectations of return or mutual benefit. *Samafal*, either as part of relief operations or outside their formal boundaries, is also neither utilitarian nor impersonal.[44] *Samafal* presents one means through which Somalis living in eastern Ethiopia cared for one another and forged relationships of solidarity. Official humanitarian relief operations or *bani'aadamnimada* are indeed occasionally and sporadically part of greater enactments of *samafal*, and global aid can affect and augment *samafal* in places where interventions recur.[45] Material and immaterial humanitarian bequests, in a Maussian sense, can fulfill *samafal*, but never perfectly.

Effective humanitarian responses therefore required local aid workers to make exotic forms of assistance their own, or, in other words, it required them to render *samafal* from *bani'aadamnimada*. Accordingly, when the aid organizations Hararge Catholic Secretariat or Oxfam dropped off bins of pills or unassembled wheelbarrows and quickly departed, as mentioned in the previous chapter, these constituted grounds for serious local critique. These projects did not meet expectations of *samafal*. On the other hand, when mobile health teams departed, like the UNICEF team deployed to Elahelay where Sara lived, residents grieved their loss.

Furthermore, global humanitarian goods, services, and ideas—including materials like medicines, food rations, and shelter materials, but also immaterial things like education, political influence, and access to populations in need— were not new. They had been circulating globally and locally and changing value for generations. As I described in the opening pages of this book, international humanitarian operations happened during the colonial and postcolonial occupations of northern Somali territories, when Italian, French, and Ethiopian clinics opened to serve Somalis they at the same time attempted to conscript, control, and assimilate. Accordingly, *samafal* cannot be interpreted as "archaic" (in Marcel Mauss's book title[46]) isolated from or a precursor to Somalis' interpolation into contemporary global and Ethiopian systems of humanitarian assistance. It does not represent a timeless artifact or inherent characteristic of a static notion of Somali culture (indeed, there is no such thing). Instead, *samafal* is articulated, enacted, and evaluated differently through time, in part through people's frequent experiences with the global and Ethiopian humanitarian industries.

Doctor Hamza, for example, the senior-level aid worker with an INGO based in Jigjiga, enacted *samafal* informally, providing regular contributions to help his family and close friends in his natal community when they needed assistance, while also, simultaneously, implementing humanitarian interventions at his job. He was involved in multiple and overlapping exchanges of generous gifts, hospitality, and care. While he was gainfully employed, and while he enjoyed giving and modeling generosity, he did so confident that when or if he faced a major crisis or lost his job, his family and friends would step in and provide for him. He was self-interested to be sure, but the "self" in this formulation included far more than his individual self—it included his family, his hometown, the transnational community of ethnic Somalis, and the Somali regional state within Ethiopia. He cared for and cared about them (in Somali, *daryeel*) all through *samafal*.

This concept of *samafal*, while in this case signified through the Somali language and described in reference to Somali politics and cultures, is not limited to eastern Ethiopia. Around the world, in places where relief operations recur, aid workers transform limited bequests from foreign relief agencies into more meaningful and effective forms of aid. *Samafal* is key to global humanitarianism, and not merely a local example or Somali interpretation of policies and programs designed elsewhere. *Samafal* is a global phenomenon and a vital characteristic of humanitarianism today.

At the same time, however, neither someone senior like Doctor Hamza nor a junior staffer like Mussa, quoted at the start of this chapter, could ever hope to reciprocate assistance with persons who work in the European headquarters of the relief agencies that employ them. The emotional, messy, politically contentious entanglements ground-level humanitarian work required remained largely unrecognized and uncompensated. Their stories, insights, expertise, and work held less power and value for aid organizations than those proffered by expats flying in to visit "the field" from donor countries or global headquarters for a few days. To donors and expats at headquarters, even though they were professional aid workers, Doctor Hamza and Mussa also remained "local" Somalis, so-called beneficiaries in a very broad sense, and the objects of their international development. And any humanitarian gift exchange between donors and beneficiaries remains an unequal exchange, as Krause points out, no matter how well the benefactor tunes his attention to the particular needs and desires of beneficiaries, or heroizes local staffers. These inequitable hierarchies and local aid workers' alienation from the means of producing *bani'aadamnimada* remain entrenched features of the contemporary aid industry.

3

HUMANITARIAN WORK

"I am happy, yes," Aden said about his work as we sat together in the peaceful hotel courtyard, looking away from me, up to a flock of birds gathering in a citrus tree overhead. "My intellectual development is satisfied. But I also have, *ideas*"—his voice suddenly low and almost whispered across the rickety plastic table between us.

Aden removed his thick-framed glasses, putting them between us, and washed his hands over his face, sighing. He, in some ways, wanted "to be an implementer again," he said with a grin on his face. "An implementer of projects," and a "provider of services directly to people" instead of being only a policy maker in a comfortable office in Jigjiga. Moving immediately and seamlessly in conversation to his family's life and situation he continued, "And the schools in Jigjiga are not that good, I think." He had tried to tutor and read with his children at home, "but this is not enough." Aden regularly traveled for meetings to Addis Ababa and saw his friends' children living there, and thought to himself, "Well, maybe my children aren't doing too badly in Jigjiga, but still, I am worried."

Aden has, by his own measures, been remarkably successful at work. Pastoralist programming was finally part of Ethiopia's national political and agricultural strategy, and this strategy was shaping new legislature and policies developed in the Somali, Afar, and Oromia regional governing councils. Mobile health and education services were finally becoming the standard for people on the move throughout the eastern lowlands, where pastoralists and semipastoralists move seasonally across geographic, regional, and international boundaries for grazing, herding, and trade. The UN had funded and coordinated conferences, policy workshops, and publications in the last year to change and improve the design of basic services to pastoralists and livestock herders, and to finally more fully recognize the importance of women to pastoralist communities and economies. "For many years we've been using the justification of an emergency," he said, "to do *pastoralist* programming," he emphasized, "and programming for mobile people. But the conditions in which people are living are normal for them, and not really emergencies. It looked like development because it got basic services out to people. The policy base for pastoralists and pastoralist regions will make implementation of development programs appropriate for these populations possible."

For Aden and so many other aid workers like him in eastern Ethiopia, humanitarian work also fulfilled religious mandates to be charitable, fulfilled his family's and neighbor's expectations of hospitality and generosity, and redistributed wealth through his kinship and community networks. It was a profoundly meaningful as well as a relatively lucrative vocation—especially when compared to jobs in local factories, governmental offices, or nomadic pastoralism. Jobs in the aid industry were some of the best jobs around in eastern Ethiopia.

Even so, jobs with international nongovernmental organizations or United Nations relief organizations remained difficult to come by, according to Aden and others who, like him, are trained in clinical medicine or humanitarian policy. And for most Somalis in Ethiopia, these jobs were only short-term, from a few months to, at most, a few years. Aden's career represented a lucky exception, in his estimation. Relief workers typically lacked union representation, collective bargaining power, and affordable legal representation when their employers violated the terms of contract.[1]

Furthermore, when jobs held by Somalis in Ethiopia with international relief agencies are viewed in relation to other positions and forms of labor within the global humanitarian workforce, greater inequities appear: staffers working out of subnational offices make far less money, hold less power, have fewer benefits, face equal if not more dangerous safety and political risks, and have relatively less control over the terms and lengths of their employment compared to their colleagues either in national offices in Addis Ababa or in regional or global headquarters in places like Nairobi, Geneva, or Washington, DC.[2] Subnational or local staffers rarely design the policies and projects they are hired to implement, monitor, and evaluate. Regardless of their educational degrees or professional training, they are mostly relegated to being "locals," affixed to "field" offices, in an industry led by globally mobile expatriates.[3] Recent political and governmental transformations in eastern Ethiopia have neither reformed this structure, nor improved how local staffers like Aden are regarded and compensated by the aid agencies that employ and depend on them. This chapter details the reality of aid work for local and national staff, and in so doing, describes the labor inequities that characterize the contemporary global humanitarian industry.

The Toll of Humanitarian Work

International or expatriate aid workers have always faced dangers and their jobs have always entailed working in impoverished and, at times, violent environments.[4] Aid workers stationed in countries and communities where crises happen face increasingly dangerous work conditions. In recent years, intractable internal conflicts, a disregard for international laws among nonstate actors, strategic attacks on aid workers, and the weaponization of aid work have all made humanitarian assistance more difficult and dangerous.[5] Additionally, reports of untreated mental illnesses, stressful work environments, and a high prevalence of post–traumatic stress disorder among international health workers abound in the occupational health and humanitarian aid literatures. The isolation and long hours so many international aid workers endure also frequently contribute to feelings of ennui and burnout.[6] Their high levels of chronic stress also contribute to their subsequent increased risk for depression, anxiety, and emotional exhaustion.[7] Consequently, persons deployed outside their home country for humanitarian work report they need and often now receive a significant amount of preparatory mental health and educational support from aid agencies and volunteer organizations.[8]

Relief work takes an immense toll on people at different levels of the industry—not just international staff but also the local staff and subcontractors that carry out work as well. To provide one example, truck drivers delivering aid commodities in eastern Ethiopia were frequently attacked, hijacked, and robbed. They often feared that reporting these incidents would incite involvement from distrusted police, revenge from armed groups involved, or the loss of their job. Consequently, most kept silent about these incidents and their struggles to recover from these traumas.[9]

In recent years, evidence about the mental toll of humanitarian work has inspired research and advocacy to rethink the way humanitarian assistance is organized and staffed—at least among international staffs.[10] Reducing aid workers' burnout, increasing their retention within organizations from one crisis to another, providing ample vacation time, and investing in initiatives designed to improve their mental health have been the focus of several effective interventions.[11] Encouraging social support and socializing among communities of expatriate aid workers seems to mitigate their risks of clinical depression, psychological distress, and perceptions that they lack personal accomplishment.[12]

According to major INGOs working in eastern Ethiopia, what few foreigners work there now require expensive security details, military escorts, security briefings, entourages of translators and cultural brokers, regular time off after fieldwork, mental health–care services, and hardship pay.

However, staff support and access to organizational resources do not exist equally across and between organizations and actors within the humanitarian industry. National and local aid workers—like the traumatized Ethiopian truck drivers—face many of the same challenges as their expatriate colleagues, but lack equal access to protection, support services, and compensation. Research on the mental health needs specifically faced by national and local staffers also remains scarce. What few systematic studies of humanitarian aid workers' health and well-being have been done, problematically fail to explicitly study or control for distinctions between national staffers headquartered in major cities and the local and subcontracted staffers who constitute the majority of the workforce in places like the Somali Region of Ethiopia.

My interviews and informal conversations with local and national staffs of relief agencies were often emotional. The head of a UN relief agency regional office noted, for example, "As a human being we feel very hard. We cry so many times when they tell you about their life. Their children, their husbands who've died, their resources and materials destroyed or burned or left." A project officer in Jigjiga who helped manage mobile teams throughout the region for an international NGO said that he loved traveling to the field to visit his mobile teams—it is his favorite part of the job. "Seeing with your eyes at the ground level all the communities you work with. Seeing your team, if they lack water, if they don't have food, etcetera, and realizing how comfortable you are here in Jigjiga. It is difficult."

While most research and resources to address the psychological and emotional tolls of aid work were directed at international aid workers, local aid workers and temporary hires also faced enormous and various forms of stress as well—and these stresses were, paradoxically, often a product of the inequities and inadequacies inherent to the aid industry itself. Furthermore, many of the solutions to expatriates' problems suggested in the occupational health literature and implemented in the Somali Region reinforced the segregation and exceptional treatment foreign workers received compared to locals.

Labor Hierarchies in the Humanitarian System

As its name suggests, humanitarianism is, if nothing else, an aspirational concept, focused narrowly on saving lives and ameliorating suffering. But it is an imperfect and paradoxical mechanism for such work.[13] "The humanitarian emergency is an awkward symbol," Craig Calhoun writes, "simultaneously of moral purity and suffering, of altruistic global response, and of the utter failure of global institutions."[14] As many scholars and advocates have noted over the years, the structure of humanitarian relief remains largely ahistorical and unresponsive to the ways in which aid itself tends to reproduce the very social inequalities and political dysfunctions underpinning recurrent crises—in the Somali Region and elsewhere.[15] In Ethiopia, it remains largely unresponsive to calls for sustainable political reforms, lasting multisectoral engagement, and peace and reconciliation work along the regional boundaries and in its political and geographic margins. Historical amnesia allows aid agencies to, in a sense, begin anew with the declaration of every new emergency. This releases the organizations that repeatedly intervene from culpability when political insecurity and poverty continue.

The human architecture of the global humanitarian industry itself also produces institutionalized forms of difference, inequalities, and new forms of segregation. Jobs in the humanitarian sector are, for local and national staffers at least, mostly precarious, short-lived, and compared to the Europeans and North Americans employed within the same relief organizations, undercompensated. Somali aid workers' idiomatic expressions and experiences of political insecurity within Ethiopia have actually intensified, alongside Prime Minister Abiy Ahmed's reforms and economic development happening elsewhere in the country.

David Rieff wrote years ago with indignation, "Only an idiot needs to be reminded that the world is as unjust in its response to disasters as it is in almost everything else."[16] In a similar vein, Beerli finds that the humanitarian system is "a social space constituted by growing socioprofessional differentiation and multiple struggles to define the most legitimate means of thinking and doing humanitarian action."[17] It is inequitable. There is a discernable, visible, embodied division of "humanitarian labor," she argues, that distinguishes and distances "the headquarters" from "the field." Local aid workers, in this case, are destined only for "field work" and cannot be promoted to and cannot work in "headquarters." Silke Roth finds that segregation between the binary category of "expat" and "national" aid workers happened within office spaces as well as outside offices, as people socialized within exclusive circles.[18] Lisa Smirl similarly finds that white SUVs, walled residential compounds, and other metaphoric green zones in "the field" provide spaces in which segregation between expatriate and local staffers is realized and differences between aid workers' and beneficiaries' subject positions are symbolized and reproduced.[19]

The humanitarian system is therefore not an exception to or an improvement upon the normal rules and functioning of government and society.[20] It instead represents an enduring network of actors engaging in professional work—work that highlights characteristics and failings of the contemporary world in which it operates.[21] Local aid workers, within this system, are not marginal to the machinations of power within the global aid industry, but rather constitute the very means by which humanitarian actions are conceived and actualized.[22] They are paradigmatic. The global humanitarian industry depends on ample supplies of cheap, temporary, flexible, and expendable labor from the localities where it intervenes—ironically to proffer a narrative of improving the lives of locals. Various symbolic and spatial forms of segregation and the inequities between differentiated, distinguishable local and national and expatriate staffers—ones so inherent to global aid work in general—reflect historical forms of segregation, military occupation, colonialism, racism, sexism, ethnolinguistic discrimination, and violence within and outside the humanitarian sector. To name one example, the international humanitarian system depends on the labor of locals from crisis-affected communities, and does nothing to challenge the inaccessibility of visas and international travel for persons from the Global South—most acutely, perhaps, Somalis from the Horn of Africa.

The chart in figure 7 represents the labor hierarchies inherent to the global humanitarian industry in eastern Ethiopia. At the top of the industry hierarchy, expatriates work for high salaries, generous work benefits, and with the added bonus of easy and frequent international mobility. They mostly live in Western donor countries and capital cities where aid agencies are headquartered. In the middle of the hierarchy exist national staffers or what Swidler and Watkins call "national elites."[23] In Ethiopia, these individuals mostly speak Amharic as a first language, and are fluent in English as well. They are part of the burgeoning middle to upper class in Addis Ababa, and occasionally travel internationally for conferences and education. The majority of the humanitarian workforce in Ethiopia, however, are locals from regions and communities in crisis, who work in offices close to where crises happen, and struggle to advance to offices in capital cities, and much less to headquarters located outside their country of origin.

The humanitarian industry is characterized by steep and inflexible gradations in power, marked by parallel gradations in racialized ethnic distinctions, international mobility, education, language use, and wealth. Race in Ethiopia is not a black and white matter. Racialized hierarchies include complex racialized differentiations between the many ethnic and linguistic groups in Ethiopia, whereby so-called highlanders, or people from the central and northern mountainous parts of the country who mostly speak Amharic or Tigrinya as a first language, are perceived to be disproportionately promoted to higher levels of authority within the humanitarian industry in Ethiopia compared to Somalis and other pastoralist groups, who mostly speak Somali as a first language and are relegated to local field posts.

What this representation of the hierarchy fails to depict are the relative numbers of persons at each job and level. In 2018, a study by ALNAP—a global

	International staff*	National staff	Local staff
Expatriate staff of global nongovernmental or United Nations relief organizations, based in cities in the Global North like Geneva, New York, or London	✓		
Expatriate staff of the regional offices for global nongovernmental or United Nations, based in major cities in the Global South	✓		
Expatriate staff of global nongovernmental or United Nations based in national-level offices in capital cities in the Global South and Expatriate consultants	✓		
National salaried staff of global nongovernmental or United Nations organizations, based in capital cities in the Global South		✓	
National salaried staff of Ethiopian federal relief agencies like the DPPC or ARRA headquartered in Addis Ababa		✓	
Local or subnational salaried project** staff of global nongovernmental or United Nations offices, based in regional capitals like Jigjiga, Ethiopia		✓	
Local or subnational salaried logistical or administrative staff of global nongovernmental or United Nations offices, based in regional capitals like Jigjiga, Ethiopia			✓
Local or subnational salaried project staff of federal relief agencies like the DPPC or ARRA in Ethiopia			✓
Local or subnational salaried logistical or administrative staff of federal relief agencies like the DPPC or ARRA in Ethiopia			✓
Temporary but contracted project, logistical, or administrative staff of global nongovernmental or United Nations offices, based in offices close to where relief operations happen			✓

→ Incomes (from lowest to largest incomes) ←

→ Job security (measured in length of work contracts or agreements, from daily to project-based, to multiyear) ←

→ Mobility (from least access to most access to opportunities to live, work, and travel globally) ←

→ Language used at work (from local to national to international languages, e.g., from Somali to Amharic to English) ←

← Racial and ethnic inequities, both nationally and globally →

Temporary but contracted project, logistical, or administrative staff of Ethiopian federal relief agencies, based in regional offices close to where relief operations happen	
Temporary subcontracted aid workers and staff of "local NGOs" whose employers have contracts with larger nongovernmental or governmental relief agencies	
Official, contracted daily or weekly hires for logistical or language support, in places where relief operations or distributions happen	
Informal, unofficial daily or weekly hires for logistical or language support, in places where relief operations or distributions happen	beneficiaries not officially employed
Participants paid on a daily or weekly basis, for participation in educational or vocational workshops, research projects with aid agencies, or cash-for-work or food-for-work labor projects where relief operations happen	

* Here I represent indistinct differences and the potential for movement between job position categories in the right column, from being a beneficiary all the way to an international aid worker. However, advancements are rare. These categories are defined differently depending on the organization, and some people move between the categories.

** What I call "project" staff were hired for their expertise or training in a humanitarian response-related field. However, some logistical staff working for the UN or an NGOs like Jama, described in the pages to follow, were in many ways overqualified for their positions. They took jobs as drivers or translators with international organizations for the higher pay than they received for work with a local NGO or governmental relief office.

FIGURE 7. Labor hierarchies within the humanitarian industry in eastern Ethiopia

network of relief agencies, donors, academics, and consultants—found approximately 86 percent of the personnel of United Nations relief agencies, 92 percent of the personnel of INGOs, and 98 percent of the personnel of the Red Cross Movement were from the countries or communities in crisis.[24] But these estimates did not include the legions of subcontracted and informally hired locals that help relief agencies implement and evaluate their interventions. To get a sense of the exact numbers of personnel hired at each level, including these subcontractors and potentially also temporary ad hoc hires, I reached out to ten prominent international aid organizations with headquarters in Washington, DC, and Addis Ababa. Beyond numbers, I was interested in the legal relationships and benefits packages offered staffers, especially locals in places where interventions unfold. None of these organizations could or would share this data. The breakdown of organizations' labor force globally or for particular countries was either "unavailable" or simply "not collected." This aporia is functional. A large proportion of humanitarian workers labor in liminality—somewhere between formal, salaried employment for aid agencies and entirely informal, even black market, noncontractual service provision.[25] Thus these workers cost organizations less money and less investment in training, salaries, and benefits. This arrangement is also convenient in that local aid workers were often asked to shoulder enormous risks but lacked the grounds to demand the kinds of protections and benefits expatriate staff performing similar tasks might demand or require. The resulting inequities and potentials for exploitation belie the humanitarian mission to "do no harm"[26] in the communities relief agencies serve.

Regardless of the exact numbers, unlike Aden and Doctor Hamza, most local aid workers in the Somali Region struggled to advance and struggled to emancipate themselves and their loved ones from the poverty and insecurity that plagued the communities in crisis around them. Humanitarian responses, according to Somali aid workers in Ethiopia at least, too often failed to represent a career for local aid workers, beyond the horizon of single interventions, projects, or crises. Humanitarian policies and projects strived to save lives, but often failed at the same time to sustain and truly nourish those lives. Humanitarian interventions did not adequately develop, promote, and invest in their staff, nor did they actively work to lessen inequities within and outside the aid industry. In the following pages, beginning with workers at the bottom on the labor hierarchy, I provide several examples of these failings.

The Labor of Beneficiaries

Aid workers are not the only people who work during emergency responses. Many beneficiaries perform labor during and after emergencies in order to qualify for aid disbursements, despite the fact that these forms of labor are not legal forms of employment and are never signified as "aid work." The contemporary popularity of various food-for-work and cash-for-work projects in eastern Ethiopia are paradigmatic. Rather than viewing this kind of labor as different or separate from aid work, these forms of beneficiary labor must be viewed within the spectrum of ways that the residents of crisis-affected communities hustle to gain work experience and make money from global aid agencies.

The labor beneficiaries perform for aid agencies in order to qualify for aid, more often than not, is either physically demanding or designed to elicit the perspective of people as locals. Maryan's many side gigs provide one example. Since I first met her in 2008, Maryan has been serving as an uncertified, but well-regarded midwife (or "traditional birth attendant" in the language of the government of Ethiopia) in Degago, in the northern Somali Region, ten miles away from the county seat of Aysha. Maryan has lived in Degago her whole life. She has four children, including one grown daughter named Ubah, who when we last spoke was twenty-one years old.

A sprawling refugee camp with as many as thirty thousand people was established on the edge of the town of Degago in 1988, when the civil war in Somalia forced migrations of people northward. The camp was open until 2005, when UNHCR withdrew its support and most displaced persons were resettled or returned home again. During the refugee camp period in Degago, Maryan was given basic medical training by Médecins Sans Frontières (MSF) and worked as a traditional birth attendant and a part-time medical assistant in the clinic first run by MSF, then later taken over by UNHCR and the Ethiopian governmental refugee relief agency (ARRA).

Ever since the camp closed and most refugees left, Maryan has continued providing care to mothers and babies on her own, but now in a private, informal practice, for which she receives mostly small gifts—as much as people can afford to give. In recent years, Maryan has benefited occasionally from participation in interviews and focus groups with various nongovernmental organizations conducting health and food security surveys in Degago. She has also received occasional stipends that compensate her for provision of testimonies for various human rights organizations about local political insecurity, local forms of gender-based violence, and abuses of civilians by the Ethiopian military forces nearby. UNICEF and the Somali Regional Health Bureau in Ethiopia have funded a few workshops and training initiatives for Maryan and Somali birth attendants like her from conflict-affected and impoverished communities around the country. As part of this, she has been funded three times to travel and stay in Jigjiga for one or two weeks, attend lectures on midwifery, and bring back home with her supplies of gloves, syringes, and caches of prescription and over-the-counter medications.

Maryan was never officially employed by any of the aid agencies that paid her various per diems and travel stipends, but instead, on a regular basis, she worked through informal mechanisms in exchange for various forms of material and monetary compensation. She and her family were also official beneficiaries of food and medical aid. During the refugee period, Maryan and her family benefited from an increased allotment of rations and from the clinic that opened to serve the needs of all people in Degago—refugee and not. Maryan and her family used to receive rations of whole wheat grains, oil, and either lentils or split dried peas as part of UN World Food Program or USAID food aid programs.

However, since 2015, the only form of food assistance her household has received has been through the government of Ethiopia's Productive Safety Net Program (PSNP)—an internationally funded governmental program to provide a safety net for chronically food insecure Ethiopians. For the last two years, Maryan and Ubah, alongside their neighbors and friends, have worked to pull out and destroy the invasive *Prosopis* trees (or mesquite trees, in English) that now proliferate along the dry riverbeds that wind around the outskirts of Degago. It would take her several hours, working in the blistering hot desert, where midday temperatures regularly top 100 degrees Fahrenheit, to remove even one tree.

Ironically, these trees were introduced by UNHCR in 1989 to control the erosion of sandy embankments and to provide refugees a source of firewood. The trees, unfortunately, soon outcompeted several other indigenous plant species consumed by livestock and used for charcoal production. Many residents and experts in local governmental offices speculated that the *Prosopis* have contributed to falling water tables as well. These invasive trees, everyone agreed, needed to go. The PSNP in Degago was designed to address this issue and was part of nationwide efforts in Ethiopia to mitigate climate change and to rehabilitate depleted landscapes.[27]

Food-for-work and cash-for-work beneficiaries with the PSNP program in Ethiopia can work only five days per month removing and hauling the invasive mesquites, and then for only a maximum of six months per year. For one day of work, often totaling realistically about five hours plus the time for transit and breaks—people in Degago received three kilograms of whole wheat grain, worth approximately 15 Ethiopian *birr*, or US$0.54. Since people were only allowed to work a total of six months in the program, that meant they could earn, at most, the equivalent of 450 Ethiopian birr per year, which in 2016 was worth a little over US$20. Compensation for the same amount of low-wage manual labor in nearby rural communities and cities at the time would have been approximately 150–200 birr per day, or for the same number of hours and days per year, 4500–6000 birr (or US$216–$288)—over ten times the PSNP rate.[28] Plus, the maximum "monthly transfer entitlement" for one household, no matter the actual size of the household, was 500 Ethiopian birr, meaning the program increased total annual household earnings a maximum of only approximately $108.00.[29]

Additionally, the work was not just "cheap," as the government of Ethiopia says in its planning documents, it was also dangerous. The district-level government office that organizes the PSNP provided beneficiaries inexpensive, rickety, and now rusty axes and shovels, but did not provide either gloves or any kind of protective equipment. During the second month of the work cycle in 2016, a woman named Ayaan, who was working with Ubah and Maryan to rid Degago of its invasive mesquites, was seriously injured. As several women pulled on one rough and sticky trunk, a large branch suddenly broke free, slamming into Ayaan's face and poking her directly in the right eye.

Her eye stung and could not open, she reported, and it bled badly for several hours. But there was no one who could provide first aid or medical care: even the small clinic in Degago was unstaffed and locked because the community health worker was several hours away attending a workshop. The nearest hospital was at least a two-hour drive farther northeast, across the international border, in Djibouti. But no one in Degago had a car. The closest ambulance that could have transported her was in a remote community over fifteen miles away, outside the range of mobile phones, so there was not even a way to hail the driver.

Ubah recalled, with emotion, Ayaan's predicament: "What could we do?"

Drawing on her years of training by humanitarian organizations and work as a midwife, Maryan helped Ayaan wash and patch her eye with bandages. The wound never became infected, but several months later, Ayaan was still blind in that eye.

The next day, this incident was reported to supervisors of the PSNP at the regional government by the local PSNP manager, a salaried government employee (making 10,000 birr or US$370.00 per month) who worked in a governmental office in the county seat of Aysha. But neither the government nor sponsoring NGOs ever followed up or checked on Ayaan. Ayaan received three kilograms of wheat for her one day of work on the day she was injured. In the future, if the government decides to renew the PSNP program in Degago, another PSNP monitor explained, she may qualify for direct support without labor due to her disability. She is no longer considered, in the words of government documents in English, "able-bodied," and she will receive the same amount of cash per year (at most US$21.00) as other qualifying adults unable to work.

As the number of people in Degago, like Maryan and Ubah, who receive regular food rations has dramatically fallen in the last five years, and at the same time, as the number of residents enrolled in the PSNP has increased, numerous residents have begun to rethink the role and potentials of aid in their communities. One of Maryan's neighbors who also worked on the PSNP described this change, "as the way organizations are now. We have to work now, there is no other way."

Mahamed, a young father who spent his teenage years in the Degago refugee camp, helped manage two different PSNP interventions like the one Maryan participated in. He also reflected on the effects of the PSNP program on local economies, compared to relief programs in the past in Degago, as we drove between towns, talking about the history of various NGOs nearby:

> We here, we were once refugees, you see, and I think at that time we expected to receive everything, all the food, all the medicine, for free. But not now. Today we must work to develop our communities; the people must work to get this aid. But the people here are not used to working to receive [aid]. I think by talking about these things, these changes, I am convincing them now. I am helping them change. We cannot just take food and things and not do any work. This is how things are now. But this is difficult to understand for the people here.

Mahamed was at the time forty-one-years old, born in a small village near Degago, and can recall working for at least six different humanitarian NGOs plus at least two governmental bureaus during his life. Sometimes he worked as a volunteer, sometimes he worked for several days, all day, for the equivalent of between five and twenty dollars in cash, and on one occasion he worked as a survey enumerator for what was then worth approximately US$300 in one week alone. Mahamed was literate and fluent in Somali, Amharic, and English and was related to at least one person in nearly every village and city in the area. He was invaluable to aid agencies. His wife and children lived in the nearby city of Dire Dawa, his mother still lived in Degago, and his father lived in another village along the border of Somaliland, and so he traveled weekly, if not more frequently, back and forth from Dire Dawa to Aysha, Degago, Jigjiga, and to other remote communities along the Somaliland border, wherever he could find work or job training or even the potential for work, sleeping on floors in the homes of his subclan relatives. Even so, in the decade I have known him, Mahamed has spent most of this time unemployed.

While Mahamed acknowledged the historical reality of refugees like himself receiving aid commodities for free, he did not complain about now having to work for assistance. Instead, echoing his role as a PSNP organizer, he acknowledged the contemporary reality that beneficiaries in Degago and elsewhere must now work to receive assistance. He explicitly encouraged people to work for aid as part of his job: "I am helping them change," he said to me again, repeating common aid discourse. "We must battle this dependency on aid."

As Mahamed acknowledged, bags of food from the PSNP were not given as unidirectional gifts or as an appropriate form of humanitarian aid (*samafal*) but rather, as compensation for work adequately performed.[30] Through beneficiaries' manual labor in the hot sun to pull out invasive vegetation, or the labor of leaving home and leaving behind children to sit in a workshop or help organize a PSNP project, Maryan, Ubah, and Ayaan embody and represent the labor inequalities inherent to the contemporary global aid industry. Their labor and the conditions in which they work were elided from most program monitoring and evaluation protocols, donor appeals, media stories, human resources departments, and occupational health and safety considerations within aid institutions.[31] The labor of these beneficiaries also existed outside the enduring social relationships and obligations inherent to *samafal*. Consequently, in addition to working with the PSNP, Maryan also continued to work as a midwife, sometimes for cash payment, but mostly without payment, as *samafal*.

Food-for-work, training workshops in midwifery, and similar interventions organized through governmental and UN relief programs are almost free gifts, and almost one-time humanitarian handouts, but not quite.[32] These required an exchange of labor, but only for a small amount of food or a small per diem, and only for a few weeks or months out of the year. These projects for people like Maryan were also almost a real job, almost a training in midwifery, almost a job in natural resources management or humanitarian response, but again, not quite.

Instead, the cheap labor supplied by beneficiaries like Maryan enabled the improvement of public landscapes and the education of rural midwives the government did not otherwise have to pay for. These forms of aid, furthermore, never supported and only existed outside locally salient systems of *samafal*. Finally, like the ineffectual attempts to erase *Prosopis* trees from the landscape, the commodification of beneficiaries' labor erased the fact of humanitarian relief's enduring presence, year in and year out, and the failures of aid organizations to affect meaningful or lasting improvements. These projects instead required the performance of absurd and Sisyphean forms of labor.

Data Production in the Gig Economy

Data collection in all its forms—enumeration, statistical reporting, the collection of illustrative anecdotes via interviews, and all the logging and tallying that accompanies every humanitarian intervention—presents significant employment opportunities in places where humanitarian interventions recur. Persons who help aid agencies collect data often work temporarily with multiple organizations, as researchers, language interpreters, logistics experts, and field monitors. And the methods and applications of data collection, in particular, are shifting. Relief organizations and the donors that fund humanitarian projects increasingly require "accountability," "local engagement," and other participatory forms of data collection in addition to quantitative surveys in crisis-affected communities around the world.[33] Perennial data collection activities are both requisite and routine, and contribute in significant ways to local economies of aid.

In addition to the persons hired to help collect data, both formally and informally, the subjects of research and monitoring also make money from data collection. Participating in research, as a human subject, is also an important side gig for beneficiaries during and after emergencies. The lines between beneficiaries, aid workers, and donors are all blurred.[34]

For example, one bright Saturday morning in Aysha, Idrias, an Amharic-speaking Ethiopian employee of an international NGO and Jamal, an Ethiopian representative of the United Nations World Health Organization (WHO), recruited a dozen local Somali men to conduct a health and food security survey in surrounding communities. Idrias and Jamal had worked for this INGO in the Addis Ababa headquarters for a few years, and had just arrived in Aysha, for the first time, the night before. It was the middle of the long winter dry season. In the preceding weeks there had been outbreaks of measles and dysentery in several *kebeles* nearby. Health extension workers in the area had reported rising numbers of severely acutely malnourished children under five years of age, and there were new calls for needs assessments and updated donor appeals from foreign and domestic relief organizations.

By eleven o'clock in the morning, after a two-hour training session with Idrias and Jamal inside a courtyard surrounded by government office buildings, the newly minted group of Somali enumerators—all holding clipboards, pens, and measuring tapes emblazoned with the NGO and the WHO logos—were organized and ready to practice their new skills. Two women and their toddlers, who had recently arrived by foot from an encampment of herders several miles away, were at the same time in Aysha shopping and catching up with relatives. The trainees confidently approached the two mothers in the center of town, and suggested they bring their children over to be weighed and measured, so the other enumerators could practice using the equipment and survey materials.

But before handing the children over to the eager line of men, the two mothers suddenly and unexpectedly demanded an immediate cash payment from Idrias and Jamal. They requested one hundred Ethiopian birr (then worth approximately US$9.00) per diem—equal at that time to an entire day's wage for manual labor in Dire Dawa and Jigjiga.

The men looked at each other and shrugged, and then, through awkward language translation, Idrias informed the women his NGO did not have any per diems for them.

The women responded, simply, "Birr. We want 100 birr" in exchange for weighing and measuring their children.

Idrias scoffed at the women's request, brushing them away with his hand. In frustration, he and Jamal adjourned the training session, and retreated to the nearest café for lunch, to mull over their options on how to proceed. Idrias told me the next day when we spoke, he felt "bad for the situation." How would he be able to recruit participants for this needs assessment if everyone wanted to be paid? Had other women in town heard the women's demands? What would they say about this in Addis Ababa?

"These women are too demanding," he concluded, as Jamal nodded in agreement. "They do not understand the situation and we are here to help. This training is necessary."

Later that afternoon, as men in town settled in to chewing khat and women settled into afternoon prayers and naps, word spread around town that this NGO would not pay anyone any money for weighing and measuring children. Their team of enumerators would be deployed first thing Monday morning, with or without first practicing their new skills.

In the last several years, international aid organizations have increasingly turned to providing monetary compensation to residents for their participation in time-consuming participatory and qualitative research methodologies—focus groups with beneficiaries, participatory mapping exercises, rapid rural appraisals, testimonials to human rights organizations, and extended individual interviews. Compensation for these activities historically included between twenty and one hundred Ethiopian birr plus additional cases of plastic disposable water bottles or emergency food aid supplements. More recently, cash or other forms of compensation in exchange for participation in research projects have increased and now sometimes exceed the mothers' 100-birr demand—even for less time-consuming forms of participation in anthropometric surveys and rapid needs assessments.

Monetary compensation for participants in research is commonplace in populations enrolled in public health interventions, randomized controlled trials, and medical experiments.[35] But this also occurs in places like the Somali Region where rapid, intensive research projects are designed to assess the need for and the effectiveness of humanitarian interventions.[36] Several expatriate and Ethiopian aid workers and bureaucrats within the Somali regional government claimed that aid organizations simply cannot conduct any qualitative or participatory research methods at all without first providing monetary compensation to local residents. It is expected.

Beneficiaries' rising demands for per diems for participation in data collection are challenges expats in Addis Ababa joke about over drinks in the evening, and something researchers including me now budget for in grant proposals. Despite these known and acknowledged changes in the way data is collected, recruitment methods, budgets, training requirements, and ethical guidelines for compensation for aid research fall outside the official purview of human resources departments within aid organizations, and outside industry-wide minimum standards and protocols for humanitarian response.[37] Similarly, Paul Geissler finds that payments and compensation for research participants during clinical trials in Africa are appreciated and recognized, but yet "excluded from the public space." They are as such an "open secret."[38]

The two mothers in Aysha, as well as the survey enumerators and all the various participants in aid research in and around Aysha, were part of a global humanitarian "audit culture."[39] Beneficiaries' bodies, finances, and personal experiences of crisis, suffering, and relief operations were repeatedly elicited, measured, monitored, evaluated, and reported—most often by other beneficiaries and local aid workers living nearby. Even so, data collection did not always or immediately result in responsive or new interventions. Humanitarian relief in the Somali Region, for the most part, remained sporadic and inadequate to meet people's needs. While emergency aid is desperately needed at times in places like the Somali Region, most beneficiaries and aid workers remained pessimistic about the promise of humanitarian relief to prevent, or improve people's ability to withstand, future crises. Consequently, the production of data itself (and not the findings or outcomes of research or individual interventions per se) was seen as beneficial to those who could make the most of the opportunities aid research provides. The hustle for data, performed by beneficiaries, aid workers, relief agencies, and donors alike, shaped crisis-affected economies, the social relations of relief work, the visibility and activity of local staffers and beneficiaries, and the professional lives and careers of everyone involved.

The newly trained group of Somali enumerators in Aysha benefited financially from the research funded by this particular relief NGO and the WHO, but these men were also each officially beneficiaries of the aid that resulted from their research. Each enumerator received per diems of 200 birr per day for their work implementing the needs assessment over the course of the one week, and in addition, the enumerators' households in Aysha regularly received from the UN World Food Program and the US Agency for International Development rations of wheat grain, corn-soy blended flour, oil, and split peas both before this particular study and the months and years after.

In another town outside Jigjiga, an aid worker named Asad, then in his mid-forties, twice since 2016 was paid 700 birr per day (at the time worth US$35) for one-week stints translating research instruments and administering a survey for a European relief NGO that subcontracted with a private research firm headquartered in Addis Ababa. Reflecting on his employment a few years ago, while driving in a crowded vehicle near the Ethiopia-Somaliland border, Asad said that aid agencies "cannot just have people from Addis [Ababa] fly in and do the research. They do not know us, and the people here will not like that. They will not answer your questions, or they will just answer however they feel and not truthfully. No, that was my job. They trusted me. They know me. And I convinced them that this was okay; the project was okay. They could tell me things, and I could come inside their house."

Conversation among three other men in the vehicle picked up on his point, repeating and laughing about the fictions Somali residents might tell an Amharic-speaking survey enumerator if not convinced by the translator to remain honest. After a pause, in a more serious tone, Asad said to all of us, looking around, "The people [in those communities] did expect something from us, I think, and nothing ever happened after that. Organizations have for a very long time been coming here and distributing things. Resources. Every time they would see a white vehicle, there would be a distribution of something."

A friend of ours in the car then said to Asad, while smiling, "Maybe the next time [the NGO] comes the people will not participate. Because they did not receive anything!"

Then facing me, Asad said, "The people here, they expect to get something. They expect to benefit in some way when you come and do a study. Food, money, a project, something. And immediately. They [the people living here] cannot see into the future."

A third man who was laughing at this exchange, said directly to Asad, "Yes, I am not sure you will be welcome the next time in their houses! You will have to deliver something to them!"

The beneficiaries Asad encountered were insightful. People realized visits and needs assessments almost never directly lead to new humanitarian programming. Instead, the research itself was the intervention. Another aid worker, on a different occasion and at a different European relief organization, said, "Many NGOs—national and international—go around and make lots of promises without carrying anything out. These promises are understood [to be promises] by people when NGOs come to their communities doing needs assessments and studies. There are so many proposals that NGOs make to their headquarters . . . then get rejected and never implemented. 'What happened?' the people will say. And the next time when that NGO shows up, the people say they will not tell you anything this time."

Despite the rising interest in localizing the aid sector, many aid organizations still only superficially engage with recipient communities in Ethiopia, and only then through predetermined methodologies and for short periods of time.[40] Plus, relief work continued to imagine itself temporary, and continued to rely on the labor of residents living in communities in crisis already struggling to make ends meet. A majority of emergency interventions during this research consisted of one-time disbursements of aid commodities or emergency medical services for a few days or months at a time, rendering the research projects and employment opportunities these interventions required—like the anthropometric study in Aysha or Asad's survey work—also sporadic and short-lived.

Asad and others provided another perspective on these per diems. Many Somalis in Ethiopia wanted and expected to benefit from intensive but rapid research methodologies, even as their expectations of the relief operations that result remained low. Data collection was not a realistic or sustainable career option for the vast majority of people living in crisis-affected places. But for some like Asad and the enumerators in Aysha, these interventions presented important and relatively lucrative side hustles, especially in places without other viable livelihood options.

Therefore per diems have risen in prominence as popular forms of cash payment in international aid.[41] The emergence of the English phrase *per diem* often signified, in the Somali Region at least, temporary, nonsalaried, negotiated, and often informal forms of payment for work, travel, or participation in research. Even so, people from communities where interventions happen, despite their increasing participation in aid, still remained largely alienated from the mechanisms and institutions that govern and design interventions. Asad, for example, never signed a contract or earned a paycheck from the NGO headquartered in Addis Ababa for his work near Aysha; he instead benefited from fluid and informal employment with private research firms. The enumerators in Aysha, as well, only received cash payments in Ethiopian birr, and never signed a legal work contract.

Additionally, regardless of how and for what compensation people agreed to work, the myriad data collection activities themselves have indelible effects on people. Rather than data producing fixed or powerless categories of people (in this case, "beneficiaries") the subjects of research as Ian Hacking argues, are "moving targets because our investigations interact with them, and change them. And since they are changed, they are not quite the same kind of people as before."[42] Continual investigations of humanitarian crises and interventions, time after time, on individuals' bodies, in their homes, and in their communities, as well as the rising prevalence of remuneration for various forms of temporary participation in these studies, entail intimate and repeated interactions and exchanges between beneficiaries, aid workers, and researchers. These activities thus change what it means to be a beneficiary and subject of humanitarian inquiry. They change how people value, perceive, and negotiate with their physiologies, diagnoses, finances, experiences, and struggles as these are variably measured, recognized, redefined, categorized, and represented during data collection activities.

The two mothers in Aysha, for example, exhibited remarkable assertiveness with the staff of the NGO, Idrias and Jamal—a move that is unimaginable without understanding the contemporary ways in which so many beneficiaries in the Somali Region of Ethiopia are regularly interpolated into data collection activities in order to receive cash benefits. Their children's biological markers and their time and consent for anthropometric measurements were, in this case, immediately valuable and marketable. The women's attempted capitalization of data collection signaled the thriving market for and value of data in and around Aysha, but this story also importantly highlights the fact that, in the end, unlike the newly trained male enumerators or like Asad and so many other local aid workers, the two mothers' potential forms of participation were not valued enough, this time, to be worthy of monetary compensation.

Even so, in this case, data collection presented a means by which Asad could be part of an aid industry that had helped his family survive for generations, as they have lived in different refugee camps and received rations and clinical care from various relief organizations through the years. As we drove between towns, Asad pulled out the official identification card and badge he had received while working as a language interpreter for a different European aid organization several months before: "Maybe they will want me again," he said, "and that would be so nice. Even though it is many hours south of here, I would go. You see, I had practice from the survey here, and I now have experience with language interpretation and with surveys. Inshallah I will go to them again."

David Mwambari and Arthur Owor write, "In order to support more informed decisions about development aid and humanitarian aid in conflict and post-conflict societies, academics, policy makers, and journalists travel to these communities to collect knowledge. To gather knowledge, they will almost always rely on local people to facilitate their research."[43] The gig economies that result from this market in knowledge production should not, however, be viewed as ends in and of themselves, or even as adequate or fair given the poverty and insecurity of so many crisis-affected populations. Instead, these gig economies should be regulated and reconfigured to ensure sustainable local investments in crisis prevention and response. After all, most humanitarian emergencies in eastern Ethiopia and around the world are not one-time events. Humanitarian crises are symptoms and manifestations of systemic vulnerabilities and structural inequities. The particular NGO that visited Aysha has visited to conduct needs assessments and deliver aid commodities almost every year since this event happened; Asad continues to work for aid organizations in the area on short-term contracts of a few weeks or a year at most; and several of the Somali enumerators trained that day in Aysha have since worked on additional surveys and studies nearby. There is a thriving market, throughout Ethiopia and around the world, for the kinds of data that can prove the existence of a crisis and the urgent need for the kinds of interventions relief agencies can readily deliver. But jobs in the data economy are at best temporarily lucrative, and often fail to offer local aid workers or beneficiaries sustainable means of employment or adequate compensation for their time and labor.

The Humanitarian *Delala*: A Fixer and Guide

Drivers, logistics managers, translators, data collectors, researchers, and field monitors and the like—were all necessary to aid operations because, essentially, they made projects happen. They were, in Amharic and other Ethiopian languages, humanitarian *delalawoch*: brokers, fixers, or guides. In general, in many sectors, a *delala* helps people understand new situations and places and helps people get all sorts of things accomplished. If you need to find an apartment in Addis Ababa, you would hire a *delala*; if you want to cross an international border without a visa or passport, you could also hire a *delala* to help. What I call a humanitarian *delala*, accordingly, is an expert in the relationships, networks, politics, and economies important for the implementation and evaluation of humanitarian response. But like other *delalawoch* in Ethiopia (in real estate, trade, migration, and the like), their work and expertise can never be fully or accurately represented in official scopes of work with relief agencies. Many of their activities and forms of expertise remained informal, ad hoc, and interpersonal, and therefore both largely invisible and potentially exploitable.[44]

Farah, for example, a staffer at a different regional UN relief agency based in Jigjiga, coordinated his organization's emergency response unit for the entire Somali Region for four years, from 2012 until 2016. But without warning, the UN suddenly hired an "international expert to come here," he told me, essentially taking over his post and demoting him to an "assistantship position." Farah said he, "felt a burden because [the expatriate] had to learn everything, internally and externally, like the culture, the history, etcetera." "Number one," he began to list for me the challenges of this restructuring of his office, "you have to introduce the new person to all the external partners, like the Somali Regional Health Bureau, and this typically takes six months for them to understand all the relationships with external and implementing partners. Especially because this is very political, and you have to know your role vis-à-vis these different offices and people." Farah showed me his impressively long contact list on the cell phone between us, demonstrating he knew the mobile phone numbers of numerous local actors at the regional, *woreda* (district), and *kebele* (village or neighborhood) levels, and he knew all his partners in Addis Ababa too. "It's your relationships with all these different people that is so important."

"Number two," he continued, "during implementation you must meet with the government—a lot. And there is a language barrier. You have to take notes, do real-time translation, and then most importantly, you have to be able to react and help correct the new coordinator when they don't understand something enough, and the person needs repetition and explanation." But this is not an issue of needing simple Somali-to-English translation. Most meetings with foreign staff can easily take place in English. Instead, the international staffer, in Farah's experience, does not understand the professional language that is common parlance for those working in humanitarian response in Ethiopia.

For example, he explained further, "The new guy once accompanied me to the Bureau during an emergency response, and during meetings there we all started talking about the C.F.R. [crude fatality rate] is this, the C.F.R. has gone up . . . and the new guy didn't know what that was! So everyone had to stop and explain the epidemiological term for C.F.R. and what it means, and the cut-offs, and so on. We had to stop the meeting for that. He didn't know!" Farah rolled his eyes at me, smiling.

Farah continued counting on his fingers, "Third, you have to do external-facing information management when there is an international staffer." I had him repeat this phrase, to make sure I understood. He repeated it for me, clearly: "External-facing information management. An example is cholera. What if the new guy actually reported cholera in an email? He would get fired, and he would get us all in trouble. You cannot do that here. The government doesn't disclose cholera statistics."

Farah then continued, "Fourth, UN and implementing partners sometimes disagree on policies and priorities," but these disagreements, he attested, "should not rise to the level of politics or endanger someone's career." Local staffers mediate and negotiate frictions between governmental agencies and the NGOs and UN agencies that partner with the government, because "people cannot easily say no to the government." "Abshir [another project officer at the same UN agency in the Jigjiga office]," Farah recounted, "had a fight with the regional government over some policy or something, and the government people got very angry, but instead of going to Abshir's superiors at [the UN agency] they called in the *ugaas* [traditional Somali leaders] to help resolve the conflict. The *ugaas* from Abshir's home community and the *ugaas* from the partner's communities discussed, and decided that Abshir should be free to push for whatever policy it was, and that their disagreement should remain professional and not get personal or engage with the superiors in either organization. This kind of mediation is not possible with international staff."

In the end, the scope of Farah's work changed after "the new guy" arrived. He was demoted from head of the emergency response department, to essentially a guide and translator for the expatriate staffer who replaced him. He organized and curated the education and experience of an expatriate aid worker who, according to him, was unprepared for the job. He drove with him to ministerial offices and introduced him to local leaders. He drove with him to field sites and the distribution sites, and introduced him to the challenges and dynamics of humanitarian response. In doing so, however, his labor and his expertise as the former head of the office were rendered invisible and less valuable, and his role as a local eclipsed his former role as a leader and expert.

Several other aid workers I spoke with in Jigjiga were tired of just being known as local experts. Every time an expatriate came for a visit or a short study, they felt obligated to put away their other work to provide the newcomer guidance, data, language interpretation, and an orientation to the politics and geography of the area. Jira, a leader at a UN relief agency office in eastern Ethiopia said, "WFP, UNOCHA, IOM, Save the Children, NRC [Norwegian Refugee Council], and so on together provide hundreds of local jobs and thousands of jobs for Ethiopians around the country." Having so many local staffers is necessary for relief operations, but also underappreciated. "Management [of the UN agency] in Addis [Ababa] sometimes does not even understand that local language is actually different than Amharic!" he exclaimed, shaking his head. "The international managers would have really struggled if I was not here. I have knowledge of the area, the regional and woreda-level officials, the languages," he said. It was vital that he could "convince the people out in the region of what they need to do. Then the higher officials at the regional and zonal levels push the people at the woreda level, and convince them to cooperate. Even if the field monitors are new, I can get things done," he stated.

Local experts like Jira were also repeatedly tasked with adjusting programs designed in faraway places like Geneva or New York to fit people's expectations and the dynamic needs and circumstances on the ground. When tasked with implementing projects, local aid workers had to represent global relief organizations to communities, and to explain the organizations' priorities, limitations, protocols, and expectations. Additionally, local staffers were tasked with forging and maintaining over long periods of time relationships with other local actors including bureaucrats in woreda and kebele offices, politicians, and traditional leaders.

Many local aid workers testified they felt invisible to the global aid agencies they worked for. Indeed, from what I could find, there had never been systematic monitoring or data collected by aid agencies on the challenges of contractual work and subcontracted work at subnational or local field offices; there were often no legal or official ties between local staff and the global aid organizations that delimited their labor; and there was little if any legal or financial recourse to settle employees' grievances. Outside humanitarian response, in many employment sectors, workers' invisibility and the informality of employment can foster both exploitation and alienation.[45] This holds true in the global humanitarian industry. The invisibility of the difficult and dangerous conditions in which local aid workers labored, and the informality of jobs to implement, manage, and monitor relief operations, obscured workers' potential exploitation by NGOs and government agencies.

So in innumerable and diverse ways, local aid workers like Jira and Farah were absolutely vital to global humanitarian assistance but they also represented the bottom rungs of the global aid industry. In the pages that follow I uncover the unjust and harmful realities of the steep and rigid hierarchies inherent to humanitarian work, and the structural, systematic mechanisms through which locals in the Somali Region struggled to access resources, decision-making power, training opportunities, and professional support within the organizations that repeatedly intervene in their communities. Local aid workers attested they at once felt lucky and blessed to have the job opportunities they did, but at times they also expressed disappointment and frustration. They felt they were sometimes exploited, underappreciated, invisible, and limited by their roles as humanitarian *delalawoch*. They filled the "local slot," or the morally righteous and responsible object of global aid encounters, and very often, they yearned for more.[46]

Two weeks after I spoke with Farah and Jira, as I was conducting interviews inside a UN compound in Jigjiga, I spotted an English consultant making appointments with these same staffers to learn about the local political situation and the challenges Farah and Jira faced reaching more remote communities. The consultant had just arrived for a two-week visit. So between all my own questions, and this new arrival's need for translation and explanation of the projects at hand, Farah and Jira and others were overwhelmed with work. My inquiry and my own research were part of the problem, so I returned home for the day.

Freedom through Nongovernmental Work

While many aid workers within UN agencies and international NGOs in the Somali Region said they felt stuck working at the local level and stuck being only seen as experts on local conditions, other staff felt this was still preferable to work within regional or district-level government agencies. Another distinction marking inequities between aid workers was, as Aden phrased it, different levels of "freedom" between nongovernmental and governmental employment. "They [aid workers in governmental agencies] often feel like they are stuck as part of a big system, and cannot be free. They cannot be free to be creative. . . . People work in aid for their basic survival," Aden said matter-of-factly, leaning forward and gesturing with his hands to his own chest, "especially government workers who are often not able to meet even their basic needs with the [relatively low] salary they are given [compared to staff at UN agencies or INGOs]."

Freedom was something several Somali aid workers in Ethiopia felt jobs with nongovernmental aid agencies could offer compared to work within government agencies. In addition to higher salaries, people desired the opportunities they felt nongovernmental jobs promised. A driver working for a European relief agency said to me once, "Lots of people want to move from the government job"—he was once a nurse in a public clinic—"to the INGO [international nongovernmental organization] in order to expand your mind, get opportunities to see and know about the whole world. When you're in a government post, you are just local. When you work for an INGO, you're part of something bigger."

Abdulahi, for example, loved his work for a UN relief agency because of its expansive vision and the opportunities he had through the UN to travel and study abroad. Abdulahi was born just outside the Jigjiga city limits, but when he was two years old his mother moved with him to Mogadishu in Somalia. The civil war in Somalia in the 1980s forced them to flee to Kenya, where he lived with extended family members in Nairobi and attended a public school. But his mother longed to live in Greater Somalia again, so they moved back to Degahabur in the Somali Region of Ethiopia. He attended the University of Khartoum and obtained his first master's degree from Haramaya University in Ethiopia, then obtained another master's from an online program at a European University. While Abdulahi loves living in the thriving Somali city of Jigjiga, he also loves travel.

"Working at the UN," he said, "you meet so many people, you have to get knowledge from each sector." For example, at the Water, Sanitation, Hygiene (WASH) program, "If there is someone who is missing in a woreda-level post, he can just fill in temporarily. I can just go. I can fill in." And through the UN Abdulahi has also met global leaders: "I remember one donor visit. I cultivated the interest of donors—shook hands with the German finance minister—that sort of thing. You are teaching them in a sense, taking them on a field visit. It is fascinating!" These are things, he says, he could never do if he worked for the government. The UN gives him the opportunities to travel and to learn. It is expansive.

Nimo, a woman introduced in previous chapters and approximately twenty-five-years old, had begun working for an international relief NGO for only a few months before we spoke. Nimo disliked employment with governmental relief agencies because she only ever worked on month-to-month contracts, and after three years, without warning, one month her contract was not renewed. "I have a family! I need to work!" she exclaimed. She also disliked the scope of her work for Ethiopia's federal Disaster Prevention and Preparedness Commission: "you are simply delivering services. Giving out the money." At her new job, she said, she was able "to increase [her] knowledge and experience. There [were] so many broad experiences there when before for the government I was just writing checks." And, she reiterated, the relief NGO offered her greater stability. She signed a one-year contract, and felt confident about its renewal the following year.

Mona, with several more years of experience both at different government posts and at the same NGO, sat next to Nimo as she spoke, nodding in agreement. Then she added, echoing Aden's and Abdulahi's sentiments as well: "The government work is also so political," she said. "For the NGOs you are free, you can be free, and you can do the big programs."

A driver named Jama who worked for a European relief NGO was a certified nurse and had also earned a bachelor's degree in sociology. Learning this, I asked him why he decided to apply for a job as a driver instead of a clinical provider, health expert, or project officer. He responded that the NGO position, even though he was only hired as a driver, had the potential to develop into "something else," something better, he said, and, "something bigger," with a higher salary than he could ever hope for as a public sector nurse. Because of his prior work experience, he speculated he might get a promotion soon from the NGO and "move up and up." He wanted to, in his words, "professionalize himself at the NGO." "People that work at NGOs," he said further, "do not do heavy or bulky work—it is easy work. They do the same thing every day, every time."

Job Insecurity—Even with One of the Best Jobs in Town

Abdirahman's workday was intense and busy. When we had last spoken, he was working as the Health and Nutrition Coordinator for a major INGO based in Jigjiga, and his salary and contract were based on renewable two-year grants for emergency response programming in the Somali Region of Ethiopia. Eighty percent of his time, he estimated, was spent writing reports to donors on his aging Dell desktop computer. He even carried his computer home sometimes, to work on Microsoft Word documents late into the night, after his two little girls fell asleep in the adjoining room.

When he arrived at his office on a typical weekday morning around nine o'clock, Abdirahman always checked his emails and responded to immediate inquiries from the office in Addis Ababa. But even before his arrival at work, while driving through Jigjiga's traffic-clogged streets, he had typically already fielded several phone calls from friends, former colleagues looking for employment opportunities, and bureaucrats and service providers in rural woredas and kebeles where his NGO organizes health and nutrition projects. During the first part of his day in the office, he organized time sheets for all the mobile teams, health-care providers, and government employees being paid from the NGO coffers. He tracked as many as forty people's hours worked, their travel and expenditures and per diems, and he made several phone calls to double-check and fill in the numbers. He coordinated and approved all these lower-level workers' vacation time, sick days, and contracts—and all this had to be completed during the morning hours, before people left work to lunch and chew khat at home.

By nine-thirty on a day when I visited, Abdirahman's smartphone on the desk between us buzzed every two or three minutes. He quickly answered a few of these calls while we talked, greeted, responded, and thanked callers in Somali, hanging up with only a few minutes before the next buzz. Most calls were about problems his different field teams encountered: fuel and electricity shortages, vehicle problems, security concerns, missing supplies, schedule confusion, and the like.

That afternoon, when I checked back in with him, he had just opened the most pressing task for the day: finishing the reports back to the INGO's global headquarters. He was writing and editing three different reports in English simultaneously, two for past projects and one for a new project they were developing, with large teams of other project officers from the same organization. He was also responsible for contributing to datasets and donor appeals and media summaries from past work. But all this—all the paperwork and phone calls and projects—were set to end abruptly the next week, on Thursday, his last day of work. After four years at this INGO, and with his phone literally buzzing all day long with inquiries and problems to be solved, the "emergency" program that funded his salary was simply going to end. Data would no longer be collected to demonstrate the long-term effectiveness of the interventions he had so carefully planned, and families would no longer receive support for feeding their children.

In fact, Abdirahman was already looking for other jobs and thinking about his future. Could he go back to school? Should he apply for another NGO position, despite the long odds? Should he instead write reports to argue for additional emergency programming at his current NGO, despite the fact this work would have to happen without pay? What would his family do, without his income? As we talked about his options, he stopped and said abruptly, "I cannot think about this yet."

The phone between us buzzed again, and he answered. A nurse from one of his mobile teams reported their safe arrival to a rural kebele experiencing continuing high rates of acute malnutrition among young children.

The precarity of jobs like Abdirahman's was compounded by the continued tightening of project budgets across the humanitarian landscape in the Somali Region over the last several years. Parallel decreases in expatriate staff doing relief work in the region accompanied increases in the number of Somalis hired, but these local hires were almost all for temporary, lower-level positions. Aid agencies often subcontracted temporary jobs out to small private companies based in Jigjiga or local NGOs lacking capacity and regular support staff. Aden said, consequently, "People are often diverted from their work, because they are doing other things." Productivity and effectiveness among these staffers flagged, he assumed, because people "are constantly looking for other jobs and not even doing their own job."

In the Somali Region, data collection, monitoring and evaluation protocols, and managing the logistics and transit of aid distributions, were tasks mostly accomplished by private companies subcontracted with relief organizations like the UN World Food Program, UNICEF, and Save the Children.[47] Employees hired from regional cities were sometimes paid much more than the subnational governmental bureaucrats and persons working with local NGOs in the crisis-affected places where they were deployed, creating tensions and perceived inequitable hierarchies between relief organizations and governmental offices. For example, UNICEF outsourced nutrition monitors, WASH (or "water, sanitation, and hygiene") information management officers, disease surveillance researchers, people who monitored and logged food distributions, and almost all the logistics experts and drivers from small companies based in Jigjiga. One project officer said, "We need so many more people on the ground than we have. The government lacks capacity. . . . They don't even have vehicles to reach remote woredas." The subcontracted workers for UNICEF will actually make several times the salary, he estimated, compared to district-level government workers. This system, he admitted, was "unsustainable, surely." International aid agencies justify this system, he said when we spoke in 2018, because there was an emergency and increasing numbers of displaced people in the region, and suddenly more staff are needed to complete the requirements for collecting data and publishing reports, but, "we can't keep this up."

Doctor Hamza, the senior adviser to an international NGO in Jigjiga and a former leader in ministerial positions in the Somali Region, admitted that since the very founding of the Somali Regional Health Bureau, the government had been hamstrung by the high turnover of its staff. People "reshuffle, reshuffle" every few months, he said. From work at governmental ministries, then they "reshuffle, reshuffle," he repeated, to NGOs, "reshuffle, reshuffle," to UN organizations, "reshuffle, reshuffle," back to governmental posts, "reshuffle, reshuffle," and to NGOs again, perhaps in their retirement founding their own local NGOs. Individuals moved from position to position based not on need but instead on funding and seemingly arbitrary project timelines. People rarely stayed in one place or one institution for more than two or three years.

Abdirahman said all this reshuffling increased "the burden of my work. It is stressful. We are trying now to complete all our activities. Plus the termination is sudden. Most of them are on emergency contracts." When I spoke with him after his own final week at work for the international NGO, Abdirahman said that in his final days on the job, he had to "release four additional mobile team workers" from their contracts. He shook his head sadly. "It is stressful." Farah, in the relief agency across town, had also watched several colleagues depart in recent months. "We need to recognize the contributions of local staff. There needs to be more motivation and position support. There is often low morale."

Glass Ceilings

Jira, for one, willingly discussed his relatively high salary and his relatively lengthy work contracts compared to others in his office, and admitted the terms of work for his employees were "not fair." He, Abdirahman, Doctor Hamza, Farah, Aden, and other aid workers in long-term positions in the aid industry in Jigjiga also recognized they still needed to remain local to retain and accomplish their jobs. Their localness was the reason they continued to work in their relatively high positions, and there were no mechanisms by which they could easily apply or campaign for promotions to the national headquarters in Addis Ababa, much less jobs outside Ethiopia, due to the need for their particular skill set in the lowlands of eastern Ethiopia.

Jira's predicament provides a window into this problem. For several years, Jira led a UN relief agency office in eastern Ethiopia, overseeing staffing and reporting problems with human resources to the national and international headquarters offices. Since 2017 the number of employees in his office has repeatedly ballooned and then dramatically declined, despite the steady increases in numbers of internally displaced persons in the area. Most of the employees in his office remained on "fixed-term" or "short-term" contracts.

But, Jira pointed out, this situation was both unsustainable and suboptimal. "Many of these staffers just get better jobs and then leave. Three people in my office just did this. They work typically three to eleven months, which means they require a lot of work and investment and training then [they] don't end up staying around very long." International staff will often stay for eleven or twelve months when they are deployed to a local office, but "then they will take a break, [or a vacation, he clarified later] often meaning they actually change their location." To counter such high turnover, Jira tried to hire logistics officers and program officers only from cities in the eastern part of the country. In other words, he tried to only hire persons who had reasons to stay in the area.

Even Jira's employment contract was short-term. He had predicted his year-to-year contract would not be renewed a few months before we met. But because of the state of emergency in eastern Ethiopia lasting until 2018, and due to increases in displaced persons streaming into camps and cities nearby, his contract was provisionally extended through the end of 2018. Jira shook his head, frowning and balling his hands into fists between us. "What will they do?" he asked, rhetorically. Despite his fifteen years of experience, he said he had no idea what would happen to him in six months, when his contract was supposed to run out. He said he felt like he was just barely holding the office together, hearing about drivers being attacked and robbed by bandits, training and deploying new staffers every few days in the middle of an unfolding humanitarian emergency, negotiating every day for more resources with the headquarters in Addis Ababa, and constantly calculating and recalculating the metric tons of aid commodities he had promised to deliver. Even with all his accomplishments over the last several years and all the moving parts he managed in the midst of repeated emergencies, he could not count on his job lasting more than a few months.

On the other hand, Farah also testified he was dissatisfied with his position and wanted to leave the UN system altogether. One point of critique he offered was that he could not, in his current assistantship position, resolve the inequities between different staffers within the country office of this UN relief agency. He no longer wanted to be a local worker. "There is much more [upward] mobility for people who are at the *national* level," he stated, meaning Ethiopians headquartered in Addis Ababa. He could think of only one person who came from a pastoralist area like the Somali Region or the Afar Region who was able to get a job internationally, "and that one job was only very temporary, I think," he lamented. Staffers in his office, including himself, Jira, and Aden, introduced in the first pages of this book, have repeatedly failed to get jobs they apply for in Addis Ababa, and without this step, they struggled to compete for jobs anywhere outside Ethiopia. Within-country differences in salaries and security were significant: staffers in the Addis Ababa office of the same UN agency typically made more money and signed longer work contracts, for as many as eight years, while at the regional office in Jigjiga just about everyone has a "fixed-term" contract, renewable every year. "I cannot advance to the national office [of the UN relief agency]. I have tried," Farah said, and paused. "I need a new and challenging environment."

Farah's skill set was valuable, he said, becoming emotional as we spoke, but in Jigjiga, he felt undercompensated and underappreciated. He knew, for example, "how to give space and recognition to local staff, and ask them about the political dynamics on the ground." He had, he said, "been in the local guy's shoes," especially in having to help orient international staff to the Somali Region. It was not impossible to give Africans chances at promotions, because he had "seen other Africans working in Ethiopia as expats": a Kenyan staffer he worked with once was very popular with the local staffers and effective at implementing international aid projects. "He played football with everyone; he was a great guy. He really got to know everyone and everyone trusted him." Having given up on getting a post in Addis Ababa, when we last spoke Farah was still applying for jobs with NGOs based in Ireland and Kenya, and thinking about attending graduate school in Europe.

Most aid workers in the Somali Region were men, by far, but increasingly, more women sought higher education and employment with aid agencies. Several men who led regional aid agencies admitted to me they struggled to respond to women's demands for equitable education, professional advancement, and participation in policy making. These structural changes took time and political will. But at least in Jigjiga, people like Aden, Doctor Hamza, and their colleagues were finally hiring and promoting more women in decision-making posts. "Females are heads of household. They are pastoralists. They care for our children. They are so important," the president of Jigjiga University in the Somali Region said as he keynoted an academic conference on pastoralism in July 2018. There were only five women (I could see) in the large ballroom listening to his speech. The room was packed from wall to wall with approximately two hundred men from just about every region in the country. It was evident, from the sessions these women led and the questions they asked to other attendees, change was afoot, and they—all but one Somali—were part of it.

Even so, at least in eastern Ethiopia, few female staffers in the humanitarian industry had ever been promoted above the local or regional level, to the office in Addis Ababa or outside Ethiopia. While Mona and Nimo and others benefited from jobs and promotions within the Somali Region, they too, they said, would have liked to effect change at the national or even international level. But like Farah, all the female staff I knew remained stuck in posts in Jigjiga.

Local staffers—very often persons who hail from minority and marginalized ethnic groups within Ethiopia and who do not speak Amharic as a first language—were disproportionately rendered valuable only as locals and were consistently walled off from opportunities for professional advancement. In general, the resulting low morale among aid workers plagued the offices of NGOs and UN relief agencies in Jigjiga and Dire Dawa; sometimes, it felt to me as if no one was focused on the pressing issues of the day, but instead, hustling and dreaming with each other about their next big move. National and expatriate staffers and leaders in Addis Ababa and in other headquarters locations, by not calling out and changing their organizations' lack of representation from minority groups and marginalized regions around the country, further cemented these disparities and insecurities and reproduced a view of Somalis as merely the so-called beneficiaries of aid rather than experts in and key to global humanitarian response.

"Staff Want to Be Developed Too"

Professionalization and localization of the global humanitarian industry require recognition that local staffers aren't just valuable as locals. Staffers likewise argued that their skills were transferable and worthy of both investment and trust. Aden spelled it out clearly for me as we sat together in the quiet courtyard, discussing his love for humanitarian work, and his struggles to advance: "The staff also have rights. And staff want to be developed too."

In addition to the wide and easily discernable inequities between non-Ethiopian expatriate and Ethiopian aid workers, intranational inequities exist between Amharic-speaking Ethiopians hailing from the highlands of the country, and ethnic minorities and people from pastoralist areas of Ethiopia's lowlands. Intranational inequities are regularly rendered invisible by data collection that only differentiates between national and international staff, or that fails to account for racialized patterns of discrimination within Ethiopia and transnational political and economic ties between people throughout the Horn of Africa.

So often seen merely as beneficiaries, and as part of this, unfairly prevented from advancing to jobs at the federal or international offices of relief agencies, Somalis in Ethiopia were as Didier Fassin phrased it, "expected to show the humility of the beholden rather than express demands for rights."[48] Similarly, Kenneth Maes's research in Addis Ababa with governmental health extension workers reveals a similar plight. Some of the health extension workers he spoke with declined to raise objections or seek better jobs. Sister Tsinkenesh, one of his interlocutors, "was reluctant to write letters of recommendation, figuring that helping volunteers get jobs would send the wrong message. From her perspective, constrained as it was by norms in the industry, the correct message was that volunteers should be happy with what they had."[49]

While not volunteers, aid workers like Farah, Abdirahman, Aden, Jira, Mona, Nimo, and so many others who dared critique the similar humanitarian system from within and place demands on well-intentioned humanitarian organizations were still inherently out of place within labor hierarchies and within the humanitarian order of things.[50] By demanding recognition, better compensation, and promotions, these workers essentially renounced their expected subject positions as objects of charity and their expected roles as locals. Their being merely locals elided their expertise and years of experience in humanitarian policy making and implementation—forms of expertise and experiences that, they argued, should be valued outside Ethiopia, at the global level too.

The humanitarian industry continues to rely on the willingness of locals to accept temporary, precarious, and flexible contracts, informal labor arrangements, and small salaries and per diems for less money than either Amharic-speaking Ethiopians or expatriates occasionally flying into the Somali Region. The informality of the aid work so often performed by locals and the popularity of tropes about the heroic local aid worker also leave unquestioned the conditions in which their labor takes place, and leave unquestioned the fact that it is often performed in unacceptable conditions with no benefits and no legal rights or recourse for workers' emotional well-being, abuse, exploitation, or injury. Locals too often only either fill the "local slot" or are portrayed as hometown heroes, but are not the recipients of equitable investment, professional development, or workers' rights. Instead, the few aid workers who do garner long-term employment doing humanitarian work in the Somali Region, like Jira, Farah, and Aden, eventually hit a low glass ceiling and struggle to advance. Finally, because the labor and expertise and critiques of most aid workers are rendered invisible, the public is left with the false impression that locals are simply lucky to be employed at all, and are therefore seemingly rescued, once again, by the benevolence of others, and not by dint of their own hard work.

4

CRISIS WORK

Proving the existence and urgency of a humanitarian crisis remains necessary in the Somali Region to fund many governmental programs in basic health care, food security, and agricultural support. Measuring, narrating, and then marketing repeated crisis events constitute an important part of local aid workers' jobs, because otherwise, their jobs and the funding for much of the regional governments' activities, would cease. People living all through the region—not just aid workers—recognize this fact.

One afternoon in the small and arid community of Elahelay, north of Jigjiga, I reclined on mats with several friends and colleagues on the shady side of a two-room health post to pass the hot part of the day. It was 2009, and it had not rained for at least four months. Local garden plots and small patches of grass had dried up, and several young men had left the area with camels and cattle to graze farther south and west. As we sat, dark clouds gathered slowly on the horizon, over the mountains along the border with Somaliland. Unaware of the change in weather, chatter between us about life and politics and music continued. Then suddenly, large drops of rain began to fall from the sky. Everyone leaped to their feet, and rushed to bring inside our mats and materials. It poured for several minutes, clearing all the dust and haze out of the air.

Responding to my obvious excitement at this turn in the weather, and the first rain in so long, so desperately needed, one of my friends said to me, laughing, "It isn't raining here—this is not a true rain!" A cluster of women nearby giggled, and another man joked, "Yes, you can't let anyone know it's raining or they'll never say it's a drought!"

The Production of Crisis

Years later, in 2018, I sat in Jigjiga with Nur as he looked around the dilapidated courtyard, knowing he was in his final days working for this international NGO. An oversize plastic umbrella shade hung askew above us, now a faded pink, and it creaked and rocked awkwardly in the wind. After a large gust, one of its panels slid off into the garden, a few feet from where we sat, startling us both and making us laugh awkwardly. Behind us, laminated posters, mounted along the exterior walls, told success stories about recent nutrition interventions and livestock projects Nur had helped organize, lead, and evaluate.

For the last two years, part of Nur's job has been to coordinate the NGO's Mobile Health and Nutrition Teams project in collaboration with the Somali Regional Health Bureau. The mobile teams provided health care, nutritional, and agricultural support in parts of the Somali Region "where pastoralists are scattered and lack access to health posts and other services," he described. For this NGO, teams of two nurses plus a community health worker (or a "health extension worker," as they are called in Ethiopia) traveled together by vehicle to where nomadic pastoralists lived or were seasonally camped, or to camps of internally displaced persons. Although this was officially an "emergency" project with what Nur called "emergency money," within the "emergency" department of this organization, in his words, the mobile team was focused instead on "primary health care, like vaccinations."

For several months, Nur had been writing grants and helping publish donor appeals calling for an extension to this project, to no avail. The state of emergency in Ethiopia was over; Prime Minister Abiy Ahmed was making sweeping and largely welcomed changes throughout the region; and in the preceding months, there had been decent rainfalls farther south and less violence to the west. Nur's work for the NGO, therefore, was about to end.

But "Thirty-eight percent of Ethiopian children are stunted!" he argued to me, rhetorically, throwing his hands in the air. "And this is a chronic problem, not an emergency!"

By the way he spoke about his work and led my tour of the different offices and posters on the walls, I could tell Nur was proud of his role in this NGO's infant and early childhood nutrition program. It was a program, he explained, that provided far more than just PlumpyNut brand therapeutic food pouches and bins of amoxicillin pills. Rather, it used emergency funding to invest in the training and deployment of mobile teams of medical providers as well as the purchase of "farming materials and small livestock like goats and sheep [for] agro-pastoralist communities." They were monitoring milk consumption as well as child weight and, "had begun to see really positive changes." He paused.

"However, donors are not interested in this sustainability. They say it lacks a theory." He threw his hands up over his head again. "When one child is dying, they rush in the money. But if you say many children *will* die," he emphasized, "nothing. They do nothing. When there is cholera, measles, they are running here to visit and send money. Now, nothing."

Pounding his right index finger on the table between us, he continued, "But chronic water shortages are very important too. Mothers are responsible for water collection, you know—they use the wheelbarrows and the big jerricans and they bring the water to the house every day. When the mobile teams arrive, one day out of seven [because mobile teams typically serve six localities at a time, traveling to a different one each day of the six-day workweek] . . . always some of the mothers are absent, gone to get water. Also women are always keeping fires in the home kitchen, they are cooking and taking care of things at home, and they miss the mobile team."

"Mobile teams provide medications for UTIs [urinary tract infections, mostly experienced by women], anti-pain medications, a few antibiotics, RDTs [rapid diagnostic tests for malaria]—but this is all. Many things fall outside their capacity. Like, [people living in] rural and urban areas are now also eating the same foods like pasta and rice and so on. So they are getting the same diseases. We are seeing hypertension for example, and other chronic diseases like diabetes too. But there is no medicine for this. We [through the mobile team program] can do referrals but we are thinking about proposing doing rapid tests with mobile teams for things like hypertension and diabetes." To echo the words of the old arthritic man from Elahelay, described in chapter 2, frustrated by the long line of children and mothers in the UNICEF-funded mobile team intervention years before, "*Ma jirto dawo oday ah*": there is no medicine for old men.

Externally funded and organized relief operations (*bani'aadamnimada*) required the effective discernment and representation of a sudden and urgent crisis event, necessitating an intervention to ameliorate suffering that is presumed to occur as a direct consequence. As Janet Roitman insists, "Crisis is constituted as an object of knowledge."[1] Crisis must be rendered knowable, measurable, material in some sense, and worthy of and appropriate for a quick institutional response. Crisis also signifies both a historical and a moral change, she argues, through the announcement of departures from the norm. In a crisis, things are both not right and not how they used to be. And that, for aid workers in eastern Ethiopia, is where the trouble with the production of crisis lies. They are tasked with proving and narrating an emergency situation to donors and representatives of their organization in headquarters, when their work actually requires they address *chronic* forms of suffering and *entrenched* poverty—not true departures from the norm. They are therefore tasked not just with implementing humanitarian interventions, but also with the production, communication, and evaluation of artificial and exotic notions of crisis itself. This is what frustrated Nur so much at work—not only the existence of suffering or crisis in this case, but the absurdity of having to provide donors an artificial notion of crisis they would care about and act on.

The diagnosis and management of chronic noncommunicable diseases, chronic malnutrition, long-standing water insecurity, prenatal and antenatal care, and women's disproportionately hard and invisible work to manage households: these problems fell outside the domain of crisis programming and so lacked for dedicated funding and long-term staff. Nur had not been able to obtain funding for these kinds of crises. Only when he could prove through quantitative research and reporting there was an emergency situation, declared by the federal government or outside organizations, an outbreak of infectious disease, a drought, a sudden spike in rates of severe acute malnutrition among children, or something similar, could humanitarian program funding be reconfigured to help meet people's continual needs. Nur later explained, "INGOs try to help local people to enhance the[ir] coping strategies," and "try to help support instead by doing income generating activities but don't have much of an impact unless they are around for three or more years."

Asha, another aid worker at a European NGO based in Jigjiga had similar frustrations. Over plates of spaghetti and salad one evening, she divulged some of her greatest frustrations. "We have the mobile teams coming to a place for six months, or an organization distributing things for a few weeks, and then they go!" She waved her hands. "They run away!"

She shook her head, and continued, "People in other places, I think they say, bring a man a fish he will eat for one day, teach [him] to fish and he will eat for a lifetime. Something like that. That is not what we do. If there is an emergency, a drought, whatever, there is an emergency response, and that is good. It is good to be quick into an emergency, but we need to also think long-term about how people are going to live in the weeks and years to come."

One of Asha's female colleagues at the same organization, a nurse who worked on several mobile teams throughout the region, said to me on another occasion, "Mostly we do not target chronic diseases. For example, the mobile teams treat mostly infectious diseases, but they don't treat throughout the lifespan. Some people do say, 'You only target things that are acute, and not things that are problems only for older people!' At the mobile team, also we saw lots of TB, diabetes, and so on, and we would help write a referral letter for those patients only. That is all we can do."

Putting on Band-Aids

Humanitarian relief has long been critiqued for its shortsighted focus on relieving immediate bodily suffering at the expense of making lasting and sustainable reforms.[2] Nongovernmental humanitarian agencies, such as the Ethiopian Red Cross and the emergency unit of UNICEF in Ethiopia, for example, represent their work in donor appeals and media stories as only a Band-Aid, focused on saving lives and protecting people, and otherwise remaining neutral to or uninvolved in more contested political movements or lasting economic and infrastructural transformations. Calling humanitarian aid a Band-Aid originally referenced Bob Geldof's studio recording to raise money for the famine in Ethiopia in the mid-1980s.[3] But beyond this pop culture use, the Band-Aid metaphor is also a useful shorthand for an intervention that only attempts to address superficial problems—as, for example, only supplying communities with antibiotics during an outbreak of diarrheal disease without piping and cleaning the water supplies. Band-Aids, as a metaphor, are inexpensive, portable, name brand, and popular. Band-Aids obscure whatever exists beneath, making it easier to ignore deeper, structural problems. And Band-Aids outwardly communicate that something has been done to ameliorate the situation. They can even have placebo effects, help people feel better, or at least, help them feel confident something has been done.

Similar metaphors abound. João Biehl and Adriana Petryna use the term "magic bullet" to signify quick-fix, technological, and narrowly imagined approaches to health problems.[4] Magic bullets aren't just a combination of magical pills and silver bullets, but beyond this, represent attempts to medicalize bigger social problems. The phrase contains within it also the image of a gun, shot quickly in spectacular fashion, and from far away, so the shooter remains distant from its target.

Peter Redfield, as well, finds that Médecins Sans Frontières' development and deployment of humanitarian "kits" to respond to outbreaks of cholera, for example, is paradigmatic of the fundamental problem with humanitarian response more broadly: "Employing essential techniques of mobility, a standardized package performs well in emergencies and outbreaks, but falters when facing chronic conditions."[5] MSF providers know this. He writes, "Members of the organization like to point out that most people die not from exotic causes, but from 'stupid things,' effectively condemned by a lack of infrastructure and care."[6]

Nur and Asha, similarly, expressed dissatisfaction with their metaphoric boxes of Band-Aids, magic bullets, and kits—short-term, technical fixes that did little to fundamentally transform the larger systems in Ethiopia that caused suffering and humanitarian crises. Aden, from the UN office in Jigjiga, explained as we waited in a governmental office for a meeting with pastoralist policy experts: "You have very few development partners in the Somali Region. . . . The Somali Region gets emergency programming but it's for the normal conditions in which pastoralists and semi-pastoralist people in remote areas live. They are mobile, they are vulnerable to destitution, and often they are very sick. But it's not a sudden disaster or emergency." Band-Aids therein represent normal modes of international engagement with places like the Somali Region of Ethiopia, but the notion of *samafal*, and what actually happens during relief operations, defy the limitations and symbolic meaning of these material objects. Likewise, aid workers very often write donor appeals and grant applications not to respond to abnormal crisis events, but instead to bring attention to chronically high rates of disease and poverty among remote and pastoralist families in politically inse-cure parts of the region. The prevalence of malnutrition or the incidence of a contagious disease might at the same time cross a threshold, rainfalls might sig-nificantly decline, or there might be a media exposé about a conflict or forced displacement. But these catalysts for emergency funding, to local staffers at least, remained largely arbitrary and exogenously determined.

Humanitarian assistance conceived and structured by outsiders was therefore appropriated, modified, and molded in eastern Ethiopia, to the greatest extent possible, to solve entrenched and basic problems local aid workers faced year in and year out. Emergency funding augmented the government of Ethiopia's efforts to decentralize health care and disaster preparedness and response. Permanent health extension workers were trained, supervised, and given materials through funding earmarked for emergency projects (funding the training and salaries of people like Ahmed, shown in figure 8). At Nur and Asha's two INGOs, emergency funding subsidized the government's mobile team program to improve vaccine coverage, distribute oral rehydration solution, provide prenatal and antenatal checkups, and provide regular screenings for children and their mothers for mal-nutrition, malaria, and intestinal parasitic diseases. Emergency responses funded educational opportunities for local women's groups on various health and nutri-tion topics, and veterinary care for pastoralists outside major cities. Ambulances purchased during relief operations served rural woredas for years following the crisis that necessitated their purchase. Relief commodities like therapeutic foods were frequently stockpiled in warehouses and clinics during emergency relief operations, so local community-based providers could continue to distribute them when needed between interventions. Aid workers in eastern Ethiopia did

FIGURE 8. Ahmed, pictured here in 2009 at nineteen years old, was then a newly minted health extension worker in Ethiopia, trained and supervised early on in his deployment to the community of Elahelay by nurses on a UNICEF-funded Mobile Health and Nutrition Team. He was left to work on his own after the six-month project ended. UNICEF's mobile teams were originally deployed there to respond to a spike in rates of severe acute malnutrition and dysentery, but they also gave Ahmed a much-needed introduction to primary health care in this rural setting. In 2017 Ahmed married the daughter of a prominent local leader, and as of 2020, had two children and was still living in and serving the same community. Photograph by Lauren Carruth.

not in fact, hardly ever, provide Band-Aids, literally or metaphorically. Staff in the Somali Region accomplished the best primary and continuing care they could, as well as crisis response, with sporadic bursts of funding and supplies.

   Band-Aids additionally hid or erased all the work done to produce, publicize, and prove the existence of crises—on which the provision of basic health and social services in the Somali Region depend. Likewise, the labor required to render *samafal* from narrowly imagined *bani'aadamnimada* remained invisible and underappreciated. And many of the relief programs in the last decade in eastern Ethiopia—including the mobile teams and deliveries of potable water via tanker truck and the like—were exorbitantly expensive and unsustainable. These programs required vehicle rentals, training new staffers, and mountains of grant writing and monitoring and evaluation paperwork. Regional and district-level bureaus abandoned these kinds of projects as soon as emergency funding subsided.

The construction and deployment of exogenous notions of crisis shaped aid work in the following case examples: first, in a typical health post (or rural public clinic), in the community of Lasarat, emergency funding and relief supplies could not address the water insecurity, chronic malnutrition, and recurrent infectious diseases residents faced. Second, while adult-onset diabetes represented a rising problem in the Somali Region, and despite the fact it caused a significant burden on the health providers whose salaries and mandates are governed in part by relief organizations, health-care providers like Ahmed, pictured on the previous page, struggled to garner support for noncommunicable disease care. Third, outbreaks of cholera have been the subject of several emergency relief operations in the Somali Region, but the roots of these outbreaks remained unaddressed. Metaphoric Band-Aids, like the provision of antibiotics, precluded other, potentially more effective and lasting improvements, like the distribution of vaccines and diagnostic equipment and more importantly, improvements to piped water and sanitation infrastructure. Finally, many women suffered from a postpartum condition called *mindheeli* (literally translated as "shifted uterus") most likely due to a combination of overexertion, injury, and reproductive mishaps. Mobile teams and other aid workers in the Somali Region, however, treated women presenting with *mindheeli* for urinary tract infections or sexually transmitted infections they assumed they were too shy to disclose. The staffs of these relief operations had supplies of antibiotics but were ill-equipped to recognize and manage the complex and chronic problems women often faced.

Crisis Responses for Chronic Problems

Child Survival in Lasarat

Lasarat is located a few miles off the main road northeast from Dire Dawa near the Djibouti border, along a historically important railroad line and an older camel caravan trail connecting the Ethiopian highlands to Lac Assal (the salt lake in what is now Djibouti) and ports along the Red Sea and Gulf of Aden. Lasarat sits between a flat field of black volcanic rocks and a sandy plain where gazelles and baboons vie for the few natural resources not claimed by livestock. In this dry, hot, and flat landscape, most residents depend on hardy livestock like goats, sheep, donkeys, and camels, as well as the relatively thriving commercial market and truck stop several miles away in Aysha. Lasarat has experienced several crises in residents' recent memory: droughts, outbreaks of measles, and spikes in the rates of diarrheal diseases and severe acute malnutrition among young children. The water table in Lasarat, residents estimated, is located deep underground, too deep for wells dug by hand. Twenty years before, the United States military dug a borehole for water, but without anyone in town who could maintain the structure, it stopped working and filled with sand. Instead, every week, residents waited for deliveries of water from a tanker truck funded by the NGO Oxfam.[7]

On the steps of the health post, one bright March day, stood a little boy. He remained indifferent to me, visiting for only a short time, and uninterested in the cool shelter the health post offered behind him.

"He has pneumonia!" a health extension worker—working alongside a UNICEF-funded mobile team of nurses—proclaimed to me from just inside the door, loudly, pointing his finger upward at the sky, and smiling, presumably, at his success in identifying the boy's distress. "You see, we have given his mother some medicines already."[8]

The boy, it turned out, was also too small for his age—chronically malnourished, or stunted, according to the basic anthropometrics they had measured inside. He had been sick for months. That day his nose was runny; his eyes were irritated, he coughed a few times and had a fever, and the extension worker said "his digestion is not good. It is not right." He reported the child most likely suffered from parasites consumed in dirty water, had a diet inadequate to promote optimal growth and immune function, and he coughed and was feverish as a consequence of pneumonia. There were a few ways to help: the mobile team had on hand generic children's formulations of amoxicillin for the pneumonia and albendazole for the intestinal worms. The health extension worker also provided the mother a stamped and signed referral letter, recommending she take her son to the closest Health Center or a hospital where he could be evaluated and treated further. "Just in case he becomes worse," he told her gently.

The boy's mother, too, was moderately malnourished according to a quick measure of her upper arm circumference, and so the whole household received as many BP-5 biscuits as she could carry, wrapped in an extra scarf at her waist. After about an hour, the mother and her children walked back toward their home, just a little over one mile away.

This child—like most persons who present to clinics large and small around the world—arrived not with one disease or one problem but with many. And the problems afflicting him were both interrelated and long-standing. The only treatments offered included short courses of medications. Nothing to make his water source cleaner, nothing to reduce the labor and time it took his mother to collect the water, nothing to improve his diet and food security in the ensuing years, and even with a paper referral in hand, there was nothing the health worker could do to make the long trip to a hospital easier or more likely. The narrow possibilities of responses like this are what frustrated Nur and Asha, back in Jigjiga, so much.

Furthermore, meaningful designations or separations between what might in this case be defined as "chronic" diseases, like the chronic malnutrition that led to the boy's compromised growth and immunity—and the "acute" infectious diseases at hand, like the pneumonia and intestinal parasites infecting his gut, were blurry and interrelated. His infections were in part a consequence of and then also made worse by his chronically undernourished state. His gastrointestinal infections may have been in part a consequence of his exposure, throughout his life, to pathogens in the water obtained from wells dug into dry wadis nearby, where livestock also gathered to drink. His gastrointestinal infections may also have been a consequence of exposure to pathogens in communal latrines, his lack of adequate supplies of soap and water, or the fact there are no latrines at all in the seasonal camps where his family grazed their goats and sheep outside Lasarat. But these deeper problems were not addressed by the relief operations that funded this clinical interaction. Humanitarian solutions there and elsewhere were typically mostly focused on discreet, categorizable, easily treatable "acute" conditions, and not the more involved and structural causes of these afflictions.

Diabetes Care through Humanitarian Programs

In February 2018, as I rode with Ahmed and a few other friends and colleagues through the town of Elahelay, just a few kilometers away from the Somaliland border, Ahmed told me about two recent cases of diabetes. Just a few months before I arrived, in February 2018, a mother of four in her midthirties, seemingly otherwise healthy, had died only a short time after being diagnosed with Type-2 diabetes mellitus. Then, to Ahmed's expressed dismay, in April 2018, a father in his forties from Elahelay died of diabetes as well.

"They both died out there," he said, and motioned toward the desert expanse just outside the small collection of buildings. These two patients had both been recently diagnosed with diabetes by another health-care provider at clinics in Dire Dawa, and both were taking prescribed courses of metformin. Ahmed had just seen them in town, he said, and nothing seemed wrong. Three other people in this remote community had also been diagnosed with diabetes; one, a local leader, told me he feared for his life. What was perceived by residents as a sudden outbreak of deadly diabetes echoed stories about outbreaks of other acute infectious diseases Ahmed had heard about and helped treat through the years, including local epidemics of measles, dysentery, and cholera.

As the only local health worker within a day's walk, Ahmed felt responsible for the health of his neighbors. But at the same time, he lacked any training in diabetes prevention or management—his training had mostly been in response to acute health crises and common childhood illnesses like diarrheal diseases or pneumonia, and his local stocks of medications did not include any prescriptions for chronic conditions. I first met Ahmed when he had been deployed to Elahelay a decade before this, in December of 2008, during an epidemic of dysentery and a sudden rise in cases of malnutrition among children. UNICEF had sent mobile team nurses to Elahelay to assist with the response, and supervise his first clinical experiences. While over the last ten years, infant mortality, child mortality, and outbreaks of deadly infectious diseases had decreased significantly, he estimated to me, the frequency and burden of noncommunicable diseases like diabetes were rising. It felt to him like a crisis.

Noncommunicable diseases (or NCDs), including diabetes, are on the rise in Ethiopia[9] and among many crisis-affected populations around the world.[10] Experiences of humanitarian crisis and population displacement increase people's subsequent risk of serious infectious diseases, and this may also potentially trigger or complicate underlying, untreated, and undiagnosed NCDs. NCDs like diabetes therefore present a number of challenges for aid work. Screenings and preventive care are more difficult during humanitarian emergencies, when health systems are stretched or collapsed. The existence of humanitarian crises may limit patients' ability to pay for their medical needs, manage their disease close to home, achieve continuity of care, and access hospitals or pharmacies. Furthermore, in places like eastern Ethiopia where health systems have been decimated by decades of governmental neglect and intermittent international aid programs, many people lacked access to even basic primary health care—much less tailored, holistic, and lasting NCD care.

In my 2018 study of diabetes in eastern Ethiopia, we found that patients who were diagnosed with diabetes initially reported having symptoms of frequent urination and thirst.[11] But in addition, all the patients we spoke to also experienced concerning weight loss, weakness, and exhaustion both before and in the months and years following their diagnosis—and even when taking prescribed medicines or insulin. Many patients complained of losing their teeth over time as well, despite not having previous problems with dental cavities or tooth decay.

The disease in English called "diabetes" (in Somali, usually called *macaanka*, or literally "the sweet") is defined differently among many Somalis in Ethiopia. *Macaanka* is not associated with fatness and unhealthy lifestyles there, as it so often is in North America, Europe, and elsewhere. Instead, diabetes is understood to be a humoral pathology usually triggered by people's exposure to crisis or distress.[12]

Many Somalis measured their health (*caafimaad*), in general, by the balance of their bodily fluids or humors, and many patients visited mobile teams and refugee camp clinics complaining of humoral imbalances or dysfunctions. Primary among these were illnesses resulting from excessive digestive bile (*dacar*),[13] managed through triggering diarrhea or vomiting (*bixin*), consuming camel milk, feasting or otherwise changing the diet (*buulee*), and sometimes consuming pharmaceutical medications. Many Somalis looked to the traditional nomadic pastoralist diet, consisting of daily camel milk, occasional goat's and cow's milk, sorghum, hot broths, and hot tea plus regular supplements of fresh meat from local livestock, to promote health and strength (*xoog*).

FIGURE 9.   Dayibo cooking a fresh pot of goat broth in Elahelay, the Somali Region of Ethiopia, 2018. Photograph by Maxwell D. Hawla.

Additionally, diets associated with urbanization and sedentarization—consisting of oily (*saliid leh*) or soft (*jilicsan*) foods such as pasta, potatoes, and rice, as well as sugar, sodas, and sweets—were generally perceived to cause adults' diabetes, hypertension, heart disease, and chronic fatigue among other ailments. Food aid and rations were not perceived as nutritious either, because these mostly consisted of corn-soy blended (highly fortified, high-protein) flours for making porridge for children, and wheat and oil for cooking breakfast crepes (a food only popular, in this area, with the advent of ration commodities in the 1970s). Instead, diabetes was perceived by residents as resulting from a combination of dramatic environmental changes, exposures to trauma, emotions like anger or worry, external political or social crises, and lack of access to traditional Somali pastoralist diets. Bodies and diseases provided corporeal evidence of histories of stress, violence, food insecurity, and international intervention.[14]

Ahmed's patients struggled to access diagnostic technologies, to get continuing medical care, and to follow dietary recommendations due to their food insecurity and long-term dependence on limited food aid rations. Among residents and health-care providers in the Somali Region, diabetes was therefore a deadly and frightening disease. Lacking reliable access to preventive care, affordable medicine, refrigerators to store insulin, and community-based and continuing medical care from trained providers, diabetes was absolutely a matter of life and death—during and long after humanitarian emergencies.

(Mis)recognizing *Mindheeli*

Several years ago, while I was shadowing a mobile team operation in another small community several miles northeast of Jigjiga, a young mother came to where a UNICEF Mobile Health and Nutrition team had set up an intake table on the cool, shady side of the two-room health post. She approached Ali, one of the male nurses, holding her hand over her abdomen.

"It is *mindheeli* I think," she said softly. "Here," she said, and showed him on the outside of her dress where it hurts and how the pain had moved.

Ali nodded quietly and wrote down her name in the logbook, her long list of symptoms, and took a measure of her weight, height, and upper arm circumference to check for potential malnutrition. "Are you pregnant now?" he asked politely, and she shook her head no. "How long since you delivered the baby?" he asked. "Over one year," she said, "and no problems with the birth." Ali again nodded and escorted her into a private room out of earshot from everyone else, where the team kept caches of medications. She exited a few minutes later.

At the end of the day, while we cleaned up, I asked Ali to tell me more about this woman's case if possible. He said he suspected she had a urinary tract infection—a UTI—but without a thorough physical exam or a laboratory he could not confirm this. Consequently, he had provided seven days of doxycycline pills and asked her to return if she continued to have pain. But over the next several weeks, we never saw this patient again.

Many women—perhaps even the woman who sought care from Ali that day—moved through cycles of pregnancy, childbirth, breastfeeding, and after weaning, in most cases, soon after, back to pregnancy again over the course of many years. Although female genital cutting practices were changing in eastern Ethiopia, most women still endured excruciating and risky infibulation and subsequent reclosure surgeries after each childbirth.[15] Most women I knew gave birth at home with a traditional midwife, and many experienced painful complications and fistulas. Maintaining fertility and managing the pain of reproduction were major concerns. A range of self-care practices and traditional healing modalities were consequently focused on pain management and the health of women's reproductive systems.

In conversations, however, many women maintained that their daily routines fetching and pouring twenty-liter jugs of water, chopping and hauling firewood, cooking over fires all day in smoky enclosures, and tending livestock presented even greater physical tribulations and vulnerabilities to disease. Numerous women presented to relief workers and clinicians like the mobile team nurses with pain in their reproductive system and difficulty conceiving—sometimes from single events such as infibulation, childbirth, or acute injuries or infections, but often in combination with wear and tear on their body over many years of hard physical labor, the stress of everyday life, and the cumulative effects of years of childbearing.

Training manuals for nurses and health extension workers in the Somali Region, provided at public universities in Jigjiga and training workshops in Dire Dawa, noted the high prevalence of urinary tract infections and sexually transmitted infections like chlamydia and gonorrhea. These diseases were part of the mobile team interventions, and components of primary health-care provision in refugee camps throughout the region. However, UTIs and STIs are difficult to treat during temporary relief operations and in remote communities. Most clinicians outside hospitals lacked for the kinds of diagnostic and laboratory equipment these diagnoses require. The mobile team nurses and health extension workers in the rural Somali Region, for example, were almost always male, and furthermore, most facilities where they practiced provided little if any space for private consultations. These factors limited women's willingness to speak openly or have physical examinations. Most women sought care from a male clinician only as a last resort and then, more often than not, only from private hospital facilities far from their home communities. The young woman's visit with Ali, he said later, was unusual.

Fardosa, a young mother from the town of Aysha, tried to explain: "All the people they have different cultures, so when the people go to the hospital, some people they are ashamed and they don't talk exactly about their problems. Like women. They don't talk about their problems. If the woman sees a female doctor she might tell them about her problem, but if she sees a male doctor, she won't tell him. If the woman . . . doesn't talk [openly], [the doctor] cannot understand them, and cannot give any medicine or help."

I then asked her, "What health problems do women feel shame about?"

"Women, if they have a problem with their vagina, they don't talk about it, and if they have stomach or uterus problems they won't tell. There are so many problems like this that women experience and they cannot talk about." Just as in the story above, one of the most common ailments women in the Somali Region was *mindheeli*, literally translated as "shifted uterus."

Maryan, the fifty-year-old midwife from Degago, the small former refugee camp town in the northern Somali Region I introduced in chapter 3, attended a training session for two weeks in Jigjiga, funded by a UN relief agency and an American NGO, to be an officially recognized traditional birth attendant by the government of Ethiopia. Many of her peers had suffered from this type of pain, and when she had worked as a medical assistant in the camp clinic run by UNHCR and MSF several years before, during the civil war in Somalia, she realized this condition was not unique to her friends and family. Many Somali women suffered from *mindheeli*, she said, and she hoped to one day understand its causes and treatments better.

"*Mindheeli* comes after the woman delivers a baby, when she tries to lift something very heavy, like a jerrican. This hurts her stomach, or her uterus, and makes her uterus move over." She then showed me with her hand on my abdomen. "The woman should have to rest, and then eventually will get better. But usually, taking this rest this is difficult. The woman will become very sick—she will have a high fever, feel cold, and then she'll want to only sleep. After that, especially in places where there is no doctor, people will call an old woman with experience in such things [a *duugto* in Somali]. This *duugto* will use an oil to massage the stomach, will feed her hot food, and then let her sleep. After she's rested, she will likely become well again. If there is a hospital, the woman might go there, and they will give her pills for the *mindheeli*. They don't have any of these pills here in Degago, and they aren't in the shop either. You have to get them in Dire Dawa."

I asked as a follow-up to this, "Do you know someone who's gone to the hospital or clinic for *mindheeli*? She answered, yes, "the doctor tests the woman's stomach with a computer. He can see the problems in the stomach with the computer, and he will say there has been a change or a movement inside, and give her two pills."

Despite consensus among women about what constituted *mindheeli*, male aid workers, nurses, and health extension workers, Somali and non-Somali alike, were unsure of its exact etiology or definition. They assumed women had many different problems they glossed as *mindheeli* in the context of awkward clinical interactions. Consequently, several women presenting to the mobile team with *mindheeli* were prescribed antibiotics primarily for the treatment of urinary tract or sexually transmitted infections, although their reported symptom was severe pain in the abdomen after lifting a heavy object or giving birth. I asked a small group of mobile team nurses at a conference if perhaps *mindheeli* was a hernia or other muscular injury to the abdomen, but the whole group nodded no, and began explaining to me the women I had spoken to likely had sexually transmitted or urinary tract infections. Several additional mobile team nurses I spoke with reported that women are too embarrassed to speak about UTIs and STIs, and so *mindheeli* was their way of expressing these problems. Plus, they maintained, UTIs and STIs are very common and important to treat. "We have medicines for that," one nurse said.

Hibo, for one, struggled to find relief for *mindheeli*, despite the wide availability of antibiotics in clinics and shops nearby. Hibo was a young mother and a friend of Maryan; her experience typified many women's dissatisfaction over lack of diagnoses and effective treatments for *mindheeli*. Hibo had two young children, but for five years had been unable to conceive again. Her infertility, she guessed, was caused by *mindheeli*—in fact, she could pinpoint two times when she had hurt herself lifting jerricans full of water and tending livestock while her second child was still a small infant. Two years before we met, a *duugto* was called from another town several miles away to massage Hibo's abdomen, but the treatment did not change anything. Hibo ended up finding two more women who could massage her, but still she found no relief.

"Before I believed [*aamina*] in other types of medicine," like traditional massages and the like. "I saw other women improved. . . . Before now, I saw a girl who had gone without a baby for a long time; she also called a *duugto* to massage her, and now this girl is pregnant. After I saw that, I tried [the massage] again too."

When the second and third massages apparently failed to provide her relief or help her get pregnant, a few months before our conversation, Maryan accompanied Hibo to a hospital in Dire Dawa, hoping that the "new" kinds of medicine there would cure her. But Hibo said, "When I went to the hospital they said I didn't have a problem. 'You are normal,' they said." She shook her head sadly, "But they did not even test me with the computer." Hibo hoped to save her money and return to Dire Dawa and visit another hospital, perhaps one in Djibouti where they spoke Somali instead of Amharic, for another private consultation and another set of diagnostic tests.

Cases of *mindheeli* highlight the difficulty treating complex medical problems in a place with limited health-care facilities, diagnostics, female clinicians, Somali physicians trained in reproductive health, and private medical consultations. It also highlights the frequent incommensurability of biomedical diagnostic or treatment procedures and the lived experiences of illness in the Somali Region. For many women, *mindheeli* simultaneously indexed a nonspecific but sharp pain in their abdomen from overexertion or lifting a heavy object too soon after childbirth, and also, in the same conversations, indexed fears of reproductive mishap and infertility. *Mindheeli* was an "idiom of distress"—or a way women verbalized their psychosocial and physical suffering in locally meaningful ways.[16] But this idiom, and the cogent, physical symptoms women described were consistently misrecognized or misunderstood by nurses, aid workers, and health extension workers unprepared to diagnose or treat the complexities of women's internal injuries, chronic pain, or infertility.

A simple, straightforward biomedical diagnostic classification or a test for *mindheeli* that (mostly) male mobile teams or nurses might accomplish—without consideration of this condition's complex meaning and chronic effects—might actually spur inappropriate medical advice or therapeutic regimens. A doxycycline or azithromycin regimen for an STI or UTI, provided without a medical examination or a laboratory test, for example, evidently did not often provide women the relief they sought. The way humanitarian operations were configured in eastern Ethiopia—as public and crowded interventions, focused on the quick distribution of material medical supplies like antibiotics—and the way these interventions were usually staffed, by young, male health-care providers, cannot adequately respond to *mindheeli* and women's other reproductive health problems.

Moreover, Maryan, the midwife from Degago, was never given educational opportunities in nursing or medicine, or hired to serve in a licensed clinical practice that might have helped her transform local reproductive health care for women. *Mindheeli* therefore represented far more than a UTI or a STI (if it is ever these diseases), or a pulled or separated abdominal muscle or hernia, but instead also signified the ambiguous embodiment of a lifetime of overexertion, the painful and personal experiences of reproduction, and the inequities of health systems in eastern Ethiopia that fail to provide adequate health care to women.[17] It highlights the fact that despite acknowledgments within the humanitarian industry and government of Ethiopia of the importance of women and gender in humanitarian response, and despite the fact Maryan was trained as a traditional birth attendant, these initiatives both failed to fully incorporate or value women like her in either relief operations or reproductive health-care initiatives.[18]

Cholera: On Declaring and Denying Crisis

Cholera is the focus of numerous humanitarian interventions—in Ethiopia and elsewhere around the world. But temporary humanitarian responses to epidemic diseases like cholera will not, in fact, eliminate the disease. It is not enough. There is no magic bullet for diarrhea, no kit comprehensive enough, and no Band-Aid appropriate.

Cholera is an infamous scourge. In books detailing its historical and social significance[19] and even in recent media reports from Yemen, for example, cholera is depicted as an effect as well as a symbol of state failure.[20] Outbreaks of cholera typically happen in extremely impoverished places also affected by conflict or disasters; consequently, there have been repeated outbreaks throughout the Horn of Africa.

Cholera disease is caused by the ingestion of the bacterium *Vibrio cholerae*, which is often present in water or food that is contaminated with fecal matter. Symptoms of cholera begin anywhere from two to five days after infection, but patients who are already severely malnourished or sick with other ailments can die within hours. Cholera is far more deadly than most other diarrheal diseases. Merely washing hands cannot prevent infection when people also lack adequate sanitation facilities, clean toileting facilities, clean water supplies, and hospitals. Cholera outbreaks occur when drinking water sources or sewage systems fail or do not exist at all, and where cholera already exists in the environment. It is a highly pathogenic, frightening, fast-moving disease that can spread like wildfire in crisis-affected communities.[21]

Cholera has a long history in Ethiopia.[22] After a successful elimination of *Vibrio cholerae 01* strains in the 1980s, it reemerged in Ethiopia in 1994. Then in 1998, an epidemic of multi-drug-resistant *V. cholerae* in Ethiopia sickened thousands of persons throughout the country.[23] Since 1998, there have been only a few reports of cholera in Ethiopia, yet at least once every year, reports emerge from NGOs or the news media about an outbreak of acute watery diarrhea or AWD, especially in refugee camps or settlements of internally displaced persons.

Governments around the world—not just Ethiopia—have attempted to suppress word of cholera outbreaks or to mislabel diseases in a way that pacifies public anxieties.[24] Due to the stigma of cholera and its potential effects on tourism and trade, Ethiopian public health authorities have euphemistically classified suspected cholera cases as merely acute watery diarrhea.[25] Media outlets have accused the Ethiopian government of hiding outbreaks of cholera from the public by terming the disease AWD rather than reporting its more specific etiology or causative agents.[26]

During the second half of the year in 2009, for example, several reports of AWD were published online and broadcast on the radio. Aid workers headquartered in Jigjiga expressed concern to me about the outbreaks, but only publicly mentioned cases of AWD. They said privately that they assumed that the reports of AWD meant there had been an outbreak of cholera even though patients were not tested for the presence of the *V. cholerae* bacterium. In November 2009, the Amharic- and English-language online news source Abbay Media published a report that read, in part:

> When Ethiopia is hit by cholera outbreaks, as often happens, the government prefers to call it acute watery diarrhea because it dislikes the bad publicity that cholera attracts. The latest cholera outbreak, which began in August, has sickened thousands of people, but the government called it AWD and minimized the numbers. When the true numbers finally surfaced in a United Nations document, the government was so furious that it suspended its co-operation meetings with the relief agencies for a month.
>
> In fear of government punishment, many agencies fall into self-censorship. "There's a whole layer of anxiety that we're all operating under," one veteran worker said. "The obsession with control has been even stronger than last year."
>
> Some Western diplomats argue that the government's euphemisms and public evasions are unimportant because the accurate assessment data is known internally to the key agencies that supply emergency aid to Ethiopia. Compared with many other African countries, they say, Ethiopia is relatively efficient in distributing aid and is introducing good programs to expand health care and food delivery in rural regions.
>
> But others say the government's sensitivities and restrictions are hampering the world's response to Ethiopia's emergencies, delaying the flow of crucial aid for months.
>
> "If you delay the life-saving response, lives don't get saved," one relief worker says. "People get weaker and less productive. And the response is a short-term Band-Aid."[27]

The BBC Somali-language radio station broadcast into Ethiopia from Djibouti City and Hargeisa in Somaliland reported on these same recent AWD cases, translating reports of what the government and aid agencies called AWD into *shuban biyoot*, which literally translates as "watery diarrhea" in the Somali language. *Shuban biyoot* describes diarrhea that is, in general, watery, and could potentially cause dehydration or develop into a more serious illness. Somali health providers and lay persons I spoke to consistently described *shuban biyoot* as caused by anything from drinking raw camel milk to drinking from contaminated water sources. By contrast, *daacuun* (and also, less frequently the word, *kalooraa*) is a more accurate translation of cholera into Somali. *Daacuun* was described by laypersons as well as health-care providers as a severe form of diarrhea that is white in color, like the starchy water left in a cooking pot after pasta has been boiled. While various forms of diarrhea including *shuban biyoot* were seen as common yet potentially dangerous for young children, *daacuun* was seen to mortally threaten everyone, even healthy adults. Local distinctions between *shuban biyoot* and *daacuun* or *kalooraa* could not have been clearer.

Reports of outbreaks of *shuban biyoot* on Somali-language radio therefore carried less weight and generated far less local collective anxiety than if the word *daacuun* had been used. This mistranslation elided the potential urgency of a cholera epidemic among the local populations involved, and left unexplained to them the rationale behind the dramatic media attention and then, following these reports, the dramatic changes in humanitarian programming and the abandonment of measles and vaccination programs nearby. I prodded one expatriate staff member at an American NGO in Jigjiga, "Have there been any reports of cholera in the Somali Region?" He did not say "no," but rather, he carefully answered, smiling, "There have been reports of AWD. You know this."

Even in 2018, Mona and Nimo, two aid workers with a relief agency and based in Jigjiga, said the same purposeful mistranslation was still commonplace. Mixing both Somali and English words Mona said, "*Shuban biyoot* is not a problem but the people *fear daacuun*" she emphasized, "and would change their behaviors if they thought that was happening. But no one is allowed to use the word *daacuun*, cholera."

"No one could say that there was a cholera problem because of the government," Mona explained. "The cause of cholera was directly the shortage of water, and lack of hygiene materials and practices. As a result, the government thought that having cholera made them look weak, poor."

Mona said she has tried to ask her colleagues, "Why can't we talk about 'cholera' instead of AWD?" and she has consistently gotten unsatisfying answers. "Most people just refuse to talk about it. In 2016," she recounted, a cholera epidemic in Ethiopia "started in Addis, not in the refugee camps!" she claimed, and from Addis she said it spread all over the country, including to Jigjiga throughout the southern part of the Somali Region. An MSF nurse in the southern Somali Region, a European woman, Mona said, "wrote an email to the government, saying this was cholera, it looked like cholera, and not just AWD, but the government wrote back and told her that no, it was just AWD and she must not use the word cholera. This happened many times all over the country."

Cholera outbreaks are now easily detectable, preventable, and controllable. Even in crisis-affected locations, refugee camps, or areas without diagnostic testing or laboratories, a new rapid diagnostic test can enable disease surveillance and provide early warning to public health officials that an outbreak is unfolding.[28] These tests were designed specifically for use in resource-constrained environments and in humanitarian emergencies at highest risk of a cholera outbreak. Additionally, oral cholera vaccines, if widely used, are proven to prevent and control an outbreak.[29] The WHO, under the leadership of Director General Dr. Tedros, formerly the minister of health in Ethiopia, has called for preventing and controlling cholera outbreaks, and as part of this, developing and disseminating ready-to-go treatment and testing kits for first responders.[30]

But the WHO's cholera control program and its kits—while potentially useful for aid workers responding to an emergency event—are only designed to detect an outbreak and then to last for the first month of a response. Cholera typically remains in an environment for years after an outbreak, never just a month. It is endemic in eastern Ethiopia and in other environments where humanitarian crises and humanitarian interventions recur. Permanent disease surveillance and laboratory infrastructure are therefore also necessary.

In places like eastern Ethiopia, cholera is not an exception to epidemiological trends, it is paradigmatic. And even with the current WHO initiative, there are still far too few investments in community-based preventive measures and sustainable infrastructural development and disease surveillance projects in places at risk of outbreaks. Cholera provides undeniable evidence of people's long-standing—not just sudden—lack of clean water and sanitation facilities. And cholera outbreaks will never cease if aid organizations and the government only focus on ad hoc humanitarian solutions, and ignore the more expensive and complex structural inequities that result in contaminated water sources.

Mona summed it up this way: "They may have a plastic sheet from us, some materials to construct a shelter, and this can save lives. Our work definitely does save lives. But the problems are so big. They are not just needing plastic. I do hygiene education, but I need to be there in the community for three months to really help people understand how to protect themselves and enjoy clean water and wash their hands and the like. But I am only in there for twenty days, and these twenty days are spent not just in one village but in ten villages or kebeles. I do not have the time to spend with people. We need more time, not just more money. There are many different projects to distribute things, but if we give them money, or just give them other things, things will end. Soap runs out. Cash runs out. We must instead give quality things first to save lives then stay for long-term projects."

Mona's colleague Nimo nodded in agreement next to her, adding, "Education is better than material support. Rather than giving things and running away, we must teach people about concepts in health, water, sanitation, etc. Especially children. You can see it—the children, the next generation, can change so many things. When you leave, and when the people go back home, they return to their old ways of doing things. Nothing sustainably changes, with one-time distributions or interventions. These NGOs are known for running around from place to place. People talk about this. The NGOs just running around all the time." Cholera is defined and addressed as if a Band-Aid could fix the enduring problems of poverty, lack of piped potable water, lack of sanitation and toilet facilities, and recurrent outbreaks of the numerous diarrheal diseases that plague populations in eastern Ethiopia. Rather than just fixing individual behaviors, cholera elimination requires long-term investments by political actors.

Beyond Band-Aids

Aid workers and policy makers like Mona, Nimo, Ahmed, and Doctor Hamza all struggled to transform narrowly conceived crisis responses to make sustainable improvements to governmental programs and people's lives. For example, organizations like Save the Children and UNICEF, in places like Lasarat, paid for the training and supervision of new governmental health extension workers to treat upticks in rates of diarrheal disease and severe acute malnutrition among children. NGOs like Catholic Relief Services and Oxfam and others frequently subsidized or gifted diagnostics, medicines, vehicles, and salaries during outbreaks of disease, through and in support of existing governmental clinics. With relief funding from other UN relief agencies, the Somali regional government built and staffed new schools to teach internally displaced children in cities and camps in and around the cities of Jigjiga, Dire Dawa, and Harar. And UN- and NGO-funded mobile teams of clinical providers, as officially Ethiopian government employees, helped stem outbreaks of infectious diseases and trained and supervised permanent health extension workers like Ahmed throughout the region.

Crisis production, in the Somali Region, enabled aid workers and clinical providers to invest in health systems and future mechanisms of emergency preparedness and response. However, their work remained limited by donor expectations, donor priorities, donor bequests, organizational mandates, short time frames, pressures to respond quickly, and pressures to provide data and statistically significant changes to "emergency" conditions. In the face of these limitations, aid workers and health-care providers refused the narrowness of most *bani'aadamnimada* and provided meaningful forms of *samafal*. They essentially provided far more than Band-Aids, but with only limited supplies of Band-Aids. In other words, aid workers, health workers, and policy makers in the subnational offices of relief agencies and governmental bureaus transformed short spurts of material resources provided as part of international humanitarian interventions into opportunities to lessen the manifold forms of suffering in their midst.

There are better ways to organize international support. As shown elsewhere, humanitarian assistance could instead primarily work to identify and fill in gaps in existing emergency responses and health systems when these have collapsed or are overwhelmed.[31] In other words, broader, multisectoral, sustainable interventions could focus not on the production of crisis itself, but on supporting complementary, long-term crisis response systems, health systems improvement, and the promotion of health equity. For example, if an outbreak of cholera occurred, while vaccines, diagnostics, and treatments would be necessary in the immediate term, most resources should be deployed to build or rebuild water and sanitation infrastructure. Clinical facilities and laboratories might also need additional staff and material supplies to deal with an uptick in workloads. Likewise, if noncommunicable diseases like diabetes threaten the lives of crisis-affected persons, this itself represents a health emergency and indicates the failure of both crisis responses and health systems. Diagnostic technologies, medications, food donations, and refrigeration may be needed, but to be effective, these must be accompanied by efforts to screen for and treat people's comorbid conditions, provide ongoing dietary advice and support, provide for continuing care in the months and years after their diagnosis, and expand the scope of medical education.

In sum, producing crisis is a major part of local aid workers' jobs. But these productions mostly respond to exogenous ideas about crisis and expectations and assumptions about what relief agencies can most easily provide and prove. Humanitarian crises and humanitarian priorities are consequently defined too narrowly—temporally and substantively. They typically fail to respond to the manifold forms of suffering and lasting needs people face on the ground. Band-Aid humanitarianism risks the lives and health of people living in places where relief operations supply much of the primary health care residents depend on.

Band-Aid humanitarianism also risks the well-being of aid workers and health-care providers who face impossible tasks. There is a mismatch between people's needs and what relief agencies can and do provide, as well as, for many aid workers like Ahmed, Abdirahman, Maryan, and the mobile teams nurses, job insecurity at the end of every project or spurt of activity. The provision of short bursts of funding and temporary Band-Aid-style projects, year after year, more problematically deflects attention from the enduring inequities Somalis in Ethiopia still face. Band-Aids provide material evidence of donors and governments and relief agencies doing something, or being humanitarian, without addressing the deeper, political problems facing crisis-affected communities. Focusing instead on solving systemic problems and redressing inequities within humanitarian response systems represent alternative ways forward.

5

HUMANITARIANISM IS ANTI-POLITICS

For years, humanitarian actors have been grappling with questions of when, where, and under what circumstances international agencies should intervene into sovereign countries to save lives in crisis. In order to gain access to people in need, often across contested borders, humanitarian interventions continue to be described by many relief organizations as focused narrowly on saving individual lives, and otherwise, staying out of the way of conflicts and messy, partisan fights. Organizations working in eastern Ethiopia, like the Red Cross, UNOCHA, UNHCR, Save the Children, Catholic Relief Services, and others, profess they remain neutral to regional conflicts and neutral to political disagreements. Relief workers, likewise, are supposed to uphold this principle, and to act without political bias or self-interest.[1]

Critics point out, however, that relief organizations' principle of neutrality acts as a strategic façade for the more controversial and political work of relief interventions.[2] International humanitarian interventions may appear on the surface as apolitical, and focused narrowly on delivering life-saving services and materials, but in fact, these actions are often driven by political interests, and often benefit wealthy and powerful donor countries.[3] The strategic use of foreign humanitarian interventions for political gain is only possible, however, when relief agencies and governments can effectively disclaim their own self-interests and appear motivated solely by the desire to end suffering. Humanitarianism, accordingly, provides a benevolent cover and a rationale for many interventions into sovereign nations and communities facing crisis.

Organizations that deny the political intents and effects of aid, and, at the same time, depend on the political savvy of local aid workers and the political support of donors, perform what James Ferguson calls "anti-politics."[4] Humanitarian intervention entails not a rejection or avoidance of political action by relief organizations, donors, and recipient governments, but rather, an external-facing denial of political intentions and effects in donor countries, in order to achieve strategic political ends.

Relief operations in Ethiopia and elsewhere are thus integral to international, national, local politics—in part through the labor of front-line nongovernmental aid workers and their government partners. Aid earmarked for humanitarian crises bolsters various governmental missions and funds governmental staffs, bureaus, and initiatives. In Ethiopia during the last decade, humanitarian interventions supported the decentralization of health care, the improvement of local disaster preparedness and response mechanisms, and the provision of various public services like community-based primary health care to rural and pastoralist households. It contributed to the popularity, power, and cohesiveness of the Somali Regional National State, as well. As Doctor Hamza proudly proclaimed in chapter 1, after many years, the Somali Regional Health Bureau was finally "100% Somali," despite the federal government's strategic efforts since to place Amharic-speaking Ethiopians from within the ruling EPRDF and Prosperity Party into prominent posts. Ethnic and regional sovereignty, autonomy, and power have been realized, in large part in eastern Ethiopia through control of humanitarian funding and operations by regional governmental entities like the Somali Regional Health Bureau in Jigjiga.

Additionally, proficient aid workers portrayed throughout this book, like Aden, Doctor Hamza, and Mona, did not talk about their neutrality to partisan concerns nor the apolitical nature of their humanitarian work. On the contrary, these aid workers were hired for their political savvy, their ability to maintain good relationships with government agencies and other powerful actors, and their personal connections with populations in need. Understanding local and national politics, and being able to communicate and work within contested local political systems, were fundamental to their jobs and to the success of the interventions they implemented. Plus, because their work required they travel and get to know people from across the eastern half of the country, in some cases, their partnerships with persons and agencies across clan and ethnic divides changed how they, individually, perceived and talked about recent hostilities and their hopes for peace and reconciliation. The Red Cross's influential Fundamental Principles of humanitarian action, discussed in the pages to follow, and the idea of maintaining a "humanitarian space" (a theater of operation free of politics) were neither objectives nor realities for locals hired to help respond to crises in communities nearby.[5] Aid workers I spoke to and shadowed at work in Ethiopia reported these were not part of their education in emergency response, nor their orientations to the organizations with which they worked. Humanitarian principles and the concept of designating and protecting humanitarian spaces free of politics were instead part of a powerful mythology within the field of humanitarian studies and the design of *bani'aadamnimada* (translated into English as externally funded and designed forms of humanitarian assistance).

Humanitarianism as Apolitical: The Origin Story

The mythology and the ideal of a politically neutral, independent, and voluntary form of international humanitarian response stretches back to the nineteenth century. In 1859, a Swiss activist and businessman named Jean-Henri Dunant realized he needed the written signature and personal support of Emperor Napoleon III to build a series of windmills in Algeria, a French colony at the time. Without reliable courier services, he had to find and convince Napoleon of the value of his business plan in person. Napoleon happened to be away from Paris at the time, in what is now northern Italy, leading the French Army in the Second Italian War of Independence alongside Victor Emmanuel II of Sardinia.

On June 24, Napoleon's alliance defeated the Austrian emperor Franz Joseph I in the Battle of Solferino. But an estimated 6,000 soldiers were killed during the nighttime battle, and at least another 30,000 were wounded. As dawn broke, thousands of men lay injured or dying in fields between the towns of Solferino and San Martino, abandoned by their respective regiments. Women and children, mostly, who happened upon the scene attempted to provide what comfort and aid they could to the wounded and dying men.[6]

According to lore, these responders, and then later Dunant when he appeared on the scene in search of Napoleon, took up and repeated the Italian phrase to anyone who could offer assistance, "*Siamo tutti fratelli!*" ("We are all brothers!"). This mantra articulated a belief that everyone deserves comfort and assistance. Everyone who can help should be responsible for aiding the injured, dead, and missing, regardless of their thoughts on the politics or conflicts at hand.

Horrified by the abandonment of so many soldiers in the wake of the battle— most of whom were young men and boys, willing to sacrifice their lives for the good of their respective nations—Dunant later proposed there should be a better, more humane way to treat people in war. In a pamphlet he published and distributed after his return, called "A Memory of Solferino," Dunant suggested that a private, protected, and neutral legion of health-care providers and other volunteers should attend to the needs of soldiers on all sides of conflicts.[7] *Tutti fratelli* in Italian, or "all brothers," became its catchphrase. This idea was fundamental to Dunant's subsequent campaign for and then founding of the International Committee of the Red Cross (ICRC) in Switzerland, and it was central to what later became the text of the Geneva Conventions and the broader body of International Humanitarian Law.

This origin story, about the founding of and inspiration for the Red Cross Movement, is still read in many training workshops, employee and volunteer orientations, and in literature published and circulated online and in hard copy. It helps to animate the idea that assistance should be given according to need alone, by persons and organizations distant from and uninvolved in conflicts and politics at hand.

However, the myth of Dunant's epiphany on the battlefield in Solferino presents only one perspective—Henri Dunant's. As such, it fails to account for the potentially important difference between himself and the other responders on the battlefield around him. The focus on Dunant's perspective and the elision of others on the scene echoes how so many expatriate aid workers, even today, intervene into faraway places, largely unfamiliar with the situations unfolding before them, and provide assistance alongside persons from local populations. The reader assumes from *A Memory of Solferino* that the volunteers attending to soldiers on the battlefield and in nearby towns were, like Dunant, disinterested in or acting above the politics at hand. But this is unlikely. The chants of "*Siamo tutti fratelli!*" ("We are all brothers!") may have been shouted, literally, by the brothers, sisters, or other loved ones of some of the soldiers dying on the fields. Residents of the area around Solferino very likely had strong feelings about Napoleon's provocations and repeated wars. Calling for unity among "all brothers" (*tutti fratelli*) might just as well have been a cry for solidarity and action in the face of violence and occupation, and not a cry for neutrality or independence. We cannot know.

Myths like this are not fictional. The Battle of Solferino did happen, and by all accounts Dunant was genuinely traumatized by the plight of the abandoned soldiers. But through the telling and retelling of Dunant's perspective on the event, over time and for various purposes, this story—his story—has overshadowed other important insights and social movements at the time.[8] The salience of this myth has transformed the figure of Dunant into the dominant model of righteous humanitarianism. Other organizations, most prominently, Médecins Sans Frontières, define and enact humanitarian principles in other ways.[9] But MSF's vision also characterizes outsiders like Dunant as the paradigmatic humanitarians—not the local residents on the scene, many perhaps also the loved ones and compatriots of fallen soldiers.

The origin story of the Red Cross, with the figure of Dunant, an outsider, at its center, still shapes ideas about what and who is "humanitarian." It discounts both the important role locals and loved ones may have played in the recovery from the Battle of Solferino, and the role persons outside Europe now play in determining and carrying out "humanitarian" actions around the world. It also obscures another, different reality about relief operations: humanitarianism has long been a political tool with which wealthy donors and governments can intervene not just onto public battlefields, but also into the most intimate of spaces—inside people's homes and in clinics, and at the site of their bodies, for example—in faraway places, over contested borders, and among traumatized people and communities.

The Anti-Politics of Neutrality, Independence, and Voluntary Service

The International Red Cross and Red Crescent Movement remains Europe's and North America's preeminent, emblematic humanitarian organization. The Red Cross Movement, as it is abbreviated, now includes the International Committee of the Red Cross (ICRC), the International Federation of Red Cross, Red Crescent Societies, and 191 national societies like the Ethiopian Red Cross and American Red Cross. In 1965 all these organizations adopted a set of seven guiding Fundamental Principles: humanity, impartiality, neutrality, independence, voluntary service, unity, and universality.[10] These principles have been adopted by many additional UN agencies and NGOs doing relief work. ICRC also authorizes and enforces the body of International Humanitarian Law, including the Geneva Conventions, which were ratified by countries around the world to uphold these fundamental principles, and to help protect the life and dignity of victims of conflict and disaster.

Most analyses of the Red Cross's fundamental principles look to the three central principles of impartiality, neutrality, and independence to examine the political strategies and effects of intervention. However, here I instead focus on the challenges of defining and maintaining the principles of neutrality, independence, and voluntarism as guiding a sense of *bani'aadamnimada*, or the temporary, unidirectional, distant, dispassionate, and voluntary notion of foreign humanitarian assistance, compared to the reciprocal, enduring, political, and compassionate relationships *samafal* entails. The contemporary reality of humanitarian work, performed not mostly by expatriates flying in from wealthy donor countries, but mostly by people from the very same communities facing emergencies, challenges the usefulness and universality of these three principles in particular.

First, the principle of neutrality, which lies at the core of the work and the identity of the Red Cross Movement, is defined as "not taking sides in hostilities."[11] Not taking sides and not appearing to take sides enables organizations to maintain access to politically contested areas and to build local partnerships during emergency responses. Beyond the Red Cross, many NGOs and United Nations relief agencies like the UN High Commission for Refugees (UNHCR), the UN World Food Program (WFP), UNICEF, and the International Organization for Migration (IOM) all realize the benefits of maintaining neutrality. Neutrality is believed to be an operational necessity—a strategic blind spot to governments' policies that can facilitate international interventions and the safety of aid workers, and can allow for the flow of money from distrustful donor countries to partner organizations in crisis-affected parts of the world.

Second, the principle of independence, by contrast, requires that organizations act autonomously according to International Humanitarian Law and the other Fundamental Principles, and must remain free from political, military, or economic influence. Independence, like neutrality, is operationally useful, because it allows aid agencies to deny partisan influences or objectives, and to partner with problematic governments or other organizations in places where crises unfold. While relief organizations publicly maintain their independence from governments and parties to conflict, very often they also rely on cooperation with these same entities to access populations in need and to defend the security of their personnel. Independence requires at least a modicum of duplicity, if not deceit.

A third principle is that of voluntary service. Voluntary service is defined as assistance "not prompted in any manner by desire for gain."[12] Voluntarism proclaims that donors, governments, and aid workers should not maintain any self-interest in humanitarian interventions. Yet this principle discounts the important financial benefits of having a job in the humanitarian sector, and the meaningful opportunities aid work offers people to more broadly and generously enact *samafal*. The principle of voluntary service also obscures the way *samafal* resembles what Marcel Mauss called a "gift exchange," discussed in detail in chapter 2.[13] "In theory these are voluntary," Mauss wrote, but "in reality they are given and reciprocated obligatorily . . . such services have taken the form of the gift, the present generously given even when, in the gesture accompanying the transaction, there is only a polite fiction, formalism, and social deceit, and when really there is obligation and economic self-interest."[14]

Hugo Slim, former head of policy at the ICRC, argues it is the duty of humanitarian aid workers, even those employed by agencies outside the Red Cross, to
partition their professional from their private lives, or their roles and identities
as humanitarian workers from their roles and identities as humanitarian people.
"Humanitarian office," he writes, "carries the specific obligations and behaviors
of humanitarian principles, but they may not be necessary or morally appropriate to humanitarian workers' personal lives when they are off-duty. . . . They are
obliged to be impartial and neutral in a way they would not necessarily be in their
private lives, in which they might have strong political views or put their family
first in a crisis."[15]

But it is nonsensical that, at the threshold of their workplaces, people can cast
off their social obligations and identities to temporarily become a neutral, independent volunteer, distributing relief. Climbing into a white SUV or putting on a
blue vest cannot change who people are, what they do, and what others expect of
them. As quoted earlier, the relief worker Mussa, from Jigjiga, said, "People would
see if I was doing this work at [the relief NGO] professionally and not living it.
What you are doing and saying in the community, it has to be what you are. If
I am not practicing, they will know. . . . You should not go to a hotel, but you
should sleep there with them [recipients of aid], and then they will know you are
serious. . . . I love to think broadly, to help all the people, not just our clan or our
region. All the people. That is humanitarian aid."

In speaking with local aid workers in NGOs and UN relief agencies throughout eastern Ethiopia, I found the expectation that they remain neutral in conflicts
and to partisan politics, and not expect to be taken up in relations of mutual
exchange and gift giving, was never part of their job training or education.[16]
It was not in the hard copies of Codes of Conduct or in the manuals and reports
they stored in their offices. Most aid workers instead enacted *samafal* through
their positions with relief organizations, with all its inherent political sensitivities
and mutually beneficial and political effects.

Additionally, aid workers in the Somali Region did not only work for international nongovernmental humanitarian organizations like the Red Cross.
Staffers constantly, "reshuffle, reshuffle," Doctor Hamza said in chapter 3, from
the governmental sector, to the nongovernmental sector, then to party politics, to traditional forms of Somali leadership, to the private sector, and then
again to work for relief agencies. Even the president of the Somali Region as
of 2019, Mustafa Muhumed Omer, had worked in international relief for various INGOs and the United Nations. Many of the people I spoke with for this
research knew each other, had worked together, and had collaborated across
multiple governmental and nongovernmental agencies. Many of these aid
workers, policy makers, and clinical providers held more than one job at a

time, in multiple sectors of the aid economy. Lower-level and temporarily hired aid workers, in particular, usually maintained side hustles in the private sector, politics, or at universities while also working for humanitarian organizations. The fact that many aid workers maintained personal connections and good relationships with governmental bureaucrats and politicians in Jigjiga or in smaller localities were perceived to be positive attributes or even necessities—not potentially unethical or corrupting. Expecting humanitarian work to be apolitical through the principles of neutrality, impartiality, and volunteerism discounts and devalues the politically savvy work aid workers perform, the political effects of aid, and the importance of aid to local economies and informal systems of crisis response.

Plus, humanitarian action also very often risked both personal and political peril for those involved—especially for the vast majority of the global humanitarian workforce who are from the communities where crises happen, and who at the same time often lacked adequate protection and legal recourse when they became the targets of violence or find themselves in dangerous situations.[17] For local aid workers in Ethiopia, maintaining the perception they were nonpartisan or neutral to the politics unfolding around them was impossible. Local staff often proudly hailed from ethnic, kinship, or national groups at times involved in internal armed conflicts or peacekeeping missions elsewhere, and they were often publicly perceived as representatives of a political or national group in their capacity as service providers. Aid workers had occasionally participated in political activism and protests as university students, and their more recent engagement in relief work represented, at times, an extension of their political and advocacy work.[18]

However, the principles of neutrality, independence, and voluntary service enshrined and enforced by dominant Western humanitarian relief organizations, as well as the legal conventions and the organizational practices on which these principles are based, were not developed primarily to protect or discipline local aid workers, but rather, primarily to protect and promote interests of these relief organizations and the governments that support them.[19] *Bani'aadamnimada* therefore represents a form of conventional global political engagement between powerful governments and nongovernmental institutions, in places where alternative policies and programs, like long-term economic development, remain challenging or impossible. Global humanitarianism therefore wields representations of principles, crisis, and compassion in order to be able to carry out a kind of government—a "politics of precarious lives," in the words of Didier Fassin—through management of lives and suffering.[20] The United States, for example, has engaged with politics in Ethiopia, very often, through humanitarian intervention.

The Politics of Being above Politics

Dunant rode onto a battlefield in Solferino because he needed Napoleon's permission to do business, and he volunteered there out of a sense of horror.[21] Since then, however, the political strategy of intervening into sovereign states to save lives, over and above political self-interests, has been taken up, ironically, by numerous politicians. Perhaps the most famous invocation of a variant on *"tutti fratelli"* was uttered by the US president Ronald Reagan who declared, in reference to the suffering of children in Ethiopia, "The hungry child knows no politics." But how did this stance, and Reagan's unlikely support for people in Ethiopia's Marxist-Leninist dictatorship in the midst of the Cold War, emerge? And why do such blatantly false pretenses or "social deceits," in Marcel Mauss's words, of neutrality, independence, and voluntary service continue? What purpose do they serve?[22]

Countries across most of North and East Africa, including Ethiopia, from 1981 through 1983, experienced repeated droughts and failed harvests. During these same years, following decades of imperial occupations, wars of independence, and violent resource extraction, most of these countries were reeling from internal conflicts over control of territory and natural resources. By the summer of 1982, it was clear to those following African politics and humanitarian affairs that millions of people in Ethiopia needed immediate help.

A year before this, in 1981, Ronald Reagan had proposed a $1 billion supplemental appropriation for humanitarian assistance for several countries affected by drought, including Ethiopia. But Ethiopia was by this time essentially a Soviet client state, led by a communist Marxist-Leninist military junta called "the Derg," and chaired by Lt. Col. Mengistu Haile Mariam. For years before this, the United States had provided regular assistance to Ethiopia, mostly in the form of food aid. Even just a decade before, in 1973, on the eve of the country's biggest modern political revolution, the United States provided humanitarian aid and supported Haile Selassie's Ethiopian Empire in many drought-affected parts of the country— at that time, in the grander scheme, to prevent the Soviets from controlling resources and ports in the Horn of Africa, and to undermine Somalia's nationalist project to unite Greater Somalia.

But in the years after the 1974 coup d'état and revolution in Ethiopia, Soviet support for Somalia's president, Mohamed Siad Barre, had waned. Ethiopia resoundingly defeated Somalia in the 1977–1978 Ogaden War, and Siad Barre's dreams of a united Greater Somalia faded. By 1983, the Soviet Union had abandoned its support for Somalia and Siad Barre altogether, and had turned its monetary investments and political support instead to Ethiopia. The United States consequently reinstated its financial, political, and military support for Somalia. By the mid-1980s, any US humanitarian support for Ethiopia would have therefore been a political anathema, and would have countered the US's commitment to deny all requests for support to any Soviet allies or communist governments. So even as famine conditions unfolded in Ethiopia, and even as Mengistu and the Derg continued to forcibly displace and dispossess hundreds of thousands of food insecure Ethiopians, the United States made the decision to withdraw its support.[23]

Several prominent international NGOs based in the US claimed the Reagan administration had proposed cuts in aid to Ethiopia "because of its politics," accusing Reagan of allowing people to starve for the sake of publicly displaying the depravity of Marxist-Leninist socialist policies.[24] The United States was in a good position to supply generous amounts of domestically grown and produced food aid to Ethiopia that year, as it had done in previous years. Yet, in order to penalize Ethiopia for its allegiance to the Soviet Union, the US administration seemed willing to forgo a humanitarian response, potentially allowing people to die.

These optics proved too politically detrimental for members of the US Congress. In a dramatic move, M. Peter McPherson, the head of USAID, then reversed the Reagan administration's position in 1983 in a speech on Capitol Hill, stating: "Our position is that we are going to respond without regard to political considerations. The hungry child knows no politics."[25]

Beginning in late 1983, food aid commodities produced in the United States began to flow again to Ethiopia. Ronald Reagan repeated this catchphrase in subsequent press conferences and became famous for siding with USAID, saying, "The hungry child knows no politics." Then in the summer of 1984, the famous "Live Aid" benefit concert organized by Bob Geldof and the "Band Aid" recordings from the concert hit radio waves and nightly newscasts, amplifying the Reagan administration's position to intervene to save lives, even into objectionable and undemocratic states. The United States was seen as acting with benevolence for all, over and above instrumentalism and Cold War politics.[26] On March 5, 1985, McPherson wrote in the *Washington Post*, "The U.S. motto has been, 'A hungry child knows no politics.' Our emergency aid will go anywhere there is hunger, regardless of our relationship with the government in question. Ethiopia, where 7 million are affected, is the largest recipient of our emergency aid to Africa, despite the Marxist character of its government. But unfortunately, politics—and war—will not leave the hungry alone."[27] Despite these official lines, and despite sending a portion of the requested aid to NGOs working in Ethiopia, however, the US government continued to delay and decrease overall foreign aid funding to Ethiopia throughout the rest of the decade.[28]

The administration's political maneuver—publicly claiming the US government's right to intervene into sovereign states to save lives, and its objective to be humanitarian and therefore above strategic politics—was not limited to foreign policy toward Ethiopia. In hearings before the Senate Committee on Finance to consider his nomination to be Deputy Secretary of the Treasury in 1987, McPherson was asked pointedly, "Why does so much assistance continue to flow to adversaries of the U.S., including Mozambique?" He defended relief to Cold War adversaries by demonstrating the political potentials of this kind of support: "The President and the Secretary of State have made a controversial but calculated decision to support the Government of Mozambique. That Government receives military support from the Soviets, votes against the U.S. in the UN, etc. However, they also liberalized their economic policy to an important degree, signed the Nkomati Accord, etc. There are problems but substantial possibilities with this policy for a country that is likely to be so important to what happens in Southern Africa. A.I.D. is an instrument that can be important in winning the gamble."[29] Humanitarian aid, he admitted, was a political tool. To gain political advantage, humanitarian aid was described to Congress and the American people as apolitical.

Reagan, McPherson, USAID, and US presidents and humanitarian agencies ever since have argued forcefully that relief operations do not themselves extend conflict and support undemocratic or abusive governments because humanitarian aid is not usually channeled directly through or in support of governments. Rather, they argue, humanitarian aid is often given as a form of protest *against* other governments' actions (or inactions), and only given through supposedly neutral relief organizations. Humanitarian aid is portrayed as directed at individuals, to save the lives of innocent people, as well as to leave open future possibilities for diplomatic engagement and economic investments, but not to benefit the abusive governments of countries in which they reside. Reagan's and McPherson's claims, at least, were that politics should not impede humanitarian programs during disasters, but rather the opposite. The point of humanitarianism, these actors argued, was that it does not concern itself explicitly with politics or politicians' electoral strategies; it is done even in the face of potential political peril to save the lives of individuals facing disasters and conflicts.

This kind of denial of explicit political objectives, highlights, ironically, the political value of this kind of humanitarianism within donor countries like the United States. Reagan benefited politically from his administration's daring and moralistic representation of its actions, and its perceived rejection and reversal of previous Cold War tactics. It served him well. Since the 1980s, US military interventions into Iraq, Afghanistan, Libya, and elsewhere have been called "humanitarian" in similar efforts to raise public support for war.[30] The veneration of the ideals of neutrality, independence, and voluntary service constitute, with different strategies and effects, what James Ferguson called an "anti-politics machine."[31] Humanitarianism is foreign policy by other means.[32]

At the same time that anti-politics rhetorics occurred in donor countries like the United States, humanitarian interventions shaped local politics and local political debates in the places like eastern Ethiopia where relief organizations recurrently intervened. These effects were often mundane and subtle. As the following pages show, international humanitarian interventions affected political dynamics throughout eastern Ethiopia in informal and professional spaces: vehicles filled with aid workers traveling to distribution sites, United Nations offices and local governmental bureaus where decisions were negotiated, in hospitals and small two-room clinics where aid workers cared for the sick and elderly, and in cafes and homes as people discussed and debated current events. Humanitarianism in these spaces was political in two important ways: first, it was intentionally and explicitly political as it so often funded local political organizations and politicized initiatives. In some cases, it funded governmental entities and programs, like the Somali Regional Health Bureau and the federal government's objective to decentralize policy making throughout the country, and other times, it funded international and local nongovernmental organizations like UNICEF and Save the Children that performed roles of the government or attempted to influence the government. Second, humanitarianism was incidentally and indirectly political, as aid workers communicated with, learned about, negotiated with, and cared for people from oppositional groups during relief operations.

Politics through Intervention

During my various research trips through eastern Ethiopia, I frequently traveled through the western edge of the Somali Region, along the Oromia regional boundary in East Hararge, through the scenic town of Babile, and then near the capital city of Jigjiga in the bucolic Fafan zone of the Somali Region. Vehicles zoomed around rocky hills, on newly paved, narrow roads lined with invasive prickly pear cactuses, giant milkweeds atop gravel pilings, and thorny bushes stretching skyward for water and light from between eroded boulders. Driving through this landscape, on two different occasions, I had telling conversations about the potential for peace and the uncertain road toward political reconciliation in the region.

First, in an SUV packed with mostly Somali government bureaucrats, professors at Jigjiga University, and non-Somalis driving and helping with logistics, I found myself in the middle of a heated conversation about incidents of violence along the regional boundaries the week before. Questions surfaced rhetorically among the group.

"Why do we have all this violence? Why is it continuing?" some of the men asked.

"Because it is always like this," another added. "It is the fault of the federal government and you [all] know it."

"Yes, they have their finger in this mess absolutely," someone chimed in from the back seat.

"Why do they [representatives of the federal government in Addis Ababa] not stop it?" Several people mumbled that Abiy Ahmed, the relatively new prime minister, was certainly trying to make peace.

"You know this is not normal," a bureaucrat and researcher from Jigjiga turned and told me directly. "We are brothers, actually, the Somalis and the Oromos. We are not that different. We actually speak almost the same language—you know I am part Oromo!"

I did not know this, because I had only heard him speak Somali, Amharic, and English. He kept going, turning so everyone could hear clearly, "My mother is Oromo, and somewhere on my father's side I am also Amhara too."

A good friend, who is Amhara, chimed in and smiled at him. "Oh! Really? I did not know that. You are everything, man."

"Yes, we would go to their house sometimes when I was a boy. To the Amhara region in the west."

In fact, this man not only visits family members throughout the country, but he has helped fund his cousins' education and their travels for high school and university. He gives them advice on career choices and research agendas. When they visit Jigjiga, they stay with him in his home. So indeed, he is "everything," and as such, he is very typically Ethiopian. He is not merely a proud Somali, although he most definitely is that, but he is also a polyglot, a product of intermarriage, a longtime resident of Jigjiga, a man who was raised farther south in the pasturelands shared by nomadic pastoralists from Somali, Oromo, and Afar regions, and student of science who has studied at universities throughout the country.

Several months before, in another large vehicle packed with two local aid workers and my research team, we were all checking our mobile phones for updates on the security situation farther south and in trade towns along the same contested Somali-Oromia regional boundaries. I began probing for people's thoughts on the roots of the violence.

"I do not understand it," one man said. "We are all one people, but the people, you see they become angry about who has control over the land." I asked for clarification on this point, to which he replied, "I don't understand it really, but I think some pastoralist people they want to be able to move freely across the border, but they can't. Or their home and grazing land has always been on the Oromo side, but they are actually Somali. Or the police they check them at the [regional] border. They cannot move like before." Indeed, in the 1990s, the regional boundary between the Somali and Oromia region arbitrarily divided an area settled by several ethnic and linguistic groups that hitherto had cooperated and shared kinship and economic ties.[33]

"And this is why fifty people were killed?" I asked again. "Over land, water rights, and checkpoints?"

"No, I actually don't think this is it." He sighed and paused, as if reconsidering. "The people are angry for some reason, but often it is the government people who are targeted, not the rural people. We are all brothers. We," he said emphatically, motioning with his hands all around the vehicle, "we all want peace. The people don't want war, they don't want to fight. It stops everything," the markets, travel, and so forth, he clarified later, "when there is fighting. But the government does want us to fight I think."

With this comment people in the car recounted another recent massacre in a bustling market town along the Somali-Oromo regional boundaries. A prominent Somali trader was "killed by the Oromos" a woman said—but at least this particular person owned businesses in that town that everyone frequented. "He was even married to an Oromo woman I think!" someone shouted up toward those of us near the front, and others nodded. The road where this massacre took place is a major transportation artery connecting cities in the Horn of Africa, and it is the location of perhaps the largest khat market in Ethiopia. Somalis and Oromos both have much to lose with the closure of the road and the intimidating presence of police and military forces. No one could understand why this particular person, who was so well known and liked, who had never been involved in politics, and who was also symbolic of intertwined ethnic identities in Ethiopia, was killed.

Regardless of these divergent narratives about the origins of the recent outbreaks of violence, during both conversations, with both groups in these two different vehicles, people emphasized the kinship and interconnectedness between supposedly oppositional and discrete ethnic groups, and the mobility across borders that necessitated constant interaction and communication there. Somali aid workers dispatched from offices in Jigjiga responded to numerous crises along these regional boundaries where both Oromo and Somali displaced persons lived without adequate water supplies, food, or medicine to treat the outbreaks of diarrheal disease, and where pastoralists and farmers continued to fight for access to diminishing natural resources. Oromo staffers also led aid agencies headquartered in Dire Dawa and organize responses to outbreaks of disease within displaced Somali communities nearby and farther south and east.

These complexities necessitated conversations between people who traveled throughout the region for aid work—they speak with all sorts of people during their journeys, at the places where they stop to rest and drink tea and eat and sleep. So in traveling to field sites to study and respond to the humanitarian crises that result from conflict and displacement, they had witnessed how ethnic and political divisions can be reified by politicians, but at the same time, undercut by everyday people reaching out to help folks potentially outside their own kinship and ethnic groups. Mobility and engaging others in debate and conversation enabled aid workers' needs assessments, access to communities in crisis, and the successful implementation and evaluation of aid. "Moving out" to "widen the heart," as discussed in chapter 2, is central to humanitarian responses in the Somali Region, but these mundane activities and their political effects remained largely invisible or unrecognizable to foreign staffers in the headquarters of global relief agencies.

More broadly, the Somali word *samafal*, in contrast to the English word *humanitarian*, signified for Somalis the political embeddedness of aid workers' subjectivities and the political potentials of the relief operations they implemented. It was, at least in this regard, without pretense. *Samafal* presented opportunities for people from oppositional ethnic and kinship groups to talk, listen, and even care for each other. *Siyaasada samafalka*, or humanitarian policy, provided means by which underfunded, marginalized governmental offices and crisis response mechanisms in eastern Ethiopia could stitch together sporadic injections of relief and meager public funding to provide basic governmental social and medical services—even across tense political divides. *Samafal* was inherently relational, and embedded in larger systems of meaning, exchange, reciprocity, hospitality, religious duty, and loving care. It was therefore by definition and by nature necessarily political. Because *samafal* entailed more than just the dispassionate distribution of relief commodities, these kinds of politically charged interpersonal interactions and consequent political shifts were necessary for humanitarian assistance to be effective.

The Somali Region Rising

Humanitarian assistance in the Somali Region did not typically involve any explicit engagements with or critiques of partisan politics, the EPRDF, or the

Prosperity Party. But as shown, in many different ways, relief operations were not apolitical—either in donor countries or in countries and communities where relief operations unfolded. Even temporary distributions of food, medicine, and potable water involved politically sensitive negotiations over what groups and individuals were most in need of assistance, and cooperation between diverse and sometimes oppositional governmental and nongovernmental agencies. Humanitarian aid was often provided in remote and underserved areas by people from cities or other parts of the Somali Region, by people with higher incomes and better access to higher education, and often, by people from different *qabiilooyinka* (clan groups) and even political parties. Very often, Somalis from *qabiilka Ogaadeen* (the Ogaden clan), for example, provided care to people from other, smaller groups outside their *qabiil* or *jilib* (extended family units). Political tensions and suspected inequities between Somali groups in the region affected the way interventions unfolded and people's subsequent evaluations of relief operations, aid workers, and clinical medical providers.[34]

More broadly, antagonisms between various Somali kinship affinities (translated into Somali as *reer, qabiil,* and *jilib*) have for decades contributed to local and regional political insecurities.[35] The Issa-Ogadeni dichotomy is paradigmatic. While approximately 98 percent of population of the Somali Region of Ethiopia identify as ethnically Somali, there are several different Somali groups in the Horn of Africa, variably divided by geography, dialect, and kinship. In the areas north of Jigjiga, a majority of Somalis identify as from the Issa family, or *Reerka Ciise.* Many Somalis in Djibouti and in the northern stretches of Ethiopia also identify as Issa, and the mayor of the city of Dire Dawa in 2019 was an Issa Somali man, but Issas remain a minority group within the Somali Region of Ethiopia as a whole.

In the last twenty years, Issa leaders and elected politicians in Ethiopia neither participated in Somali secession movements nor aligned with the Ogaden National Liberation Front (ONLF) in opposition to the Ethiopian government. Issas frequently described themselves as "closer" and "more cooperative" with the federal government in Addis Ababa, especially compared to other groups like the Ogaden. Recent conflicts between pastoralist groups were discussed locally as fights between "the Issas" and "the Afar"—not as between ethnic Somalis and ethnic Afars as united contingents.[36] And while a majority of Issas in the Somali Region vote for and align with the EPRDF, many of these same persons express lingering distrust of the Ethiopian government due to allegations of voter fraud, graft, unlawful detentions, lack of sustainable investments in health or development, and long local histories of abuse at the hands of (mostly Amharic-speaking, *Habesha* Ethiopian) military and police forces.

Many Issas expressed lingering distrust of individual Ogadeni politicians in Jigjiga as well. Self-identified Ogadenis, in contrast to Issas, dominated the Somali regional government based in Jigjiga. Back in 1991, Ogadenis within the Ogaden National Liberation Front (ONLF) famously led fights against the Derg and helped topple its regime east of the Rift Valley; the ONLF subsequently helped found and support the original Somali regional government; and since the 1990s, Ogadenis have held a majority of the elective offices and appointed bureaucratic positions in Jigjiga. While the EPRDF continued to appoint most leaders within regional government, many Ogadenis also advocated whenever possible for more meaningful autonomy and independence from the EPRDF. Conflicting allegiances and violent histories complicated politics in the Somali Region as well as efforts to foster interclan and interethnic relations of trust.

In August 2018, when Abdi Iley, the president of the Somali Region, was arrested in Jigjiga, his loyalists within and outside the government exacted revenge on many non-Somali residents of the city by burning churches, killing priests, and encouraging violent protests in neighborhoods dominated by businesses and homes owned by non-Somali *Habesha* and Oromo residents. While as many as 150,000 people fled the city in response, many of these were Issa Somalis, threatened by the common presumption among residents of the region that they are aligned with the EPRDF and federal government in Addis Ababa. Hundreds of Issa Somali residents escaped from Jigjiga at night, walking by foot across the arid plateau, or hailing trucks, minibuses, and cars, and arriving into the outskirts of Dire Dawa by dawn.

These antagonisms affected subsequent relief programs. During my interviews with staffers and policy makers within the regional government and their partner relief organizations, several Somalis in power highlighted their predominant interests in expanding the material apparatus and centralized power of a regional governmental system, rather than enhancing equal representation across all social, economic, kinship, and livelihood groups within the region. The representation of Issas and other minority *qabiilooyinka*, were not a matter of advocacy or discussion. Doctor Hamza, for example, was proud of the fact the Somali Regional Health Bureau was "100% Somali." He did not see a problem with the lack of ethnic or kinship diversity in this and other governmental or nongovernmental offices. Issas, he said, were a "small, minority group," already favored by the government in Addis, and he did not therefore think they suffered inequities within the regional government. These sorts of denials of inequities from powerful residents of Jigjiga and from Ogadeni Somalis did not always sit well with Issa traditional leadership (the *ugaas*).

At the same time, interclan differences and animosities were also being progressively undercut across the region—often in the process of international humanitarian aid. Regional bureaus of the government and major INGOs organized their own humanitarian responses, without micromanagement or domination by federal offices in Addis Ababa, and used aid funding to improve the functioning of local governmental services "for all Somalis as a people," Doctor Hamza insisted to me, echoing the words of Article 39 of the Ethiopian Constitution. Instead of conceiving of themselves either narrowly as Ogadenis or Issas, or as equal and deserving citizens of Ethiopia, Somali aid workers, bureaucrats, and policy makers proudly implemented policies tailored to their expectations of *samafal* and the unique needs of pastoralists and traders in the region. By these means, leaders in Jigjiga and Dire Dawa like Doctor Hamza and Aden sought to repair political wounds and undo historical injustices through mechanisms within the relief industry. Humanitarian responses in eastern Ethiopia did not entail exceptional forms or actions of government, but were integral to the functioning, power, cohesiveness, and reputation of the regional state itself, and the palpable, and yet of course still contested, rise of the Somali National Regional State.

Realistically, however, humanitarian aid remained too sporadic and inadequate to address the enduring poverty and marginality many residents and the region as a whole faced. People survived crises largely due to salient notions of *samafal* during and long after humanitarian interventions, and not only narrow distributions of aid commodities or *bani'aadamnimada*. Much of aid workers' enactments of *samafal* still happened outside governmental offices and clinics, and further, what happened inside offices and clinics was mostly still contingent on their notions of *samafal*. *Samafal* augmented intergenerational relationships of reciprocity and mutual obligation, religious forms of charity, traditions of hospitality, and generous kinship networks. These facets of humanitarianism continued to thrive in the Somali Region, alongside burgeoning political and governmental responses. Thus the fundamental principles of the Red Cross may be operational necessities for expatriates and INGOs, and may help politicians and relief organizations located in Western donor countries make the case for foreign intervention to their audiences, taxpayers, and donors. But these pretenses remained nonsensical and obscure to local aid workers.

Other principles and other political strategies structured the implementation and evaluation of relief operations. In contrast to Reagan's deceit of the "hungry child" knowing "no politics," *samafal* depended on the political savvy of its staffers and shaped the development and reputation of political institutions like the Somali regional government. Interpersonal acts of *samafal* reflected but also often undermined the divisive nature of politics in eastern Ethiopia.

And interventions helped solidify power and shape governance in the region; it often united Somalis in Jigjiga to provide aid to "those in greatest need" across historically contentious *qabiil*, ethnic, and partisan divisions. Recognizing the legitimacy and necessity of Somalis' inherently political and yet also principled forms of *samafal* to the success of global humanitarian interventions—and the interdependence and complementarity of these two epistemologies—are necessary to truly "localize" humanitarian work.

6

FROM CRISIS TO LIBERATION

Relief operations in the Somali Region of Ethiopia, even when short-lived or chaotic, were intimate and emotionally tenuous affairs. Injured, exhausted, or sick
persons, very often at the end of a long journey in search of help, and facing a crisis or recovering from a traumatic event, frequently had to divulge details about
potentially embarrassing or private symptoms, disclose their worries about infertility or possession by malevolent jinns, discuss the personal effects of drought
and their poverty, or admit to ignorance of biomedical terminology. They often
feared judgment, rebuke, and neglect.

Most encounters with aid workers lacked for privacy as well. Due to the limited capacity of indoor spaces, persons usually consulted with aid workers and
clinical providers in cramped shelters filled with dozens of other people impa-
tiently waiting around, or outdoors, in the presence of family and other community members. Relief operations frequently also lacked for peace. During the first
days of a response, crowds often pushed toward intake tables and distribution
points, and people sometimes argued over what constituted a fair distribution of
food, medicine, or water.

In order to foster calm, aid workers like Canab, in figure 10, opened spaces for
private conversations and private examinations, and sought the advice of community leaders on how to best address local expectations and apprehensions.
Aid workers forged friendships and shared meals and khat with families in the
hours after work as a way to encourage people to participate in relief operations and open up about their problems. Aid workers frequently expanded or

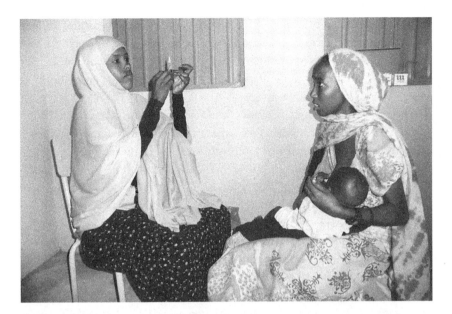

FIGURE 10.   Canab, a health extension worker in the Somali Region of Ethiopia, provided care during a relief operation in a town several miles from her home, to improve rates of severe acute malnutrition in children. She answered questions and assuaged fears about the purpose, process, and risks of immunization for over twenty minutes talks with a worried, first-time mother, and is preparing to give her baby a vaccine. Photograph by David Machledt.

modified relief operations to dispense food and medicine to persons deemed unfairly excluded from disbursements of aid. Even if interventions were paid for or supported by global relief agencies, aid workers typically acted as representatives of burgeoning governmental and nongovernmental aid agencies not always trusted by or familiar to the people with whom they worked.

Furthermore, the health extension workers, nurses, disaster preparedness and response bureaucrats, veterinary technicians, researchers, language interpreters, drivers, and enumerators administering surveys and focus groups, like Aden, Ahmed, Jira, and so many others, had at some point in their lives been recipients of global humanitarian assistance. Unlike the international aid workers and Ethiopians from the western highlands of the country who only visited or worked in the Somali Region for short periods of time, most aid workers' parents, children, cousins, and colleagues received humanitarian assistance from the same organizations that also hired them to work. Local aid workers were tasked with comforting and caring for children sickened from the same infectious diseases that threatened their own children; they watched livestock herders much like their own uncles and cousins walk for days in search of verdant pastures for their animals, only to fall sick of pneumonia or dehydration upon their arrival; they witnessed how the loss of livestock or access to land can devastate families like their own; and they had, very often, fled across borders leaving everything they knew and loved behind.

These experiences and memories transformed people, like Canab, Mona, Maryan, and others, who, when asked, narrated their own jobs and identities in response to and intertwined with long histories of humanitarianism. In addition, the mobile teams of health-care providers and the distributions of aid commodities and water supplies across the region did not just forge familial, intraclan, or local relationships of care, but rather also, at the same time, indirectly helped foster Somali solidarity across political divides, helped foster peace and reconciliation between pastoralist and farming families across regional and ethnolinguistic boundaries, and even, occasionally, helped lessen animosities between Somalis and Amharic-speaking *Habesha* Ethiopians from farther west. "Moving out widens the heart," Bashiir said. "Moving out," geographically and experientially, away from one's home, traveling, exploring, meeting new people, seeing their ways of life, learning their languages, understanding their situations, and caring for them, brought people a sense of freedom, a fulfillment of religious injunctions, and a sense of meeting expectations of reciprocity.

Caring for people in need and in moments of crisis presented aid workers opportunities to, in a sense, "build themselves anew," as Catherine Panter-Brick phrases it, to fashion themselves as the powerful agents of global aid, and therein to rebuild their communities, families, and identities after so many years and generations of partition, conflict, imperialism, and marginalization.[1] Humanitarian aid moreover allowed providers and residents to coconstruct how a government, and a *Somali* government at that, might govern, respond to crises, save lives, and fulfill people's basic needs. Through aid encounters people were "making citizens" as Lahra Smith finds elsewhere in Ethiopia—citizens who expected their government to both care for and care about its people.[2]

The Limits of *Samafal*

But humanitarian responses were never panaceas. There remained a tension between the freedom and power Somalis sometimes achieved through their humanitarian work, and the mercurial nature of the interventions themselves and the steep labor hierarchies that prevented workers' professional mobility and true emancipation. The aspirational goals and idealistic potentials Aden and Doctor Hamza and others in the humanitarian industry hoped for—to use humanitarian funding to improve primary health care and disaster preparedness in the Somali Region, to foster Somali cohesiveness, and in parallel, as the government of Ethiopia professes, to decentralize the public health and crisis response systems—have not been fully realized. These objectives were impossible to fully achieve because, like Band-Aids, global humanitarian funding and single relief operations never lasted, and therefore could not heal deeper bureaucratic and societal frictions. *Samafal* could not, even with international support, solve greater inequities, either within the Ethiopian political system or within the global humanitarian industry. "Being present," Abshir insisted, was crucial for the success of relief operations, but it would take far more than visits once per week for a few months, or occasional distributions of material goods and medical services, to catalyze a transformation of the global humanitarian enterprise.

With the rise in local forms of power came an increase in risk as well. The growing authority of a handful of Somali aid workers in Ethiopia, and their efforts to expand and transform relief operations, continued to be seen by their supervisors in Addis Ababa as the activity of locals, humanitarian *delalas*, or "rule-breakers," untrustworthy and undeserving of national or international leadership.[3] Their reliance on personal relationships and political savvy to get things done were sometimes interpreted by outsiders as bias or corruption, further entrenching negative stereotypes of Somalis.[4] Furthermore, the precarity and ephemerality of most local aid jobs, and the fact aid workers often negotiate partnerships with rigid or compromised governmental authorities, meant they continued to "lack for freedom," as Aden explained it on several occasions, to say no to something, or to try different and innovative approaches to humanitarian response.

Somali staffers remained relegated to being locals within Ethiopia and within the global humanitarian industry, reinforcing the notion of Somalis and their articulations of *samafal* as somehow fundamentally different from or opposed to humanitarian responses happening elsewhere. It reinforced ideas of Somalis as inferior, marginal to the developments and reforms happening elsewhere in Ethiopia, and marginal players in the global humanitarian industry. Local aid workers including the Somalis portrayed throughout this book were both the object and the subject of global humanitarianism, and they represented its most important output and its workforce. At the same time, these local aid workers were still too often treated like beneficiaries, fortunate to have any job at all, and not agents of a changing humanitarian system.

Humanitarianism as Liberation

Much of the work Somali aid workers in Ethiopia accomplished was dutifully enumerated, reported, and paid for: the number of patients they examined, their distributions of food aid, vaccines, and liters of water, and the miles they traveled through the region. But in addition to this quantifiable work, the care, comfort, and compassion aid workers provided were what they and the recipients of their assistance remembered and missed most when interventions repeatedly subsided. Tensions between people unraveled as aid workers stopped, exited their vehicles, and stayed to strike up conversations and engage with people from other ethnic groups, rival kinship groups, oppositional political parties, and neighboring districts. These affective elements of humanitarian response happened outside the boundaries of *bani'aadamnimada* and lacked official mechanisms of recognition and valuation. Additionally, policy makers like Aden and Abdirahman used limited and temporary project funds aimed at infectious disease outbreaks or spikes in the rates of severe acute malnutrition among children to attend to patients' chronic conditions, to provide education to uncertified midwives like Maryan, to assist adults with disabilities find services and get the food they needed, and to train and supervise permanent community-based health-care providers like Ahmed. But these achievements, too, were rendered outside the boundaries of humanitarian missions, and therefore lacked for dedicated financial investments.

Throughout my research in Ethiopia, I have invited colleagues and friends to imagine with me a new and better global humanitarian system, in the face of all the critiques and challenges they identify. "What would it look like?" I have asked them, and "What should be the most important thing to your work?" Their answers were typically straightforward. "Be with people," "Be present with them," "Just care for people in greatest need," different aid workers said.

The feminist political theorist Joan C. Tronto argues that the provision of care alone—even trustworthy, high-quality, care—is insufficient to ameliorate the larger systems and histories of injustice people face.[5] In other words, in the case of humanitarian assistance to Somalis in Ethiopia, improving interventions and increasing the sizes of aid packages are insufficient. An "ethic of care," Tronto states, must be accompanied by "a concept of justice, a democratic and open opportunity for discussion, and more equal access to power." Therefore, "only if we understand care as an explicitly political idea will we be able to change its status and the status of those who do caring work in our culture."[6]

So for aid workers in eastern Ethiopia, *samafal*, caring for people, caring about them, and beyond the mandates of relief operations, forging new political solidarities and governmental institutions, help Somalis in Ethiopia turn the page on the conflicts and suffering of the past. *Samafal* provides antidotes to violent colonial partitions, foreign military occupations, years of interethnic and inter-clan conflict, and contemporary forms of political and economic marginalization at the hands of more powerful Ethiopians. Through local humanitarian work and global humanitarian support, Somalis are decolonizing and rebuilding their government in the margins of the Ethiopian state. *Samafal* saves lives, but for aid workers and humanitarian policy makers, it also presents a first step toward Somali liberation.

An Atonement and Way Forward

The global humanitarian system—itself a product of imperialism, a mechanism of disclaiming self-interested foreign political strategies, and a reflection of global labor inequities—remains in need of an atonement. People like Aden, Mussa, Mona, and Asha loved their work, but remained immured in an industry not of their own making.

Christina Sharpe finds it ironic that a hospital ship named *Comfort*, deployed by the United States government to respond to the humanitarian crisis in Puerto Rico after Hurricane Maria in 2018, is also the name of the battleship that led the United States' invasion of Grenada, nearby in the Caribbean, only thirty-five years before. "The same instruments used to kill us are imagined as the ones that will save us," she writes. "Saving and killing often look a lot the same as far as black people are concerned."[7]

Sharpe's provocative juxtaposition of the humanitarian vessel once used for state violence and imperial conquest demands a more thorough reckoning with the injustices fundamental to the founding and the continuation of the global humanitarian industry. Her image of the *Comfort* harkens back to the small Italian clinic built in the town of Aysha nearly a century ago, at the edges of empires, used through the years to supply and house colonial administrators, military troops, police forces, and most recently surplus food aid emblazoned with American flags. Contemporary humanitarian aid agencies and interventions continue to rely on material spaces and human architectures originally designed for conquest and occupation. They continue to rely on the hard, undervalued, and often invisible work of people in communities and countries in crisis, without offering them equitable chances to advance or make decisions about these policies and programs.

In the wake of long histories of colonization and conflict in places where relief organizations still intervene, and in the midst of continuing racialized inequities in these same institutions and parts of the world, Sharpe asks, "How are we to attend to and refuse these presents and make new ones in accountable and meaningful ways?"[8] In other words, she says, echoing the words of aid workers in Jigjiga, "How are we to practice care?"

Professional humanitarians characterized throughout this book suggested that mundane practices of care, actions already happening in small clinics and the subnational offices of relief agencies in communities throughout eastern Ethiopia, model at the interpersonal scale the kind of repair needed within relief agencies and governments. Their acts of care were not only interpersonal, as they worked to relieve suffering and provide basic material and medical goods and services, their actions were also affective and designed to enhance the power and cohesiveness of the Somali regional government within Ethiopia.

This unorthodox notion of humanitarianism, articulated by Somalis as *samafal*, while sometimes ignored, unrecognized, or undervalued, is in fact essential to the implementation of humanitarian missions around the world. *Samafal* is humanitarianism, and not merely a Somali artifact or a local way of doing business. *Samafal* indexes a powerful and effective way of implementing aid in places where crises recur and where people from communities in crisis (and not expatriates or experts flown in from wealthier capital cities) staff the NGOs, UN agencies, and governmental relief bureaus. *Samafal*, through the labor of locals, makes global humanitarian response work. Global humanitarian actions are thus particularly Somali, both in their appropriations of global aid to support expansive, mobile, and politically liberating forms of care, and in their interventions that, in the end, help build a humanitarian system defined through affect, mutuality, reciprocity, and political action. And conversely, politics and political transformations in the Somali Region are also inherently humanitarian, funded and supported as they are by the global humanitarian industry.

Recognizing the fact that global humanitarianism is *samafal*—a term emic to beneficiaries and aid workers on the front lines of humanitarian crises in the Horn of Africa, but perhaps strange to policy makers or researchers elsewhere— elevates the vernacular, ethics, expertise, and labor of locals, and renders exotic the projects and materials that arrive in crisis-affected communities as the result of donor bequests. Centering *samafal* to the idea of humanitarianism also effectively challenges the dominance and narrowness of International Humanitarian Law, the fundamental principles of the International Committee of the Red Cross, and the missions of global aid agencies in defining and delimiting what humanitarian response can and should be. It elevates humanitarian epistemologies that value love and liberation above all.

But can the global humanitarian industry trust the Somali aid worker, the local, and the beneficiary to be the authors and agents of their own survival? Will foreign policy makers and politicians living and working outside communities in crisis recognize that *samafal*—with its emotional, social, religious, and political entanglements—can legitimately and effectively structure relief operations? To carry Christina Sharpe's metaphor of the *Comfort* forward again, can locals and Somalis and the many Adens and Canabs of the world be the ones to not just right the metaphorical ship, but to be given the materials and the freedom to build a new ship altogether? As Safia Aidid asks, "Can the Somali speak?"[9] If localization and the devolution of power are serious objectives in transforming the global humanitarian system, as so many in the aid industry now profess, it should mean recognizing *samafal* for what it is, recognizing subaltern concepts like *samafal* through which global humanitarian missions are realized, uplifting them, trusting them, and in so doing, beginning to undo legacies of imperialism and inequity.

Notes

PROLOGUE

1. Aden is a pseudonym. A few people and aid organizations are named in this book, at their own request, but most proper nouns remain ambiguous to ensure interlocutors' anonymity. The names of public figures and precise locations are provided whenever these do not otherwise compromise the confidentiality of private conversations.

2. In other words, humanitarian responses are temporary, short-lived international interventions designed to save and protect human lives in the wake of conflicts, population displacements, or other social, political, or economic upheavals.

3. Statistics demonstrating the current and historical changes and regional disparities in child survival rates and immunization rates in the Somali Region and in Ethiopia may be found in Federal Democratic Republic of Ethiopia, Central Statistical Agency, "Ethiopia: Demographic and Health Survey 2016," June 2017, https://dhsprogram.com/pubs/pdf/FR328/FR328.pdf; and in United Nations Children's Fund (UNICEF), "Ethiopia: Key Demographic Indicators," accessed May 31, 2020, https://data.unicef.org/country/eth/.

4. Historical trends in malnutrition rates in Ethiopia may be found in the database United Nations Children's Fund (UNICEF), "UNICEF/WHO/World Bank Joint Child Malnutrition Estimates," last updated March 2020, https://data.unicef.org/wp-content/uploads/2020/03/Joint-Malnutrition-Estimates-by-country-March2020.xlsx.

5. Some popular examples of this genre include Jessica Alexander, *Chasing Chaos: My Decade in and out of Humanitarian Aid* (New York: Broadway Books, 2015); Kenneth Cain, Heidi Postlewait, and Andrew Thomson, *Emergency Sex (and Other Desperate Measures): True Stories from a War Zone* (London: Ebury, 2006); Yael Danieli, ed., *Sharing the Front Line and the Back Hills: International Protectors and Providers; Peacekeepers, Humanitarian Aid Workers and the Media in the Midst of Crisis* (Boca Raton, FL: CRC Press, 2018); John Norris, *The Disaster Gypsies: Humanitarian Workers in the World's Deadliest Conflicts* (Westport, CT: Praeger Security International, 2007). See also recent media stories such as Nurith Aizenman and Malaka Gharib, "American with No Medical Training Ran Center for Malnourished Ugandan Kids. 105 Died," National Public Radio, August 9, 2019, https://www.npr.org/sections/goatsandsoda/2019/08/09/749005287/american-with-no-medical-training-ran-center-for-malnourished-ugandan-kids-105-d.

6. Several texts and edited volumes by social scientists investigate the cultures of humanitarian work, including Renée C. Fox, *Doctors Without Borders: Humanitarian Quests, Impossible Dreams of Médecins Sans Frontières* (Baltimore: Johns Hopkins University Press, 2014); Liisa Malkki, *The Need to Help: The Domestic Arts of International Humanitarianism* (Durham, NC: Duke University Press, 2015); Peter Redfield, *Life in Crisis: The Ethical Journey of Doctors Without Borders* (Berkeley: University of California Press, 2013); Silke Roth, *The Paradoxes of Aid Work: Passionate Professionals* (London: Routledge, 2015).

7. This turn of phrase has been used by several scholars including: Leslie Butt, "The Suffering Stranger: Medical Anthropology and International Morality," *Medical Anthropology* 21, no. 1 (2002): 1–24, https://doi.org/10.1080/01459740210619; Craig Calhoun,

"The Idea of Emergency: Humanitarian Action and Global (Dis)order," in *Contempo-rary States of Emergency: The Politics of Military and Humanitarian Interventions*, ed. Didier Fassin and Mariella Pandolfi (Brooklyn, NY: Zone Books, 2010), 33–34; Liisa Malkki, "A Tale of Two Affects: Humanitarianism and Professionalism in Red Cross Aid Work," in *Radical Egalitarianism: Local Realities, Global Relations*, ed. Felicity Aulino, Miriam Goheen, and Stanley J. Tambiah (New York: Fordham University Press, 2013), 209–19.

8. A phrase introduced into popular lexicon by Teju Cole, "The White-Savior Indus-trial Complex," *The Atlantic*, March 21, 2012.

9. P. Knox Clarke, *The State of the Humanitarian System 2018* (London: ALNAP, 2018), 101–8.

10. For examples see Inter-Agency Standing Committee, "The Grand Bargain: A Shared Commitment to Better Serve People in Need," May 23, 2016, https://interagencystanding-committee.org/system/files/grand_bargain_final_22_may_final-2.pdf; Charter4Change, "Localisation of Humanitarian Aid: The Charter," accessed June 2, 2020, https://charter4 change.org/; Yves Daccord, "From 'Victims' to 'Consumers'? Changing Perceptions of Humanitarian Aid Beneficiaries," Humanitarian Practice Network, Overseas Development Institute, March 2, 2015, http://odihpn.org/blog/from-victims-to-consumers-changing-perceptions-of-humanitarian-aid-beneficiaries/; and content organized on the website Overseas Development Institute, Localising Aid, accessed June 2, 2020, https://www.odi. org/projects/2696-localising-aid-budget-support-southern-actors.

11. Discussed in the following reports and briefing papers: P. Knox Clarke, *The State of the Humanitarian System 2018*; Christina Bennett, Matthew Foley, and Sara Pantu-liano, "Time to Let Go: Remaking Humanitarian Action for the Modern Era," Humani-tarian Policy Group, Overseas Development Institute, April 2016, https://www.odi. org/publications/10381-time-let-go-remaking-humanitarian-action-modern-era; Jer-emy Konyndyk and Rose Worden, "People-Driven Response: Power and Participation in Humanitarian Action," Center for Global Development Policy Paper 155, September 2019, https://www.cgdev.org/people-driven-response; United Nations Office for the Coordi-nation of Humanitarian Affairs (UNOCHA), "Safety and Security for National Humani-tarian Workers," 2011, https://www.unocha.org/sites/unocha/files/Safety%20and%20 Security%20for%20National%20Humanitarian%20Workers%2C%20PDSB%2C%20 2011%2C%20English.pdf; Oxfam, "Accountability and Ownership: The Role of Aid in a Post-2015 World," Oxfam Briefing Paper, September 2016, https://www.oxfamamerica. org/static/media/files/bp-accountability-and-ownership-11-16.pdf.

12. See Fiona Fox, "New Humanitarianism: Does It Provide a Moral Banner for the 21st Century?," *Disasters* 25, no. 4 (2001): 275–89. She argues here that the appropriation and use of humanitarian assistance by local and national political actors potentially rep-resent new moral and ethical standards. Also, see for example the representation of this idea on social media in the Twitter hashtags #localizeaid or #localiseaid; see the publica-tion Oxfam, "Local Aid Workers, Heroes of World Humanitarian Day," August 19, 2014, https://politicsofpoverty.oxfamamerica.org/2014/08/local-aid-workers-heroes-world-humanitarian-day/.

13. Quoted from Ilana Feldman, "The Quaker Way: Ethical Labor and Humanitarian Relief," *American Ethnologist* 34, no. 4 (2007): 689.

14. For a thorough critique of the idea of dependency on humanitarian assistance, see Paul Harvey and Jeremy Lind, "Dependency and Humanitarian Relief: A Critical Analy-sis," Humanitarian Policy Group, Report 19, Overseas Development Institute, July 2005, https://www.odi.org/sites/odi.org.uk/files/odi-assets/publications-opinion-files/277. pdf. This idea is also discussed in Antonio Donini, "The Far Side: The Meta Functions of

Humanitarianism in a Globalised World," *Disasters* 34, no. 1 (2010): S220–37; discussed in the Horn of Africa by Gaim Kibreab, "The Myth of Dependency among Camp Refugees in Somalia, 1979–1989," *Journal of Refugee Studies* 6, no. 4 (1993): 321–49; and critiqued through research in Ethiopia in Peter D. Little, "Food Aid Dependency in Northeastern Ethiopia: Myth or Reality?," *World Development* 36, no. 5 (2008): 860–74; Jenny Edkins, *Whose Hunger? Concepts of Famine, Practices of Aid* (Minneapolis: University of Minnesota Press, 2000); Jeremy Lind and Teriessa Jalleta, "Poverty, Power and Relief Assistance: Meanings and Perceptions of 'Dependency' in Ethiopia," Humanitarian Policy Group, Overseas Development Institute, July 2005, https://www.odi.org/sites/odi.org.uk/files/odi-assets/publications-opinion-files/428.pdf. Dependency and participatory aid are discussed in greater detail in chapter 1.

15. For example, see G. Hancock, *Lords of Poverty: The Power, Prestige, and Corruption of the International Aid Business* (London: Macmillan, 1989).

16. A term referring to the private capitalist industries enabled and distributed globally through international military and humanitarian responses, coined by Naomi Klein, *The Shock Doctrine: The Rise of Disaster Capitalism* (New York: Macmillan, 2007), 14–15. She says: "In only a few short years, the [disaster capitalism] complex has already expanded its market reach from fighting terrorism to international peacekeeping, to municipal policing, to responding to increasingly frequent natural disasters. The ultimate goal for the corporations at the center of the complex is to . . . privatize the government." For a critical discussion of the implications of this, see: Mark Schuller and Julie K. Maldonado, "Disaster Capitalism," *Annals of Anthropological Practice* 40, no. 1 (2016): 61–72; and for an example that contrasts with aid workers in the Somali Region, see Vincanne Adams, Taslim Van Hattum, and Diana English, "Chronic Disaster Syndrome: Displacement, Disaster Capitalism, and the Eviction of the Poor from New Orleans," *American Ethnologist* 36, no. 4 (2009): 615–36.

17. A man I call Doctor Hamza, a physician and a former leader within the Somali regional government in Ethiopia said, "Today the [governmental] Health Bureau here is 100% Somali. . . . Most INGOs [international nongovernmental organizations] are headed by Somalis now too, and before five years the heads of office were mostly either white or highlander. This is a big change for us now, and it really helps us to be free."

INTRODUCTION

1. For specific examples, see Craig Calhoun, "The Idea of Emergency: Humanitarian Action and Global (Dis)order," in *Contemporary States of Emergency: The Politics of Military and Humanitarian Interventions*, ed. Didier Fassin and Mariella Pandolfi (Brooklyn, NY: Zone Books, 2010), 29–30; Joanna Macrae, "Humanitarianism: Facing New Challenges," Great Decisions, Overseas Development Institute, 2000, https://www.odi.org/sites/odi.org.uk/files/odi-assets/publications-opinion-files/6319.pdf; Lila Abu-Lughod, "Do Muslim Women Really Need Saving? Anthropological Reflections on Cultural Relativism and Its Others," *American Anthropologist* 104, no. 3 (2002): 783–90; Miriam Ticktin, "A World without Innocence," *American Ethnologist* 44, no. 4 (2017): 577–90; Fiona Terry, *Condemned to Repeat? The Paradox of Humanitarian Action* (Ithaca, NY: Cornell University Press, 2013); Mark Duffield, *Development, Security and Unending War: Governing the World of Peoples* (Cambridge: Polity, 2007); David Rieff, *A Bed for the Night: Humanitarianism in Crisis* (New York: Simon and Schuster, 2003).

2. Michael Barnett calls this "emergency humanitarianism," and compares this narrow definition to more expansive efforts by aid organizations to address suffering, or what he calls, "alchemical humanitarianism." An examination of the difficulties organizations

have in deciding what to do and when to intervene is beyond the scope of this book. For more on these ideas and questions, see Michael Barnett, *Empire of Humanity: A History of Humanitarianism* (Ithaca, NY: Cornell University Press, 2011), 22.

3. Humanitarian response is defined by and for many leading global relief organizations in the following texts: International Committee of the Red Cross, "War & Law," accessed June 2, 2020, https://www.icrc.org/en/war-and-law; Françoise Bouchet-Saulnier, *The Practical Guide to Humanitarian Law*, trans. Laura Brav and Clémentine Olivier (Lanham, MD: Rowman & Littlefield, 2007); Sphere, "The Sphere Handbook: Humanitarian Charter and Minimum Standards in Humanitarian Response," November 2018, https://spherestandards.org/handbook-2018/.

4. Rieff, *A Bed for the Night*, 86.

5. Human Rights Watch, "'We Are Like the Dead': Torture and Other Human Rights Abuses in Jail Ogaden, Somali Regional State, Ethiopia," July 4, 2018, https://www.hrw.org/report/2018/07/04/we-are-dead/torture-and-other-human-rights-abuses-jail-ogaden-somali-regional.

6. Federal Democratic Republic of Ethiopia, Central Statistical Agency, "Ethiopia: Demographic and Health Survey 2016," accessed January 19, 2020, https://dhsprogram.com/publications/publication-FR328-DHS-Final-Reports.cfm; United States, Central Intelligence Agency, "Africa: Ethiopia," in World Factbook, Central Intelligence Agency, accessed June 11, 2020, https://www.cia.gov/library/publications/the-world-factbook/geos/print_et.html.

7. A term defined and described with regard to Ethiopia both in René Lefort, "Free Market Economy, 'Developmental State' and Party-State Hegemony in Ethiopia: The Case of the 'Model Farmers,'" *Journal of Modern African Studies* 50, no. 4 (2012): 681–706; and in Christopher Clapham, "The Ethiopian Developmental State," *Third World Quarterly* 39, no. 6 (2018): 1151–65.

8. Clapham, "The Ethiopian Developmental State." However, Daniel Mains finds that Ethiopia's narrative of progress and faith in the "developmentalist state" remain seductive. See Daniel Mains, "Blackouts and Progress: Privatization, Infrastructure, and a Developmentalist State in Jimma, Ethiopia," *Cultural Anthropology* 27, no. 1 (2012): 3–27.

9. Prime Minister Abiy Ahmed earned a PhD and is colloquially called Dr. Abiy by other Ethiopians. However, here I use his given name or his given name plus his father's given name in the Ethiopian tradition. This is discussed in Abukar Arman, "Transformation Euphoria in the Horn of Africa," *Africa at LSE* (blog), August 9, 2018, https://blogs.lse.ac.uk/africaatlse/2018/08/09/transformation-euphoria-in-the-horn-of-africa/.

10. See Scott W. Lyons, "Joint Declaration of Peace and Friendship between Eritrea and Ethiopia," *International Legal Materials* 58, no. 1 (2019): 237–39.

11. See "The Nobel Peace Prize," October 24, 2019, https://www.nobelprize.org/prizes/peace/2019/summary/; and see a discussion of these trends in Judd Devermont and Jon Temin, "Africa's Democratic Moment? The Five Leaders Who Could Transform the Region," *Foreign Affairs*, July/August 2019, https://www.foreignaffairs.com/articles/africa/2019-06-11/africas-democratic-moment.

12. See discussions and evidence of dynamic authoritarianism in Ethiopia in the following texts: Addisu Lashitew, "Ethiopia Will Explode If It Doesn't Move beyond Ethnic-Based Politics," *Foreign Policy*, November 8, 2019, https://foreignpolicy.com/2019/11/08/ethiopia-will-explode-if-abiy-ahmed-doesnt-move-beyond-ethnic-based-politics/; Jon G. Abbink and Tobias Hagmann, *Reconfiguring Ethiopia: The Politics of Authoritarian Reform* (London: Routledge, 2016); Leonardo R. Arriola, "Protesting and Policing in a Multiethnic Authoritarian State: Evidence from Ethiopia," *Comparative Politics* 45, no. 2 (2013): 147–68.

13. More detailed histories of Somalis in the Horn of Africa may be found in Safia Aidid, "Pan-Somali Dreams: Ethiopia, Greater Somalia, and the Somali Nationalist Imagination," (PhD diss., Harvard University, 2020); Lee Cassanelli, *The Shaping of Somali Society: Reconstructing the History of a Pastoral People, 1600–1900* (Philadelphia: University of Pennsylvania Press, 1982); David D. Laitin and Said S. Samatar, *Somalia: Nation in Search of a State* (Boulder, CO: Westview Press, 1987); Abdi Sheik-Abdi, "Somali Nationalism: Its Origins and Future," *Journal of Modern African Studies* 15, no. 4 (1977): 657–65.

14. Logan Cochrane and Davin O'Regan, "Legal Harvest and Illegal Trade: Trends, Challenges, and Options in Khat Production in Ethiopia," *International Journal of Drug Policy* 30 (2016): 27–34, https://doi.org/10.1016/j.drugpo.2016.02.009.

15. William Eckersley, Ruth Salmon, and Mulugeta Gebru, "Khat, Driver Impairment and Road Traffic Injuries: A View from Ethiopia," *Bulletin of the World Health Organization* 88 (2010): 235–36.

16. Federal Democratic Republic of Ethiopia, Central Statistical Agency, "Population Projection of Ethiopia for All Regions at Wereda Level from 2014–2017," Addis Ababa, Ethiopia. August 2013.

17. Aidid, "Pan-Somali Dreams"; Cassanelli, *The Shaping of Somali Society*.

18. Abdi Ismail Samatar, "Ethiopian Federalism: Autonomy versus Control in the Somali Region," *Third World Quarterly* 25, no. 6 (2004): 1131–54, https://doi.org/10.1080/0143659042000256931.

19. Found in Sylvia Pankhurst, "His Imperial Majesty's Speech to the Ogaden," *Ethiopia Observer* 1, no. 1 (1956): 5–8.

20. Abbink and Hagmann, *Reconfiguring Ethiopia*; Kidane Mengisteab, "New Approaches to State Building in Africa: The Case of Ethiopia's Ethnic-Based Federalism," *African Studies Review* 40, no. 3 (1997): 111–32; Sarah Vaughan, "Ethiopia, Somalia, and the Ogaden: Still a Running Sore at the Heart of the Horn of Africa," in *Secessionism in African Politics: Aspiration, Grievance, Performance, Disenchantment*, ed. Lotje de Vries, Pierre Englebert, and Mareike Schomerus (Cham, Switzerland: Palgrave Macmillan, 2019), 91–123.

21. Tobias Hagmann and Mohamud Hussein Khalif, "State and Politics in Ethiopia's Somali Region since 1991," *Bildhaan: An International Journal of Somali Studies* 6, no. 1 (2008): 27.

22. For more on this, see Samatar, "Ethiopian Federalism;" Vaughan, "Ethiopia, Somalia, and the Ogaden"; Abdi M. Abdullahi, "The Ogaden National Liberation Front (ONLF): The Dilemma of Its Struggle in Ethiopia," *Review of African Political Economy* 34, no. 113 (2007): 556–62; International Crisis Group, "Ethiopia: Prospects for Peace in Ogaden," Africa Report no. 207, August 6, 2013, https://d2071andvip0wj.cloudfront.net/ethiopia-prospects-for-peace-in-ogaden.pdf.

23. For evidence and discussion, see Abbink and Hagmann, *Reconfiguring Ethiopia*; Benedikt Korf, Tobias Hagmann, and Rony Emmenegger, "Re-Spacing African Drylands: Territorialization, Sedentarization and Indigenous Commodification in the Ethiopian Pastoral Frontier," *Journal of Peasant Studies* 42, no. 5 (2015): 881–901; Tobias Hagmann and Benedikt Korf, "Agamben in the Ogaden: Violence and Sovereignty in the Ethiopian-Somali Frontier," *Political Geography* 31, no. 4 (2012): 205–14; Simon Richards and Gezu Bekele, "Conflict in the Somali Region of Ethiopia: Can Education Promote Peace-Building?," Feinstein International Center, Tufts University, March 2011, https://fic.tufts.edu/assets/Conflict-Somali-Ethiopia.pdf; Bamlaku Tadesse et al., "The Dynamics of (Agro) Pastoral Conflicts in Eastern Ethiopia," *Ethiopian Journal of the Social Sciences and Humanities* 11, no. 1 (2015): 29–60.

24. Irregular migrants and contraband traders—even non-Somali Ethiopians and Djiboutians—often cross international borders without visas or passports, off the main roads and far from the official checkpoint locations.

25. Tobias Hagmann, "Beyond Clannishness and Colonialism: Understanding Political Disorder in Ethiopia's Somali Region, 1991–2004," *Journal of Modern African Studies* 43, no. 4 (2005): 509–36; Hagmann and Korf, "Agamben in the Ogaden."

26. Talal Asad, "Where Are the Margins of the State?," in *Anthropology in the Margins of the State*, ed. Veena Das and Deborah Poole (Santa Fe, NM: School of American Research Press, 2004), 279.

27. Veena Das and Deborah Poole, eds. *Anthropology in the Margins of the State* (Santa Fe, NM: School of American Research Press, 2004).

28. See for example, from ethnographic research in Ethiopia, Meron Zeleke, "Too Many Winds to Consider: Which Way and When to Sail! Ethiopian Female Transit Migrants in Djibouti and the Dynamics of Their Decision-Making," *African and Black Diaspora: An International Journal* 12, no. 1 (2019): 49–63. For discussion of how an anthropological study of humanitarian assistance necessitates this kind of critical and ethnographic work, see Alexander de Waal, "Anthropology and the Aid Encounter," in *Exotic No More: Anthropology on the Front Lines*, ed. J. MacClancy (Chicago: University of Chicago Press, 2002), 251–69; Pierre Minn, "Toward an Anthropology of Humanitarianism," Journal of Humanitarian Assistance 6 (2007), https://sites.tufts.edu/jha/archives/51.

29. Reports by humanitarian relief agencies that discuss these successive crises include: James Jeffrey, "Ethiopia Survives Its Great Drought, but a Way of Life May Not," Integrated Regional Information Networks (IRIN), June 13, 2016, http://www.irinnews.org/feature/2016/06/13/ethiopia-survives-its-great-drought-way-life-may-not; United Nations Office for the Coordination of Humanitarian Affairs (UNOCHA), "Ethiopia: Humanitarian Response," Report no. 16, November 2017, https://reliefweb.int/sites/reliefweb.int/files/resources/situation_report_no.16_november_2017_-_final.pdf.

30. Tamer Afifi et al., "Climate Change, Vulnerability and Human Mobility: Perspectives of Refugees from the East and Horn of Africa," Report 1, UNU-EHS and UNHCR, June 2012, https://www.unhcr.org/uk/4fe8538d9.pdf.

31. Elders in the Somali Region spoke to me about this repeatedly during research, and it is documented in the ongoing reporting project, ReliefWeb, "Ethiopia: Drought—2015–2020; Disaster Description," ReliefWeb and UNOCHA, accessed June 2, 2020, https://reliefweb.int/disaster/dr-2015-000109-eth.

32. For example, see the following reports: Human Rights Watch,"'We Are Like the Dead'"; United States Agency for International Development (USAID), "Ethiopia—Complex Emergency," Fact Sheet #5, USAID, September 30, 2018, https://www.usaid.gov/sites/default/files/documents/1866/ethiopia_ce_fs05_09-30-2018.pdf; United Nations Office for the Coordination of Humanitarian Affairs (UNOCHA), "Ethiopia: Oromia-Somali Conflict-Induced Displacement," Situation Report no. 4, June 2018, https://reliefweb.int/sites/reliefweb.int/files/resources/ethiopia_-_oromia_somali_conflict_induced_displacement_june_2018c.pdf.

33. United Nations Children's Fund (UNICEF) Ethiopia, "Ethiopia Humanitarian Situation," UNICEF Ethiopia, Report #12, December 2018, https://reliefweb.int/report/ethiopia/unicef-ethiopia-humanitarian-situation-report-12-january-december-2018#:~:text=In%202018%2C%20UNICEF%20Ethiopia's%20Humanitarian,cent%20of%20those%20in%20need).

34. International Organization for Migration (IOM), "Displacement Tracking Matrix (DTM) Somali, Ethiopia," Round 12, July/August 2018, https://displacement.iom.int/system/tdf/reports/R12%20Somali%20Regional%20Report.pdf?file=1&type=node&id=4459; International Organization for Migration (IOM), "Humanitarian Needs Overview," February 2019, https://www.humanitarianresponse.info/sites/www.humanitarianresponse.info/files/2019/03/02_HNO_Summary_030619.pdf.

35. This phenomenon is also noted by Andy Catley and Alula Iyasu, "Moving Up or Moving Out? A Rapid Livelihoods and Conflict Analysis in Mieso-Mulu Woreda, Shinile Zone, Somali Region, Ethiopia," Feinstein International Center, Tufts University, April 2010, http://technicalconsortium.org/wp-content/uploads/2014/05/Moving_up_or_moving_out.pdf.

36. Community health workers in Ethiopia are called health extension workers (HEWs). For more information on Ethiopia's countrywide health extension worker program, and how these health-care providers are usually paid little or no wages to serve their communities, see Kenneth Maes, *The Lives of Community Health Workers: Local Labor and Global Health in Urban Ethiopia* (New York: Routledge, 2016). Ahmed, unlike other HEWs in Ethiopia, was paid a monthly salary. However, his salary was subsidized by relief organizations and funding initiatives organized at the Somali Regional Health Bureau in Jigjiga (not through the federal Ministry of Health in Addis Ababa), in partnership with UNICEF and other international aid agencies. The regional arm of the Ministry of Health in Jigjiga enjoyed fairly autonomous administration of its HEW program.

37. Aidid, "Pan-Somali Dreams," 39. This manuscript traces in detail the histories of imperialism and conflict across Greater Somalia, and how the territorial partition of Somalis shapes Ethiopian political, economic, and even symbolic forms of power.

38. See Didier Fassin, *Humanitarian Reason: A Moral History of the Present* (Berkeley: University of California Press, 2012); Calhoun, "The Idea of Emergency," 41; and in the Ethiopian context by Tanja R. Müller, "'The Ethiopian Famine' Revisited: Band Aid and the Antipolitics of Celebrity Humanitarian Action," *Disasters* 37, no. 1 (2013): 61–79.

39. Antonio Donini, "The Far Side: The Meta Functions of Humanitarianism in a Globalised World," *Disasters* 34, no. 1 (2010): S227.

40. The inequitable labor hierarchies inherent to global humanitarian response are discussed at length in chapter 3.

41. As defined by Taye Assefa and Tegegne Gebre-Egziabher, eds., *Decentralization in Ethiopia* (Addis Ababa, Ethiopia: Forum for Social Studies, 2007), and discussed in greater detail in this book in chapters to follow.

42. I discuss this phenomenon in greater detail, and its implications for global health security, in an article I authored, "Peace in the Clinic: Rethinking 'Global Health Diplomacy' in the Somali Region of Ethiopia," *Culture, Medicine, and Psychiatry* 40, no. 2 (2016): 181–97.

43. Here I look to the following work on decolonization within the discipline of anthropology: Faye V. Harrison, *Decolonizing Anthropology: Moving Further toward an Anthropology for Liberation* (Arlington, VA: American Anthropological Association, 2011); Linda Tuhiwai Smith, *Decolonizing Methodologies: Research and Indigenous Peoples* (London: Zed Books, 2013); Jafari Sinclaire Allen and Ryan Cecil Jobson, "The Decolonizing Generation: (Race and) Theory in Anthropology since the Eighties," *Current Anthropology* 57, no. 2 (2016): 129–148; Maya J. Berry et al., "Toward a Fugitive Anthropology: Gender, Race, and Violence in the Field," *Cultural Anthropology* 32, no. 4 (2017): 537–65.

44. Harrison, *Decolonizing Anthropology.*

45. In, for example, Charter4Change, "Localisation of Humanitarian Aid: The Charter," accessed June 2, 2020, https://charter4change.org/; Overseas Development Institute, "Localising Aid," accessed June 2, 2020, https://www.odi.org/projects/2696-localising-aid-budget-support-southern-actors.

46. The trope of the aid worker–hero is evident in the following: UNICEF, "Thank These Humanitarian Heroes," accessed June 20, 2019, https://www.unicefusa.org/pledge/thank-these-humanitarian-heroes; Oxfam, "Local Aid Workers, Heroes of World

Humanitarian Day," August 19, 2014, https://politicsofpoverty.oxfamamerica.org/2014/08/local-aid-workers-heroes-world-humanitarian-day/.

47. This is acknowledged by many experts, including in Christina Bennett, Matthew Foley, and Sara Pantuliano, "Time to Let Go: Remaking Humanitarian Action for the Modern Era," Humanitarian Policy Group, Overseas Development Institute, April 2016, https://www.odi.org/publications/10381-time-let-go-remaking-humanitarian-action-modern-era; Jeremy Konyndyk and Rose Worden, "People-Driven Response: Power and Participation in Humanitarian Action," Center for Global Development Policy Paper no. 155, September 2019, https://www.cgdev.org/people-driven-response.

48. Here I draw on insights in Antonio Donini, ed., *The Golden Fleece: Manipulation and Independence in Humanitarian Action* (West Hartford, CT: Kumarian Press, 2012).

49. Discussed for example in International Committee of the Red Cross, "War & Law," accessed June 2, 2020, https://www.icrc.org/en/war-and-law; Françoise Bouchet-Saulnier, *The Practical Guide to Humanitarian Law*, trans. Laura Brav and Clémentine Olivier (Lanham, MD: Rowman & Littlefield, 2007); Sphere Project, "The Sphere Handbook: Humanitarian Charter and Minimum Standards in Disaster Response," November 2018, https://spherestandards.org/handbook-2018/; P. Knox Clarke, *The State of the Humanitarian System 2018* (London: ALNAP, 2018), 101–8.

50. Aden and other aid workers in Ethiopia were never formally educated in humanitarian policy or international humanitarian law. And so the terms I used in interviews and conversations contained multiple meanings, tacking back and forth between different and related English and Somali words (assistance, intervention, help, humanity, kindness, charity, help, *samafal, siyaasada bani'aadamnimada, sadaqad, caawin*)—and these were kept ambiguous throughout the course of this research.

51. Carole McGranahan wrote, even more simply, "ethnography is both something to know and a way of knowing" in her essay, "Explaining Ethnography in the Field," Savage Minds: Notes and Queries in Anthropology, September 25, 2017, https://savageminds.org/2017/09/25/explaining-ethnography-in-the-field-a-conversation-between-pasang-yangjee-sherpa-and-carole-mcgranahan/.

52. See Alexander de Waal, Alemayou Seyoum Taffesse, and Lauren Carruth, "Child Survival during the 2002–2003 Drought in Ethiopia," *Global Public Health* 1, no. 2 (2006): 125–32.

53. Lauren Carruth, "The Aftermath of Aid: Medical Insecurity in the Northern Somali Region of Ethiopia" (PhD diss., University of Arizona, 2011).

54. Lauren Carruth et al., "Zoonotic Tuberculosis in Africa: Challenges and Ways Forward," *The Lancet* 388, no. 10059 (2016): 2460–61; Lauren Carruth et al., "Antimicrobial Resistance and Food Safety in Africa," *Lancet Infectious Diseases* 17 (2017): 575–76. Building on this work, I am currently part of a collaborative project to study the ecology of MERS-Coronavirus in Ethiopia, focusing on how the disease emerges and spreads in livestock, wildlife, and humans along camel trade routes. Amira A. Roess et al., "Camels, MERS-CoV, and Other Emerging Infections in East Africa," *Lancet Infectious Diseases* 16, no. 1 (2016): 14–15, https://doi.org/10.1016/S1473-3099(15)00471-5.

55. Lauren Carruth et al., "Diabetes in a Humanitarian Crisis: Atypical Clinical Presentations and Challenges to Clinical- and Community-Based Management among Somalis in Ethiopia," *Global Public Health* 15, no. 6 (2020): 828–39, https://doi.org/10.1080/17441692.2020.1718735; Lauren Carruth and Emily Mendenhall, "'Wasting Away': Diabetes, Food Insecurity, and Medical Insecurity in the Somali Region of Ethiopia," *Social Science & Medicine* 228 (2019): 155–63, https://doi.org/10.1016/j.socscimed.2019.03.026.

56. Lisa Smirl, *Spaces of Aid: How Cars, Compounds and Hotels Shape Humanitarianism* (London: Zed Books, 2015).

57. Nicholas J. Long and Henrietta L. Moore, "Introduction," in *Sociality: New Directions*, ed. Nicholas J. Long and Henrietta L. Moore (New York: Berghahn Books, 2013), 2.

58. See for example, João Guilherme Biehl, Byron Good, and Arthur Kleinman, eds., *Subjectivity: Ethnographic Investigations* (Berkeley: University of California Press, 2007); Erica Bornstein and Peter Redfield, eds., *Forces of Compassion: Humanitarianism between Ethics and Politics* (Santa Fe, NM: School for Advanced Research Press, 2011); Peter Redfield, *Life in Crisis: The Ethical Journey of Doctors Without Borders* (Berkeley: University of California Press, 2013); Ramah McKay, *Medicine in the Meantime: The Work of Care in Mozambique* (Durham, NC: Duke University Press, 2017); Alisse Waterston, "Intimate Ethnography and the Anthropological Imagination: Dialectical Aspects of the Personal and Political in My Father's Wars," *American Ethnologist* 46, no. 1 (2019): 7–19.

59. For another example of how humanitarian crises are never one-time events, and how the enduring social, economic, and political effects of humanitarian crises affect the lives of everyday people, see Elizabeth Cullen Dunn, *No Path Home: Humanitarian Camps and the Grief of Displacement* (Ithaca, NY: Cornell University Press, 2018).

60. I use the concept of methodological dialectics here by drawing on the work of Alisse Waterston in the aforementioned article, "Intimate Ethnography," 7–19; and the commensurate definition in Bertell Ollman and Tony Smith, eds., *Dialectics for the New Century* (New York: Palgrave Macmillan, 2008). Waterston's description of the intimacy involved in ethnography with people one cares about helped me recognize how important the feelings of love, solidarity, and belonging were both to my ethnographic practice and the humanitarian assistance so many staffers offered to people in need.

61. Anand Pandian's book titled, *A Possible Anthropology: Methods for Uneasy Times* (Durham, NC: Duke University Press, 2019) argues that anthropology is, at its best, a potential tool for speculating and imaging possible alternative futures in collaboration with others. Tim Ingold similarly discusses the difference between ethnography (a method to describe the lives people live) and anthropology (a form of inquiry into what it means to be human, and what it could potentially mean as well) in "Anthropology contra Ethnography," *HAU: Journal of Ethnographic Theory* 7, no. 1 (2017): 21–26. This book uses ethnography to represent an anthropology of humanitarianism, here called *samafal*.

1. HUMANITARIANISM IS LOCAL

1. Liisa H. Malkki, *Purity and Exile: Violence, Memory, and National Cosmology among Hutu Refugees in Tanzania* (Chicago: University of Chicago Press, 1995), 296.

2. For a discussion and timeline of the history of conflicts and displacements in the Somali Region of Ethiopia, see Tobias Hagmann and Mohamud Hussein Khalif, "State and Politics in Ethiopia's Somali Region since 1991," *Bildhaan: An International Journal of Somali Studies* 6, no. 1 (2008): 25–49.

3. Antonio Donini, "The Far Side: The Meta Functions of Humanitarianism in a Globalised World," *Disasters* 34, no. 1 (2010): S220.

4. I use the phrase "white gaze" in the ideological and racialized senses described by Sara Ahmed, "A Phenomenology of Whiteness," *Feminist Theory* 8, no. 2 (2007): 149–68; and Erica Caple James, *Democratic Insecurities: Violence, Trauma, and Intervention in Haiti* (Berkeley: University of California Press, 2010).

5. Here I temper any tendency I might have to "essentialise and romanticise 'the local,'" as called for in Giles Mohan and Kristian Stokke, "Participatory Development and Empowerment: The Dangers of Localism," *Third World Quarterly* 21, no. 2 (2000): 249.

6. Defined in Jesse C. Ribot, "African Decentralization: Local Actors, Powers and Accountability," UN Research Institute for Social Development, December 2002, http://www.unrisd.org/unrisd/website/document.nsf/(httpPublications)/3345AC67E6875754C1256D12003E6C95?OpenDocument.

7. Lovise Aalen, "Ethnic Federalism in a Dominant Party State: The Ethiopian Experience, 1991–2000," CMI Report 2 (2002), https://www.cmi.no/publications/769-ethnic-federalism-in-a-dominant-party-state; Taye Assefa and Tegegne Gebre-Egziabher, eds., *Decentralization in Ethiopia* (Addis Ababa, Ethiopia: Forum for Social Studies, 2007); Edmond J. Keller and Lahra Smith, "Obstacles to Implementing Territorial Decentralization: The First Decade of Ethiopian Federalism," in *Sustainable Peace: Power and Democracy after Civil Wars*, ed. Philip G. Roeder and Donald S. Rothchild (Ithaca, NY: Cornell University Press, 2005), 265–92; Jon G. Abbink and Tobias Hagmann, *Reconfiguring Ethiopia: The Politics of Authoritarian Reform* (London: Routledge, 2016).

8. Tigrinya (or Trigraya) is an ethnolinguistic group residing in Ethiopia and Eritrea, and Tigray is an ethnic autonomous region in Ethiopia. Former Prime Minister Meles Zenawi, once head of the TPLF and then EPRDF, was from the Tigray Region. Tigrayan Ethiopians make up a majority of the population in northern Ethiopia along the border with Eritrea.

9. Meles Zenawi gained power during the coup in 1991 and was elected prime minister by the Ethiopian Parliament in 2005 and again in 2010. He died in 2012 while in office. For more of the history of the TPLF and EPRDF see Kidane Mengisteab, "New Approaches to State Building in Africa: The Case of Ethiopia's Ethnic-Based Federalism," *African Studies Review* 40, no. 3 (1997): 111–32; Terrence Lyons, "Ethiopian Elections: Past and Future," *International Journal of Ethiopian Studies* 5, no. 1 (2010): 107–21; Aalen, "Ethnic Federalism in a Dominant Party State."

10. As of August 2019, the ethnic autonomous regions included: Afar, Amhara, Benishangul-Gumuz, Gambella, Harar, Oromia, Somali, Southern Nations Nationalities and Peoples, and Tigray. In addition, two special administrative cities were formed and are represented in Parliament like the other regions: Addis Ababa and Dire Dawa. The Somali Region as an ethnic regional state is discussed in Abdi Ismail Samatar, "Ethiopian Ethnic Federalism and Regional Autonomy: The Somali Test," *Bildhaan: An International Journal of Somali Studies* 5 (2005): 44–76.

11. Federal Democratic Republic of Ethiopia, Constitution, Part Two, Article 39, paragraphs 1–5 (1994).

12. Alemseged Abbay, "Diversity and State-Building in Ethiopia," *African Affairs* 103, no. 413 (2004): 593–614.

13. See Abdi Ismail Samatar, "Ethiopian Ethnic Federalism." However, there has always been a gap between the ideals enshrined in the constitution and the reality of politics and policy making, as demonstrated in Assefa Fiseha, "Theory versus Practice in the Implementation of Ethiopia's Ethnic Federalism," in *Ethnic Federalism: The Ethiopian Experience in Comparative Perspective*, ed. David Turton (Athens, OH: Ohio University Press, 2006), 131–64. Therefore, while the constitution nominally guarantees a right of any nation or people to secede, secession is made extremely difficult and unlikely (if not impossible) by the bureaucratic process of referendums and votes the constitution requires (paragraph 4, Article 39).

14. Hagmann and Khalif, "State and Politics," 27.

15. See reports about this in Abdur Rahman Alfa Shaban, "Ethiopia's Somali Regional Politics: New Leader, Abdi Illey Charged, Liyu Police," Africa News, August 30, 2018, accessed September 1, 2019, https://www.africanews.com/2018/08/30/ethiopias-somali-regional-politics-new-leader-abdi-illey-charged-liyu-police/; Human Rights Watch, "'We Are Like the Dead': Torture and Other Human Rights Abuses in Jail Ogaden, Somali Regional

State, Ethiopia," July 4, 2018, https://www.hrw.org/report/2018/07/04/we-are-dead/torture-and-other-human-rights-abuses-jail-ogaden-somali-regional.

16. Giulia Paravicini, "Ethiopian Who Demanded Justice Now Has Half a Year to Deliver It," Reuters, January 28, 2020, https://www.reuters.com/article/us-ethiopia-justice/ethiopian-who-demanded-justice-now-has-half-a-year-to-deliver-it-idUSKBN1ZR10K.

17. Jon G. Abbink, "Dervishes, 'Moryaan' and Freedom Fighters: Cycles of Rebellion and the Fragmentation of Somali Society, 1900–2000," in *African Dynamics*, ed. Jon G. Abbink, K. van Walraven, and M. E. de Bruijn (Leiden: Brill, 2003), 328–65; Virginia Luling, "Somali," in *Muslim Peoples: A World Ethnographic Survey*, ed. Richard Weekes (Westport, CT: Greenwood Press, 1978), 364–69; David D. Laitin and Said S. Samatar, *Somalia: Nation in Search of a State* (Boulder, CO: Westview Press, 1987).

18. Hagmann and Khalif, "State and Politics," 42.

19. Virginia Luling, "Come Back Somalia? Questioning a Collapsed State," *Third World Quarterly* 18, no. 2 (1997): 289.

20. Abbink, "Dervishes, 'Moryaan' and Freedom Fighters."

21. Laitin and Samatar, *Somalia*, 42–43.

22. Lee Cassanelli, *The Shaping of Somali Society: Reconstructing the History of a Pastoral People, 1600–1900* (Philadelphia: University of Pennsylvania Press, 1982), 103.

23. Peter D. Little, *Somalia: Economy without State* (Bloomington: Indiana University Press, 2003), 167.

24. John Markakis, "Ethnic Conflict and the State in the Horn of Africa," in *Ethnicity and Conflict in the Horn of Africa*, ed. Katsuyoshi Fukui and John Markakis (London: James Currey, 1994), 217–38.

25. Hagmann and Khalif, "State and Politics," 35.

26. The following texts make this argument in greater detail: Tobias Hagmann, "Beyond Clannishness and Colonialism: Understanding Political Disorder in Ethiopia's Somali Region, 1991–2004," *Journal of Modern African Studies* 43, no. 4 (2005): 509–36; Hagmann and Khalif, "State and Politics"; Abdi Ismail Samatar, *Africa's First Democrats: Somalia's Aden A. Osman and Abdirazak H. Hussen* (Bloomington: Indiana University Press, 2016).

27. Hagmann, "Beyond Clannishness and Colonialism," 524.

28. See humanitarian organizations' reports here: International Organization for Migration (IOM), "Humanitarian Needs Overview," February 2019, https://www.humanitarianresponse.info/sites/www.humanitarianresponse.info/files/2019/03/02_HNO_Summary_030619.pdf; United States Agency for International Development (USAID), "Ethiopia—Complex Emergency," Fact Sheet #5, USAID, September 30, 2018, https://www.usaid.gov/sites/default/files/documents/1866/ethiopia_ce_fs05_09-30-2018.pdf.

29. Research on food aid in Ethiopia, in particular, warns that people have become problematically "dependent" on injections of international assistance: e.g., T. Elliesen, "Imported Dependency: Food Aid Weakens Ethiopia's Self Help Capacity," *Development and Cooperation* 1 (2002): 21–23. Other scholars are critical of the contention that relief causes a disincentive for people to work or provide for themselves in the absence of assistance, in the Ethiopian context and elsewhere. Articles and books that critique the idea of dependency (and "dependency theory") in general and in Ethiopia, respectively, include: Paul Harvey and Jeremy Lind, "Dependency and Humanitarian Relief: A Critical Analysis," Humanitarian Policy Group Report 19, Overseas Development Institute, July 2005, https://www.odi.org/sites/odi.org.uk/files/odi-assets/publications-opinion-files/277.pdf; Peter D. Little, "Food Aid Dependency in Northeastern Ethiopia: Myth or Reality?," *World Development* 36, no. 5 (2008): 860–74; Jenny Edkins, *Whose Hunger? Concepts of Famine, Practices of Aid* (Minneapolis: University of Minnesota Press, 2000); Kay Sharp and Stephen Devereux, "Destitution in Wollo (Ethiopia): Chronic Poverty as a Crisis of

Household and Community Livelihoods," *Journal of Human Development* 5, no. 2 (2004): 227–47; and from outside Ethiopia, Samuel Hickey and Giles Mohan, eds., *Participation: From Tyranny to Transformation? Exploring New Approaches to Participation in Development* (London: Zed Books, 2004), 5–9; Mohan and Stokke, "Participatory Development and Empowerment"; David Mosse, "The Making and Marketing of Participatory Development," in *A Moral Critique of Development*, ed. Philip Quarles van Ufford and Anata Kumar Giri (London: Routledge, 2003), 57–89.

30. Mohan and Stokke, "Participatory Development and Empowerment," 247; Fiona Fox, "New Humanitarianism: Does It Provide a Moral Banner for the 21st Century?," *Disasters* 25, no. 4 (2001): 275–89.

31. As argued throughout the edited volume, Hickey and Mohan, *Participation: From Tyranny to Transformation?*

32. John Gaventa, "Towards Participatory Governance: Assessing the Transformative Possibilities," in Hickey and Mohan, *Participation: From Tyranny to Transformation?*, 25–41.

33. For examples see: Ramin Asgary and Ronald J. Waldman, "The Elephant in the Room: Toward a More Ethical Approach with Accountability toward Intended Beneficiaries in Humanitarian Aid," *International Health* 9, no. 6 (2017): 343–48; Jonathan Fox, "The Uncertain Relationship between Transparency and Accountability," *Development in Practice* 17, nos. 4–5 (2007): 663–71; John Gaventa and Rosemary McGee, "The Impact of Transparency and Accountability Initiatives," *Development Policy Review* 31 (2013): s3–s28.

34. Several critiques and counterexamples are detailed in this conference volume: Bill Cooke and Uma Kothari, eds., *Participation: The New Tyranny?* (London: Zed Books, 2001).

35. This is discussed in detail in James Ferguson, *The Anti-Politics Machine: "Development," Depoliticization, and Bureaucratic Power in Lesotho* (Minneapolis: University of Minnesota Press, 1994).

36. For more on this movement in humanitarian assistance, see the following sources: Inter-Agency Standing Committee, "The Grand Bargain—a Shared Commitment to Better Serve People in Need," May 23, 2016, https://interagencystandingcommittee.org/system/files/grand_bargain_final_22_may_final-2.pdf; Charter4Change, "Localisation of Humanitarian Aid: The Charter," accessed June 2, 2020, https://charter4change.org/; content organized on the website Overseas Development Institute, "Localising Aid," accessed June 2, 2020, https://www.odi.org/projects/2696-localising-aid-budget-support-southern-actors; Jeremy Konyndyk and Rose Worden, "People-Driven Response: Power and Participation in Humanitarian Action," Center for Global Development Policy Paper 155, September 2019, https://www.cgdev.org/people-driven-response; Tara R. Gingerich and Marc J. Owen, "Turning the Humanitarian System on Its Head: Saving Lives and Livelihoods by Strengthening Local Capacity and Shifting Leadership to Local Actors," Oxfam, July 2015, https://s3.amazonaws.com/oxfam-us/www/static/media/files/rr-turning-humanitarian-system-local-capacity-270715-en.pdf; Oxfam, "Accountability and Ownership: The Role of Aid in a Post-2015 World," Oxfam Briefing Paper, September 2016, https://www.oxfamamerica.org/static/media/files/bp-accountability-and-ownership-11-16.pdf.

37. United Nations Office for the Coordination of Humanitarian Affairs (UNOCHA), "Resolution 46/182, Which Created the Humanitarian System, Turns Twenty-Five," December 19, 2016, https://www.unocha.org/story/resolution-46182-which-created-humanitarian-system-turns-twenty-five#:~:text=On%2019%20December%201991%2C%20the,when%20they%20need%20it%20most.

38. International Committee of the Red Cross (ICRC), "Code of Conduct for Employees of the International Committee of the Red Cross," May 2018, https://www.icrc.org/sites/default/files/wysiwyg/code_of_conduct_may_2018.pdf.

39. Core Humanitarian Standard Alliance, Group URD, and the Sphere Project, "Core Humanitarian Standard on Quality and Accountability," Core Humanitarian Standard, 2014, https://corehumanitarianstandard.org/files/files/Core%20Humanitarian%20Standard%20-%20English.pdf.

40. Sphere, "The Sphere Handbook: Humanitarian Charter and Minimum Standards in Humanitarian Response," November 2018, https://spherestandards.org/handbook-2018/.

41. Christina Bennett, Matthew Foley, and Sara Pantuliano, "Time to Let Go: Remaking Humanitarian Action for the Modern Era," Humanitarian Policy Group, Overseas Development Institute, April 2016, https://www.odi.org/publications/10381-time-let-go-remaking-humanitarian-action-modern-era.

42. Two examples, already mentioned in the introductory chapter of this book, include: Oxfam, "Local Aid Workers, Heroes of World Humanitarian Day," August 19, 2014, https://politicsofpoverty.oxfamamerica.org/2014/08/local-aid-workers-heroes-world-humanitarian-day/; United Nations Children's Fund (UNICEF), "Thank These Humanitarian Heroes," accessed June 20, 2019, https://www.unicefusa.org/pledge/thank-these-humanitarian-heroes.

43. This definition is taken from: Timothy Donais, *Peacebuilding and Local Ownership: Post-Conflict Consensus-Building* (London: Routledge, 2012), 1. There is a rich literature beyond the scope of this book on local ownership in conflict settings, as a way of achieving the goals of peace building and development. For example, see Sung Yong Lee and Alpaslan Özerdem, eds., *Local Ownership in International Peacebuilding: Key Theoretical and Practical Issues* (London: Routledge, 2015).

44. Susanna P. Campbell, *Global Governance and Local Peace: Accountability and Performance in International Peacebuilding* (Cambridge: Cambridge University Press, 2018), 4–8.

45. One example of this kind of program is the Productive Safety Net Program (PNSP) in Ethiopia, described in Federal Democratic Republic of Ethiopia, Ministry of Agriculture, "Productive Safety Net Programme Phase IV: Programme Implementation Manual," December 2014, https://srbofed.gov.et/wp-content/uploads/2019/09/PSNP-IV-Programme-Implementation-Manual-Final-14-Dec-14-1.pdf.

46. Campbell, *Global Governance*, 260–61.

47. This argument is discussed in Hugo Slim, *Humanitarian Ethics: A Guide to the Morality of Aid in War and Disaster* (Oxford: Oxford University Press, 2015).

48. Ilana Feldman, "The Quaker Way: Ethical Labor and Humanitarian Relief," *American Ethnologist* 34, no. 4 (2007): 689.

49. See Marit Tolo Østebø, Megan D. Cogburn, and Anjum Shams Mandani, "The Silencing of Political Context in Health Research in Ethiopia: Why It Should Be a Concern," *Health Policy and Planning* 33, no. 2 (2018): 258–70; Kenneth Maes, *The Lives of Community Health Workers: Local Labor and Global Health in Urban Ethiopia* (New York: Routledge, 2016).

50. I use the phrase "developmental state" the way Clapham and Lefort do in Christopher Clapham, "The Ethiopian Developmental State," *Third World Quarterly* 39, no. 6 (2018): 1151–65; and René Lefort, "Free Market Economy, 'Developmental State' and Party-State Hegemony in Ethiopia: The Case of the 'Model Farmers,'" *Journal of Modern African Studies* 50, no. 4 (2012): 681–706.

51. See for example the amounts of Official Development Assistance between countries in the following database: Organization for Economic Co-operation and Development

(OECD), "Aid at a Glance Charts," accessed June 19, 2020, http://www.oecd.org/countries/ethiopia/aid-at-a-glance.htm#recipients.

52. Data on the Somali Region compared to other regions with regard to infant and child mortality, food security, malnutrition, and other indicators may be found in reports and databases linked on the following websites: United Nations Children's Fund (UNICEF), "Situation Analysis of Children and Women: Somali Region," accessed June 5, 2020, https://www.unicef.org/ethiopia/media/2401/file/Somali%20region%20.pdf; Federal Democratic Republic of Ethiopia, Central Statistical Agency, "Ethiopia: Demographic and Health Survey 2016," Addis Ababa, Ethiopia, 2016, https://dhsprogram.com/publications/publication-FR328-DHS-Final-Reports.cfm.

53. Akhil Gupta and Aradhana Sharma, "Introduction: Rethinking Theories of the State in an Age of Globalization," in *The Anthropology of the State: A Reader*, ed. Aradhana Sharma and Akhil Gupta (Oxford: Blackwell, 2009), 11.

54. Lahra Smith, *Making Citizens in Africa: Ethnicity, Gender, and National Identity in Ethiopia* (Cambridge: Cambridge University Press, 2013).

55. For example, see the media story: Caelainn Barr, "Abuse and Terror in the Ogaden," August 4, 2011, https://www.thebureauinvestigates.com/stories/2011-08-04/abuse-and-terror-in-the-ogaden. Also see the aid report by Iván Navarro Milián et al., "Alert 2019! Report on Conflicts, Human Rights and Peacebuilding," February 2019, https://reliefweb.int/report/world/alert-2019-report-conflicts-human-rights-and-peacebuilding.

56. A few (self-identified) ethnic *Habesha* Ethiopian staff I met were committed to investigating and solving health-care and other policy problems in the Somali Region, in particular a few persons I met through the Feinstein International Center at Tufts University and at the UN World Health Organization. These individuals' work and attitudes, unfortunately, in my experience, were the exception. Most *Habesha* Ethiopian staff who had lived most of their lives outside the Somali Region regularly characterized and even joked about "lowlanders," pastoralists, and ethnic Somalis as corrupt, recalcitrant, and ignorant.

57. Hagmann and Khalif, "State and Politics," 38.

58. United Nations Office for the Coordination of Humanitarian Affairs (UNOCHA), "Ethiopia: Humanitarian Response," Situation Report no. 23, June 2019, https://www.humanitarianresponse.info/en/operations/ethiopia/document/ethiopia-humanitarian-response-situation-report-no-23-june-2019.

2. HUMANITARIANISM IS *SAMAFAL*

1. For histories and definitions of the term "localization" used by relief agencies and scholars see: Inter-Agency Standing Committee, "The Grand Bargain—a Shared Commitment to Better Serve People in Need," May 23, 2016, https://interagencystandingcommittee.org/system/files/grand_bargain_final_22_may_final-2.pdf; Charter4Change, "Localisation of Humanitarian Aid: The Charter," accessed June 20, 2020, https://charter4change.org/; content organized on the website Overseas Development Institute, "Localising Aid," accessed June 2, 2020, https://www.odi.org/projects/2696-localising-aid-budget-support-southern-actors; Jemilah Mahmood, "Opinion: Yes, the Humanitarian Sector Really Is Going to Localize," Devex, June 16, 2017, https://www.devex.com/news/opinion-yes-the-humanitarian-sector-really-is-going-to-localize-90487. For a detailed explanation and review of studies of decentralization in Ethiopia, see Taye Assefa and Tegegne Gebre-Egziabher, eds., *Decentralization in Ethiopia* (Addis Ababa, Ethiopia: Forum for Social Studies, 2007).

2. As described in, for example, Sphere Association, "The Sphere Handbook: Humanitarian Charter and Minimum Standards in Humanitarian Response," 4th ed., Geneva, Switzerland, November 2018, https://spherestandards.org/handbook-2018/;

International Committee of the Red Cross, "War & Law," accessed June 2, 2020, https://www.icrc.org/en/war-and-law; Hugo Slim, *Humanitarian Ethics: A Guide to the Morality of Aid in War and Disaster* (Oxford: Oxford University Press, 2015).

3. See Erica Bornstein and Peter Redfield, eds., *Forces of Compassion: Humanitarianism between Ethics and Politics* (Santa Fe, NM: School for Advanced Research Press, 2011), 3–30; Didier Fassin, *Humanitarian Reason: A Moral History of the Present* (Berkeley: University of California Press, 2012).

4. Betsey Behr Brada, "The Contingency of Humanitarianism: Moral Authority in an African HIV Clinic," *American Anthropologist* 118, no. 4 (2016): 756.

5. This language choice did not seem to represent a "productive misunderstanding" as in Julie Livingston, "Productive Misunderstandings and the Dynamism of Plural Medicine in Mid-Century Bechuanaland," *Journal of Southern African Studies* 33, no. 4 (2007): 801. Rather this seems to be a repetition of common aid jargon, derived from English. The word *humanitarian* is used in jargon less than other terms like *emergency* or *crisis* perhaps because of its broader, moralistic, and sentimental connotations. However, the linguistics of humanitarianism-cum-*samafal* will have to be the subject for a future project.

6. Franco Barchiesi, *Precarious Liberation: Workers, the State, and Contested Social Citizenship in Postapartheid South Africa* (Albany: State University of New York Press, 2011), 11.

7. *The Holy Qur'an*, trans. Abdullah Yusuf Ali (Durban, South Africa: Islamic Propagation Centre International, 1946), Part 2, Section 22, Verse 177.

8. Lauren Carruth and Scott Freeman, "Aid or Exploitation? Food-for-Work, Cash-for-Work, and the Production of 'Beneficiary-Workers' in Ethiopia and Haiti," *World Development* 140 (2021): 105283, https://doi.org/10.1016/j.worlddev.2020.105283.

9. Championing "need-based" aid has additional benefits for Somalis working in the aid industry: within Ethiopia, they have a relatively small population compared to other ethnic groups and regions, but because of the history of conflict, harsh environment, long distances between towns, and lack of infrastructure, all forms of aid, travel, and research are perceived to be more costly there.

10. Also discussed with regard to Chinese Muslims' pluralistic practices of charity in Matthew S. Erie, "Sharia, Charity, and Minjian Autonomy in Muslim China: Gift Giving in a Plural World," *American Ethnologist* 43, no. 2 (2016): 311–24. This is similar to charitable programs described as well in Amira Mittermaier, "Beyond Compassion: Islamic Voluntarism in Egypt," *American Ethnologist* 41, no. 3 (2014): 518–31.

11. For another description of jinns, see Barbara Drieskens, *Living with Djinns: Understanding and Dealing with the Invisible in Cairo* (London: Saqi Books, 2008). In this book, Drieskens defines jinns as, "invisible creatures, not absolutely evil but rather unpredictable. The Qur'an states that Allah created three kinds of intelligent creatures: angels made of light, humans made of clay and djinns created from smokeless fire. Belief in djinns is therefore not really superstition; it is an integral, though somewhat controversial, part of religion." Here she is speaking of jinns affecting Egyptians, but the definition she provides aptly describes Somalis' invocations as well.

12. Spiritual disorders primarily affected women, as women's bodies are perceived to be more prone to openness and attack, interlocutors told me. This phenomenon is noted elsewhere, in other Islamic societies, as described in Janice Boddy, "Spirit Possession Revisited: Beyond Instrumentality," *Annual Review of Anthropology* 23, no. 1 (1994): 407–34; Amal Hassan Fadlalla, "Modest Women, Deceptive Jinn: Identity, Alterity, and Disease in Eastern Sudan," *Identities: Global Studies in Culture and Power* 12, no. 2 (2005): 143–74; Marcia C. Inhorn, *Quest for Conception: Gender, Infertility and Egyptian Medical Traditions* (Philadelphia: University of Pennsylvania Press, 1994); Gerda

Sengers, *Women and Demons: Cult Healing in Islamic Egypt* (Leiden: Brill, 2003); Drieskens, *Living with Djinns*.

13. Sengers, *Women and Demons*, 175, discusses a similar phenomenon in Egypt.

14. This was also found in Tanzania as part of the main thesis of the book, Stacey Ann Langwick, *Bodies, Politics, and African Healing: The Matter of Maladies in Tanzania* (Bloomington: Indiana University Press, 2011).

15. Lauren Carruth, "Camel Milk, Amoxicillin, and a Prayer: Medical Pluralism and Medical Humanitarian Aid in the Somali Region of Ethiopia," *Social Science & Medicine* 120 (2014): 405–12.

16. Somali "clans" are defined and discussed in the following texts: Ioan Myrddin Lewis, *Blood and Bone: The Call of Kinship in Somali Society* (Lawrenceville, NJ: Red Sea Press, 1994); Ioan Myrddin Lewis, "Visible and Invisible Differences: The Somali Paradox," *Africa* 74, no. 4 (2004): 489–515.

17. Catherine Besteman, *Unraveling Somalia: Race, Class, and the Legacy of Slavery* (Philadelphia: University of Pennsylvania Press, 2014); Abdi Ismail Samatar, "Debating Somali Identity in a British Tribunal: The Case of the BBC Somali Service," *Bildhaan: An International Journal of Somali Studies* 10, no. 8 (2011): 36–88; Virginia Luling, "Genealogy as Theory, Genealogy as Tool: Aspects of Somali 'Clanship,'" *Social Identities* 12, no. 4 (2006): 471–85.

18. Samatar, "Debating Somali Identity," 43.

19. Rachel Sabates-Wheeler, Jeremy Lind, and John Hoddinott, "Implementing Social Protection in Agro-Pastoralist and Pastoralist Areas: How Local Distribution Structures Moderate PSNP Outcomes in Ethiopia," *World Development* 50 (2013): 1–12; Ben Watkins and Michael L. Fleisher, "Tracking Pastoralist Migration: Lessons from the Ethiopian Somali National Regional State," *Human Organization* 61, no. 4 (2002): 328–38.

20. Lauren Carruth, "Kinship, Nomadism, and Humanitarian Aid among Somalis in Ethiopia," *Disasters* 42, no. 1 (2018): 149–68, https://doi.org/10.1111/disa.12236.

21. For a definition of and information on BP-5 biscuits, see this guide for use from the United Nations World Food Programme: "BP-5 Compact Food," accessed June 2, 2020, https://documents.wfp.org/stellent/groups/public/documents/manual_guide_proced/wfp260004.pdf. For a definition of and description of UNICEF's use of PlumpyNut in Ethiopia, see this document: UNICEF, "Ready-to-Use Therapeutic Foods Scale-Up," November 2019, https://www.unicef.org/evaldatabase/files/8._EOI_Case_Study_Ready-to-Use_Therapeutic_Foods_Scale-Up.pdf.

22. Discussed in David D. Laitin and Said S. Samatar, *Somalia: Nation in Search of a State* (Boulder, CO: Westview Press, 1987).

23. Sabates-Wheeler, Lind, and Hoddinott, "Implementing Social Protection"; Watkins and Fleisher, "Tracking Pastoralist Migration."

24. Carruth, "Kinship."

25. Hospitality as a core Somali value and a feature of politics has been noted by other scholars as well, including Abdi Sheik-Abdi, "Somali Nationalism: Its Origins and Future," *Journal of Modern African Studies* 15, no. 4 (1977): 657–65; Cawo M. Abdi, *Elusive Jannah: The Somali Diaspora and a Borderless Muslim Identity* (Minneapolis: University of Minnesota Press, 2015).

26. These points also discussed in Lauren Carruth, "Peace in the Clinic: Rethinking 'Global Health Diplomacy' in the Somali Region of Ethiopia," *Culture, Medicine, and Psychiatry* 40, no. 2 (2016): 193–94.

27. Annemarie Mol, *The Logic of Care: Health and the Problem of Patient Choice* (London: Routledge, 2008), 1.

28. Annemarie Mol, Ingunn Moser, and Jeannette Pols, "Care: Putting Practice into Theory," in *Care in Practice: On Tinkering in Clinics, Homes and Farms*, ed. Annemarie Mol, Ingunn Moser, and Jeannette Pols (Bielefeld: Transcript Verlag, 2010), 10.

29. This dual meaning of the word "care" is discussed in: Lenore Manderson and Narelle Warren, "'Caring for' and 'Caring about': Embedded Interdependence and Quality of Life," in *Reframing Disability and Quality of Life*, ed. Narelle Warren and Lenore Manderson (Dordrecht: Springer, 2013), 179–93; Heike Drotbohm and Erdmute Alber, "Introduction," in *Anthropological Perspectives on Care: Work, Kinship, and the Life-Course*, ed. Erdmute Alber and Heike Drotbohm (New York: Palgrave Macmillan, 2015), 1–20.

30. Arthur Kleinman, "Caregiving as Moral Experience," *The Lancet* 380, no. 9853 (2012): 1550–51.

31. Michael Hardt and Antonio Negri likewise argue, "Caring labor certainly is entirely immersed in the corporeal, the somatic, but the affects it produces are nonetheless immaterial." The immateriality of emotional work is described in both Michael Hardt and Antonio Negri, *Empire* (Cambridge, MA: Harvard University Press, 2000), 292–93; and Michael Hardt, "Affective Labor," *Boundary* 2, no. 26 (Summer 1999): 89–100.

32. This is discussed throughout the following edited volume, including the introduction chapter written by the editors: Erdmute Alber and Heike Drotbohm, eds., *Anthropological Perspectives on Care: Work, Kinship, and the Life-Course* (New York: Palgrave Macmillan, 2015). The authors in this volume demonstrate how nurses, childcare providers, and home health aides for persons with disabilities perform "care work," and this resembles in important ways the labor of local aid workers.

33. Eva Feder Kittay, *Love's Labor: Essays on Women, Equality and Dependency* (London: Routledge, 2019); Mol, Moser, and Pols, "Care: Putting Practice into Theory," 7–26; Joan C. Tronto, *Moral Boundaries: A Political Argument for an Ethic of Care* (New York: Routledge, 1993), 155).

34. Mol, Moser, and Pols, "Care: Putting Practice into Theory," 14.

35. For example, see Tony Vaux, *The Selfish Altruist: Relief Work in Famine and War* (London: Routledge, 2001).

36. Marcel Mauss, *The Gift: The Form and Reason for Exchange in Archaic Societies*, trans. W. D. Halls (New York: W. W. Norton, 1990), 3.

37. Mary Douglas, an anthropologist, wrote at the start of Halls's translation of Marcel Mauss's book, "Foreword: No Free Gifts," in *The Gift: The Form and Reason for Exchange in Archaic Societies*, by Marcel Mauss, trans. W. D. Halls (New York: W. W. Norton, 1990), vii–xviii.

38. Mary Douglas argued that Mauss would think that the existence of a gift devoid of social obligation and social meaning, "Nonsense!" "Even the idea of a pure gift is a contradiction," she wrote. "By ignoring the universal custom of compulsory gifts we make our own record incomprehensible to ourselves: right across the globe and as far back as we can go in the history of human civilization, the major transfer of goods has been by cycles of obligatory returns of gifts." See Douglas, "Foreword," viii.

39. The Fundamental Principles of the ICRC including "voluntary service" are discussed again, and in greater depth, in chapter 5. See International Committee of the Red Cross, "Fundamental Principles of the Red Cross and Red Crescent Movement," April 11, 2016, https://www.icrc.org/en/document/fundamental-principles-red-cross-and-red-crescent.

40. Monika Krause, *The Good Project: Humanitarian Relief NGOs and the Fragmentation of Reason* (Chicago: University of Chicago Press, 2014), 58.

41. Krause, *The Good Project*, 58–59.

42. This is a point also made by Benedetta Rossi, "Aid Policies and Recipient Strategies in Niger," in *Development Brokers and Translators: The Ethnography of Aid and Agencies*, ed. David Lewis and David Mosse (Bloomfield, CT: Kumarian Press, 2006), 27–50.

43. Mauss, *The Gift*.

44. See also Thomas Yarrow, "Maintaining Independence: The Moral Ambiguities of Personal Relations amongst Ghanaian Development Workers," in *Inside the Everyday Lives*

of Development Workers: The Challenges and Futures of Aidland, ed. Anne-Meike Fechter and Heather Hindman (Sterling, VA: Kumarian Press, 2011), 41–58; Silke Roth, *The Paradoxes of Aid Work: Passionate Professionals* (London: Routledge, 2015).

45. Liisa Malkki examines Mauss's conception of the gift as related to humanitarian actions, but her important analysis focused on aid workers from donor countries in *The Need to Help: The Domestic Arts of International Humanitarianism* (Durham, NC: Duke University Press, 2015). In addition, for discussions about how Maussian gift exchanges differ from and also shape contemporary humanitarian responses in Greece and Italy, respectively, see: Katerina Rozakou, "Socialities of Solidarity: Revisiting the Gift Taboo in Times of Crises," *Social Anthropology* 24, no. 2 (2016): 185–99; and Andrea Muehlebach, *The Moral Neoliberal: Welfare and Citizenship in Italy* (Chicago: University of Chicago Press, 2012).

46. Mauss, *The Gift*.

3. HUMANITARIAN WORK

1. In this way, humanitarian aid workers' difficulties benefiting from unions and legal regimes resembled Ethiopian health extension workers working elsewhere in the country, described by Kenneth Maes, *The Lives of Community Health Workers: Local Labor and Global Health in Urban Ethiopia* (New York: Routledge, 2016), 117–31.

2. Additionally, within eastern Ethiopia, there are disparities in the status, security, and compensation of governmental versus nongovernmental or United Nations employees. Salaries for local and national staffers of NGOs or the UN are capped so as to not exceed the top salaries earned by the leaders of regional governmental bureaus. The additional nonsalary benefits, per diem payments, job security, and status that accompany NGO or UN work, however, far exceed what is offered to governmental employees—even top politicians.

3. Peter Redfield, "The Unbearable Lightness of Ex-Pats: Double Binds of Humanitarian Mobility," *Cultural Anthropology* 27, no. 2 (2012): 358–82.

4. Arnaud Dandoy and Marc-Antoine Pérouse de Montclos, "Humanitarian Workers in Peril? Deconstructing the Myth of the New and Growing Threat to Humanitarian Workers," *Global Crime* 14, no. 4 (2013): 341–58.

5. Attacks on aid workers and the weaponization of aid were relatively rare occurrences in eastern Ethiopia (compared to other parts of the world), and more aid workers faced dangers of traffic crashes than anything else, according to the directors of the regional and zonal offices of major UN relief agencies and NGOs. For more information on the global problem of aid workers' safety and security, see Abby Stoddard, Adele Harmer, and Monica Czwarno, "Aid Worker Security: Figures at a Glance, 2018," Humanitarian Outcomes, August 2018, https://www.humanitarianoutcomes.org/publications/aid-worker-security-figures-glance-2018; Silke Roth, "Dealing with Danger—Risk and Security in the Everyday Lives of Aid Workers," in *Inside the Everyday Lives of Development Workers: The Challenges and Futures of Aidland*, ed. Anne-Meike Fechter and Heather Hindman (Sterling, VA: Kumarian Press, 2011); Larissa Fast, "Characteristics, Context and Risk: NGO Insecurity in Conflict Zones," *Disasters* 31, no. 2 (2007): 130–54; Larissa Fast, "Mind the Gap: Documenting and Explaining Violence against Aid Workers," *European Journal of International Relations* 16, no. 3 (2010): 365–89; Koenraad Van Brabant, "Mainstreaming the Organisational Management of Safety and Security: A Review of Aid Agency Practices and a Guide for Management," Humanitarian Policy Group, Report 9, Overseas Development Institute, March 2001, https://www.odi.org/sites/odi.org.uk/files/odi-assets/publications-opinion-files/297.pdf.

6. For more on these outcomes and experiences, see: Barbara Lopes Cardozo et al., "Factors Affecting Mental Health of Local Staff Working in the Vanni Region, Sri Lanka," *Psychological Trauma: Theory, Research, Practice, and Policy* 5, no. 6 (2013): 581–90; Renée C. Fox, *Doctors Without Borders: Humanitarian Quests, Impossible Dreams of Médecins Sans Frontières* (Baltimore: Johns Hopkins University Press, 2014).

7. Lopes Cardozo et al., "Factors Affecting Mental Health."

8. See these several studies: Mary Morrison Bennett and Stephanie Eberts, "The Experiences of Short-Term Humanitarian Aid Workers in Haiti," *Mental Health, Religion & Culture* 18, no. 5 (2015): 319–29; Magdalena Bjerneld, Gunilla Lindmark, Patricia Diskett, and Martha J. Garrett, "Perceptions of Work in Humanitarian Assistance: Interviews with Returning Swedish Health Professionals," *Disaster Management & Response* 2, no. 4 (2004): 101–8; Cynthia B. Eriksson et al., "Social Support, Organisational Support, and Religious Support in Relation to Burnout in Expatriate Humanitarian Aid Workers," *Mental Health, Religion and Culture* 12, no. 7 (2009): 671–86; Liza Jachens, Jonathan Houdmont, and Roslyn Thomas, "Effort-Reward Imbalance and Burnout among Humanitarian Aid Workers," *Disasters* 43, no. 1 (2019): 67–87; Saif Ali Musa and Abdalla A. R. M. Hamid, "Psychological Problems among Aid Workers Operating in Darfur," *Social Behavior and Personality: An International Journal* 36, no. 3 (2008): 407–16.

9. I know this from speaking with aid workers and policy makers in eastern Ethiopia, but data were not available on the numbers of persons affected by hijackings, robberies, and the like.

10. Abby Stoddard, *Necessary Risks: Professional Humanitarianism and Violence against Aid Workers* (Cham, Switzerland: Palgrave Macmillan, 2020), xix–xxii.

11. For example, see Alessandra Pigni, "Building Resilience and Preventing Burnout among Aid Workers in Palestine: A Personal Account of Mindfulness Based Staff Care," *Intervention* 12, no. 2 (2014): 231–39; Zeina Chemali et al., "Reflections from the Lebanese Field: 'First, Heal Thyself,'" *Conflict and Health* 12, no. 8 (2018), https://doi.org/10.1186/s13031-018-0144-2.

12. Hannah Strohmeier and Willem F. Scholte, "Trauma-Related Mental Health Problems among National Humanitarian Staff: A Systematic Review of the Literature," *European Journal of Psychotraumatology* 6, no. 1 (2015): 28541.

13. See Monique J. Beerli, "Saving the Saviors: Security Practices and Professional Struggles in the Humanitarian Space," *International Political Sociology* 12, no. 1 (2018): 70–87.

14. Craig Calhoun, "The Idea of Emergency: Humanitarian Action and Global (Dis)order," in *Contemporary States of Emergency: The Politics of Military and Humanitarian Interventions*, ed. Didier Fassin and Mariella Pandolfi (Brooklyn, NY: Zone Books, 2010), 29.

15. Sue Lautze, Angela Raven-Roberts, and Teshome Erkineh, "Humanitarian Governance in the New Millennium: An Ethiopian Case Study," Humanitarian Policy Group, Overseas Development Institute, February 2009, https://www.odi.org/publications/3190-humanitarian-governance-new-millennium-ethiopian-case-study; Alexander de Waal, *Famine Crimes: Politics and the Disaster Relief Industry in Africa* (Bloomington: Indiana University Press, 1997); Alexander de Waal, "The Humanitarians' Tragedy: Escapable and Inescapable Cruelties," *Disasters* 34 (2010): S130–37, https://doi.org/10.1111/j.1467-7717.2010.01149.x.

16. David Rieff, "Kosovo's Humanitarian Circus," *World Policy Journal* 17, no. 3 (2000): 25.

17. Beerli, "Saving the Saviors," 74.

18. See a thorough discussion of this phenomenon of special segregation and differential mobility patterns in Silke Roth, *The Paradoxes of Aid Work: Passionate Professionals* (London: Routledge, 2015).

19. Lisa Smirl, *Spaces of Aid: How Cars, Compounds and Hotels Shape Humanitarianism* (London: Zed Books, 2015), 47–113.

20. Cf. Giorgio Agamben, *Homo Sacer: Sovereign Power and Bare Life* (Palo Alto, CA: Stanford University Press, 1998).

21. Beerli, "Saving the Saviors," 74–75.

22. This has different manifestations in different places. In theorizing this hierarchy I draw on Ann Swidler and Susan Cotts Watkins, "'Teach a Man to Fish': The Sustainability Doctrine and Its Social Consequences," *World Development* 37, no. 7 (2009): 1182–96, https://doi.org/10.1016/j.worlddev.2008.11.002. They describe three "strata" in Malawian society that work together to make aid work: the beneficiaries, the local elites or subnational employees of aid agencies, and the national staffs of development organizations who then liaise with expatriates. I expanded and built on this influential model, but in this case, highlighting especially how *intra*national power inequities and histories of discrimination between Somalis and other Ethiopians affect the labor hierarchy of humanitarian assistance. The societal and institutional effects of aid in our cases differ.

23. Swidler and Watkins, "'Teach a Man to Fish,'" 1191.

24. P. Knox Clarke, *The State of the Humanitarian System 2018* (London: ALNAP, 2018), 101–8.

25. David Mwambari and Arthur Owor, "The 'Black Market' of Knowledge Production," April 2, 2019, https://oxfamblogs.org/fp2p/the-black-market-of-knowledge-production/.

26. A phrase explained in the text of Mary B. Anderson, *Do No Harm: How Aid Can Support Peace—or War* (Boulder, CO: Lynne Rienner, 1999).

27. For details, see the guidance in: Federal Democratic Republic of Ethiopia, Ministry of Agriculture, "Productive Safety Net Programme Phase IV: Programme Implementation Manual," December 2014, https://srbofed.gov.et/wp-content/uploads/2019/09/PSNP-IV-Programme-Implementation-Manual-Final-14-Dec-14-1.pdf.

28. "Productive Safety Net Programme," 4–5 and 4–6. If families received a cash benefit instead of food, the official "wage" amount per person per day of work is based, according to guidance documents, on the "cheapest" price of three kilograms of cereal and 0.8 kilograms of either lentils or split peas in local markets. Elsewhere in Ethiopia, PSNP recipients may receive cash based on the number of days worked per month, with again, a maximum of six months worked per year. The basis of these calculations is a wage rate of twenty birr per day, as per information on pages 3–8.

29. "Productive Safety Net Programme," 3–8.

30. Here I refer to gifts and charity following Erica Bornstein, *Disquieting Gifts: Humanitarianism in New Delhi* (Palo Alto, CA: Stanford University Press, 2012).

31. I also discuss this point in Lauren Carruth and Scott Freeman, "Aid or Exploitation? Food-for-Work, Cash-for-Work, and the Production of 'Beneficiary-Workers' in Ethiopia and Haiti," *World Development*, forthcoming.

32. Marcel Mauss, *The Gift: The Form and Reason for Exchange in Archaic Societies*, trans. W. D. Halls (New York: W. W. Norton, 1990). This is a play on words by postcolonial social theorist Homi Bhabha, *The Location of Culture* (London: Routledge, 2012), 131: "The ambivalence of colonial authority repeatedly turns from *mimicry*—a difference that is almost nothing but not quite—to *menace*—a difference that is almost total but not quite."

33. For examples, see the following reports and websites: Active Learning Network for Accountability and Performance in Humanitarian Action (ALNAP), "Our Role," accessed June 12, 2017, http://www.alnap.org/who-we-are/our-role; HAP International

and Oxfam, "The Guide to the HAP Standard: Humanitarian Accountability and Quality Management," 2008, https://reliefweb.int/sites/reliefweb.int/files/resources/hap-guide. pdf; Oxfam, "Accountability and Ownership: The Role of Aid in a Post-2015 World," Oxfam Briefing Paper, September 2016, https://s3.amazonaws.com/oxfam-us/www/static/media/files/bp-accountability-and-ownership-11-16.pdf.

34. For more on this, see Lauren Carruth, "The Data Hustle: How Beneficiaries Benefit from Continual Data Collection and Humanitarian Aid Research in the Somali Region of Ethiopia," *Medical Anthropology Quarterly* 32, no. 3 (2018): 340–64.

35. See, for example: C. Biruk, *Cooking Data* (Durham, NC: Duke University Press, 2018); Ann H. Kelly and Paul Wenzel Geissler, "The Value of Transnational Medical Research," *Journal of Cultural Economy* 4, no. 1 (2011): 3; Adriana Petryna, *When Experiments Travel: Clinical Trials and the Global Search for Human Subjects* (Princeton: Princeton University Press, 2009).

36. See also Carruth, "The Data Hustle."

37. As described in websites like these: World Health Organization (WHO), "Health Workforce," accessed June 8, 2020, http://www.who.int/hrh/en/; Sphere Project, "The Sphere Handbook: Humanitarian Charter and Minimum Standards in Humanitarian Response," 2018, https://spherestandards.org/handbook-2018/.

38. Paul Wenzel Geissler, "'We Are Not Paid—They Just Give Us': Liberalisation and the Longing for Biopolitical Discipline around an African HIV Prevention Trial," in *Rethinking Governance and Biomedicine in Africa*, ed. Paul Wenzel Geissler, Richard Rottenburg, and Julia Zenker (Bielefeld: Transcript Verlag, 2012), 216.

39. See Carruth, "The Data Hustle," referencing Marilyn Strathern, *Audit Cultures: Anthropological Studies in Accountability, Ethics and the Academy* (London: Routledge, 2003).

40. Christian Els, Kholoud Mansour, and Nils Carstensen, "Funding to National and Local Humanitarian Actors in Syria: Between Sub-Contracting and Partnerships," Local to Global Protection Initiative, May 2016, http://www.local2global.info/wp-content/uploads/L2GP_funding_Syria_May_2016.pdf; Mary B. Anderson, Dayna Brown, and Isabella Jean, "Time to Listen: Hearing People on the Receiving End of International Aid," CDA Collaborative Learning Projects, December 2012, http://cdacollaborative.org/publication/time-to-listen-hearing-people-on-the-receiving-end-of-international-aid/.

41. James Ferguson, *Give a Man a Fish: Reflections on the New Politics of Distribution* (Durham, NC: Duke University Press, 2015).

42. Ian Hacking, "Making Up People: Clinical Classifications," *London Review of Books* 28, no. 16 (2006): 23.

43. Mwambari and Owor, "The 'Black Market' of Knowledge Production."

44. See similar findings and characterizations of local development aid workers in David Lewis and David Mosse, eds., *Development Brokers and Translators: The Ethnography of Aid and Agencies* (Bloomfield, CT: Kumarian Press, 2006); and in the Ugandan context in David Mwambari, "Local Positionality in the Production of Knowledge in Northern Uganda," International Journal of Qualitative Methods 18 (August 2019), https://doi.org/10.1177/1609406919864845. See also the analysis in Jonathan Corpus Ong and Pamela Combinido, "Local Aid Workers in the Digital Humanitarian Project: Between 'Second Class Citizens' and 'Entrepreneurial Survivors,'" *Critical Asian Studies* 50, no. 1 (2018): 86–102. This mirrors inequities evident in global research agendas as well, as argued in Yolande Bouka, "Collaborative Research as Structural Violence," Political Violence at a Glance, July 12, 2018, https://politicalviolenceataglance.org/2018/07/12/collaborative-research-as-structural-violence/.

45. Found globally in industries like agriculture, sex work, and domestic housework, as discussed in the following texts: Seth Holmes, *Fresh Fruit, Broken Bodies: Migrant*

Farmworkers in the United States (Berkeley: University of California Press, 2013); Prabha Kotiswaran, *Dangerous Sex, Invisible Labor: Sex Work and the Law in India* (Princeton: Princeton University Press, 2011; Pierrette Hondagneu-Sotelo, *Doméstica: Immigrant Workers Cleaning and Caring in the Shadows of Affluence*, with a new preface (Berkeley: University of California Press, 2007); Marion Crain, Winifred Poster, and Miriam Cherry, *Invisible Labor: Hidden Work in the Contemporary World* (Berkeley: University of California Press, 2016).

46. This phrase is a play on the phrase "suffering slot," in Joel Robbins, "Beyond the Suffering Subject: Toward an Anthropology of the Good," *Journal of the Royal Anthropological Institute* 19, no. 3 (2013): 447–62. Here I use "local slot" to signify the functions and value of defining and empowering not a "suffering" position, but instead, workers deemed merely "local," the processes of defining a crisis through the experiences and data collection of locals, and the conceptions and communications of ethical, righteous, and effective humanitarian responses designed with the help of locals.

47. This phenomenon is noted elsewhere, outside relief operations, in Anne-Meike Fechter and Heather Hindman, eds., *Inside the Everyday Lives of Development Workers: The Challenges and Futures of Aidland* (Sterling, VA: Kumarian Press, 2011).

48. See Didier Fassin, *Humanitarian Reason: A Moral History of the Present* (Berkeley: University of California Press, 2012), 4.

49. Kenneth Maes, *The Lives of Community Health Workers: Local Labor and Global Health in Urban Ethiopia* (New York: Routledge, 2016), 120.

50. Here I echo Mary Douglas's discussion of dirt as not inherently unclean or pathogenic, but rather, "matter out of place," in *Purity and Danger: An Analysis of Concepts of Pollution and Taboo*, vol. 2 of *Mary Douglas: Collected Works* (London: Routledge, 2003), 36–41; and I also echo Michel Foucault, *The Order of Things: An Archaeology of the Human Sciences* (London: Routledge, 2002).

4. CRISIS WORK

1. Janet Roitman, *Anti-Crisis* (Durham, NC: Duke University Press, 2013), 3.

2. Fiona Terry, *Condemned to Repeat? The Paradox of Humanitarian Action* (Ithaca, NY: Cornell University Press, 2013); Elizabeth Cullen Dunn, *No Path Home: Humanitarian Camps and the Grief of Displacement* (Ithaca, NY: Cornell University Press, 2018).

3. See Antonio Donini, "The Far Side: The Meta Functions of Humanitarianism in a Globalised World," *Disasters* 34, no. 1 (2010): S227; Tanja R. Müller, "'The Ethiopian Famine' Revisited: Band Aid and the Antipolitics of Celebrity Humanitarian Action," *Disasters* 37, no. 1 (2013): 61–79; Michael Barnett and Thomas G. Weiss, *Humanitarianism Contested: Where Angels Fear to Tread* (London: Routledge, 2013), 103.

4. See João Biehl and Adriana Petryna, "Critical Global Health," in *When People Come First*, ed. João Biehl and Adriana Petryna (Princeton: Princeton University Press, 2013), 1–22.

5. Peter Redfield, "Vital Mobility and the Humanitarian Kit," in *Biosecurity Interventions: Global Health & Security in Question*, ed. Andrew Lakoff and Stephen J. Collier (New York: Columbia University Press, 2008), 149.

6. Redfield, "Vital Mobility," 166.

7. Between 2000 and 2003, the United States military dug several boreholes, built schools, and helped repair other infrastructure in Dire Dawa and several remote communities between there and the Djibouti and Somaliland borders.

8. Health extension workers, even with help from mobile team nurses, do not "diagnose" diseases, but rather categorize them to provide the best possible treatment or to

refer them to a higher clinical facility. These providers used the Integrated Management of Childhood Illness (IMCI) implementation guidelines, published by the World Health Organization and distributed during their vocational training programs, as described in: World Health Organization, "Child Health in the Community: Community IMCI; Briefing Package for Facilitators," https://apps.who.int/iris/handle/10665/43006.

9. Data on diabetes in the Somali Region is available here: Kinfe G. Bishu et al., "Diabetes in Ethiopia: A Systematic Review of Prevalence, Risk Factors, Complications, and Cost," *Obesity Medicine* 15 (September 2019): 100132, https://doi.org/10.1016/j. obmed.2019.100132.

10. For additional data on diabetes in humanitarian emergencies, see Sylvia Kehlenbrink et al., "The Burden of Diabetes and Use of Diabetes Care in Humanitarian Crises in Low-Income and Middle-Income Countries," *Lancet Diabetes & Endocrinology* 7, no. 8 (August 2019): 638–47, https://doi.org/10.1016/S2213-8587(19)30082-8. Research in the aftermath of hurricanes in the Caribbean in 2017, in conflict-affected Syria since 2011, and in the Democratic Republic of Congo in recent years, all underscore the urgent need for chronic disease prevention and care as part of the acute phase of medical humanitarian response. This is discussed in Philippa Boulle et al., "Challenges Associated with Providing Diabetes Care in Humanitarian Settings," *Lancet Diabetes & Endocrinology* 7, no. 8 (August 2019): 648–56, https://doi.org/10.1016/S2213-8587(19)30083-X; Éimhín Mary Ansbro et al., "Management of Diabetes and Associated Costs in a Complex Humanitarian Setting in the Democratic Republic of Congo: A Retrospective Cohort Study," BMJ Open 9, no. 11 (2019): e030176, https://doi.org/10.1136/bmjopen-2019-030176.

11. See Lauren Carruth et al., "Diabetes in a Humanitarian Crisis: Atypical Clinical Presentations and Challenges to Clinical- and Community-Based Management among Somalis in Ethiopia," *Global Public Health* 15, no. 6 (2020): 828–39, https://doi.org/10.10 80/17441692.2020.1718735.

12. Outside Ethiopia, in places around the world, combinations of stress, anxiety, clinical depression, and violence play a causal role in the diagnosis and experience of diabetes. For example, see Emily Mendenhall, *Rethinking Diabetes: Entanglements with Trauma, Poverty, and HIV* (Ithaca, NY: Cornell University Press, 2019); Carolyn Smith-Morris, *Diabetes among the Pima: Stories of Survival* (Tucson: University of Arizona Press, 2008).

13. *Dacar* has several meanings: it refers to yellow digestive bile, an aloe plant, a bitter taste, or a disease of excess bile in the body. For more discussion of *dacar*, see Lauren Carruth, "Camel Milk, Amoxicillin, and a Prayer: Medical Pluralism and Medical Humanitarian Aid in the Somali Region of Ethiopia," *Social Science & Medicine* 120 (2014): 405–12.

14. Lauren Carruth and Emily Mendenhall, "'Wasting Away': Diabetes, Food Insecurity, and Medical Insecurity in the Somali Region of Ethiopia," *Social Science & Medicine* 228 (2019): 155–63, https://doi.org/10.1016/j.socscimed.2019.03.026.

15. Definitions of and data on female genital cutting (FGC) in eastern Ethiopia may be found here: Kidanu Gebremariam, Demeke Assefa, and Fitsum Weldegebreal, "Prevalence and Associated Factors of Female Genital Cutting among Young Adult Females in Jigjiga District, Eastern Ethiopia: A Cross-Sectional Mixed Study," *International Journal of Women's Health* 8 (2016): 357–65, https://doi.org/10.2147/IJWH.S111091. Among Somalis in Ethiopia, most cutting took the form of infibulation, and many women I met complained of suffering infections and the painful buildup of blood as a result. Cutting was the subject of NGO interventions in the 1990s and the first decade of the twenty-first century in Somali communities in Ethiopia, but these efforts were male-dominated and fragmented (for an interesting comparison on this matter, see Saida Hodžić, *The Twilight*

of Cutting: African Activism and Life after NGOs (Berkeley: University of California Press, 2017). While the popularity of infibulation is declining, FGC remains commonplace in Somali communities throughout the Horn of Africa.

16. For the full, original definition of this term, see: Mark Nichter, "Idioms of Distress: Alternatives in the Expression of Psychosocial Distress; A Case Study from South India," *Culture, Medicine and Psychiatry* 5, no. 4 (1981): 379–408. This phrase has been taken up by various scholars and disciplines including psychology and clinical psychiatry to better understand patient presentations and language. See Mark Nichter, "Idioms of Distress Revisited," *Culture, Medicine, and Psychiatry* 34, no. 2 (2010): 405 for details on how "[idioms of distress] are indicative of psychopathological states" and utilized in the DSM-IV as "cultural idioms of distress." Complaints of *mindheeli* among Somalis in Ethiopia may, in Nichter's words, "index past traumatic memories as well as present stressors, such as anger, powerlessness, social marginalization and insecurity, and possible future sources of anxiety, loss and angst."

17. Also see: Alison Heller, *Fistula Politics: Birthing Injuries and the Quest for Continence in Niger* (New Brunswick, NJ: Rutgers University Press, 2019).

18. See for example, UN Women, "Preliminary Gender Profile of Ethiopia," November 2014, https://www.usaid.gov/sites/default/files/documents/1860/Preliminary%20Gender%20Profile%20of%20Ethiopia%20Nov%202017%20final.pdf; United Nations World Food Programme (UNWFP), "Gender Equality and WFP," January 22, 2019, https://docs.wfp.org/api/documents/5389e10f4fb74c2fab08db1f725d3965/download/.

19. Charles L. Briggs with Clara Martini-Briggs, *Stories in the Time of Cholera: Racial Profiling during a Medical Nightmare* (Berkeley: University of California Press, 2003); Steven Johnson, *The Ghost Map: The Story of London's Most Terrifying Epidemic—and How It Changed Science, Cities, and the Modern World* (New York: Penguin, 2006).

20. Reuters, "Filth Spreads Yemen's Deadly Cholera Outbreak," July 27, 2017, https://www.reuters.com/article/us-yemen-cholera-sanitation-idUSKBN1AC1W9?il=0.

21. See Hannah G. Davies, Conor Bowman, and Stephen P. Luby, "Cholera—Management and Prevention," Supplement 1, *Journal of Infection* 74 (2017): S66–73, https://doi.org/10.1016/S0163-4453(17)30194-9.

22. For historical references to cholera see: Richard Pankhurst, "The History of Cholera in Ethiopia," *Medical History* 12, no. 3 (1968): 262–69; and for more recent outbreaks, Maria Scrascia et al., "Cholera in Ethiopia in the 1990s: Epidemiologic Patterns, Clonal Analysis, and Antimicrobial Resistance," *International Journal of Medical Microbiology* 299, no. 5 (2009): 367–72.

23. Scrascia et al., "Cholera in Ethiopia."

24. For examples outside Ethiopia, see a discussion of cholera in Venezuela in Briggs, *Stories in the Time of Cholera*. And in India, clinical presentations of cholera were reported as "gastroenteritis" and other nonspecific forms of severe diarrhea by the government: Ishita Ghosh and Lester Coutinho, "Normalcy and Crisis in Time of Cholera: An Ethnography of Cholera in Calcutta," *Economic and Political Weekly*, February 26, 2000, 684–96.

25. Sara Jerving, "Why Governments Tiptoe around the Word 'Cholera,'" Devex, March 21, 2018, https://www.devex.com/news/why-governments-tiptoe-around-the-word-cholera-92348; Kerina Tull, "Humanitarian Interventions in Ethiopia Responding to Acute Watery Diarrhoea," K4D Helpdesk Report, Brighton, UK, Institute of Development Studies, January 10, 2018, https://opendocs.ids.ac.uk/opendocs/bitstream/handle/20.500.12413/13568/14576?sequence=1.

26. Donald G. McNeil, "Candidate to Lead the W.H.O Accused of Covering Up Epidemics," *New York Times*, May 13, 2017, https://www.nytimes.com/2017/05/13/health/candidate-who-director-general-ethiopia-cholera-outbreaks.html.

27. Girum Yilma, "Ethiopia: Land of Silence and Starvation," Abbay Media, November 8, 2009, http://amharic.abbaymedia.info/archives/3019.

28. Demonstrated in the following articles: Christine M. George et al., "Evaluation of Enrichment Method for the Detection of *Vibrio cholerae* O1 Using a Rapid Dipstick Test in Bangladesh," *Tropical Medicine & International Health* 19, no. 3 (2014): 301–7, https://doi.org/10.1111/tmi.12252; Amanda K. Debes et al., "Clinical and Environmental Surveillance for Vibrio cholerae in Resource Constrained Areas: Application during a 1-Year Surveillance in the Far North Region of Cameroon," *American Journal of Tropical Medicine and Hygiene* 94, no. 3 (2016): 537–43.

29. See the paper Qifang Bi et al., "Protection against Cholera from Killed Whole-Cell Oral Cholera Vaccines: A Systematic Review and Meta-Analysis," *Lancet Infectious Diseases* 17, no. 10 (2017): 1080–88.

30. See these resources: World Health Organization (WHO), "Cholera," accessed June 9, 2020, https://www.who.int/cholera/en/; World Health Organization (WHO), "Revised Cholera Kits," accessed June 13, 2020, https://www.who.int/emergencies/emergency-health-kits/revised-cholera-kits.

31. See Karl Blanchet et al., "Evidence on Public Health Interventions in Humanitarian Crises," *The Lancet* 390, no. 10109 (2017): 2287–96, https://doi.org/10.1016/S0140-6736(16)30768-1; Margaret E. Kruk et al., "Rebuilding Health Systems to Improve Health and Promote Statebuilding in Post-Conflict Countries: A Theoretical Framework and Research Agenda," *Social Science & Medicine* 70, no. 1 (2010): 89–97; William Newbrander, Ronald Waldman, and Megan Shepherd-Banigan, "Rebuilding and Strengthening Health Systems and Providing Basic Health Services in Fragile States," *Disasters* 35, no. 4 (2011): 639–60.

5. HUMANITARIANISM IS ANTI-POLITICS

1. The Red Cross's principle of neutrality is defined in International Committee of the Red Cross, "Fundamental Principles of the Red Cross and Red Crescent Movement," April 11, 2016, https://www.icrc.org/en/document/fundamental-principles-red-cross-and-red-crescent; neutrality is discussed in Hugo Slim, *Humanitarian Ethics: A Guide to the Morality of Aid in War and Disaster* (Oxford: Oxford University Press, 2015).

2. The principle of neutrality is more critically evaluated, however, in Adia Benton and Sa'ed Atshan, "'Even War Has Rules': On Medical Neutrality and Legitimate Non-Violence," *Culture, Medicine, and Psychiatry* 40 (2016): 151–58; Peter Redfield, "Clinic in Crisis Response: Imagined Immunities," *Culture, Medicine, and Psychiatry* 40, no. 2 (2016): 263–67; Sherine F. Hamdy and Soha Bayoumi, "Egypt's Popular Uprising and the Stakes of Medical Neutrality," *Culture, Medicine, and Psychiatry* 40, no. 2 (2016): 223–41.

3. Alexander de Waal, *Famine Crimes: Politics and the Disaster Relief Industry in Africa* (Bloomington: Indiana University Press, 1997); Mark Duffield, *Development, Security and Unending War: Governing the World of Peoples* (Cambridge: Polity, 2007); Mark Duffield, "Challenging Environments: Danger, Resilience and the Aid Industry," *Security Dialogue* 43, no. 5 (2012): 475–92; Didier Fassin, *Humanitarian Reason: A Moral History of the Present* (Berkeley: University of California Press, 2012); Miriam Ticktin, "A World without Innocence," *American Ethnologist* 44, no. 4 (2017): 577–90; Antonio De Lauri, *The Politics of Humanitarianism: Power, Ideology and Aid* (London: I. B. Tauris, 2016), http://hdl.handle.net/11250/2475398.

4. James Ferguson analyzes the "anti-politics" of development interventions in Lesotho in *The Anti-Politics Machine: "Development," Depoliticization, and Bureaucratic Power in Lesotho* (Minneapolis: University of Minnesota Press, 1994), 249–78.

5. To carry out humanitarian missions, relief organizations defend what is called their "humanitarian space," or a literal and metaphoric field in which they can intervene, all the while remaining silent on or denying involvement in the political actions and stances of the organizations and countries funding and assisting their operations. A more detailed definition of humanitarian space may be found in Overseas Development Institute, Humanitarian Policy Group, "Humanitarian Space: Concept, Definitions and Uses," October 20, 2010, https://www.odi.org/sites/odi.org.uk/files/odi-assets/events-documents/4648.pdf. This concept is also discussed in Mark Duffield, *Global Governance and the New Wars: The Merging of Development and Security* (London: Zed Books, 2014).

6. For more extensive histories of the Battle of Solferino, the Red Cross Movement, and other related social movements in Europe at the time, see: John F. Hutchinson, *Champions of Charity: War and the Rise of the Red Cross* (London: Routledge, 2018); Caroline Moorehead, *Dunant's Dream: War, Switzerland and the History of the Red Cross* (London: Harper Collins, 1998); Michael Barnett, *Empire of Humanity: A History of Humanitarianism* (Ithaca, NY: Cornell University Press, 2011).

7. Dunant's account is published here: J. Henry Dunant, *A Memory of Solferino* (Geneva: International Committee of the Red Cross, 1986), https://www.icrc.org/en/doc/assets/files/publications/icrc-002-0361.pdf.

8. Including the important work of abolitionists at the time, but also others, as described by John F. Hutchinson, "Rethinking the Origins of the Red Cross," *Bulletin of the History of Medicine* 63, no. 4 (1989): 557–78.

9. See, for example, Renée C. Fox, *Doctors Without Borders: Humanitarian Quests, Impossible Dreams of Médecins Sans Frontières* (Baltimore: Johns Hopkins University Press, 2014); Peter Redfield, *Life in Crisis: The Ethical Journey of Doctors Without Borders* (Berkeley: University of California Press, 2013).

10. International Committee of the Red Cross (ICRC), "Fundamental Principles of the Red Cross and Red Crescent Movement," April 11, 2016, https://www.icrc.org/en/document/fundamental-principles-red-cross-and-red-crescent.

11. See ICRC, "Fundamental Principles"; Slim, *Humanitarian Ethics.*

12. ICRC, "Fundamental Principles."

13. See Marcel Mauss, *The Gift: The Form and Reason for Exchange in Archaic Societies,* trans. W. D. Halls (New York: W. W. Norton, 1990). Mauss's concept of the gift is discussed in greater detail in previous chapters of this book.

14. Mauss, *The Gift,* 3.

15. Slim, *Humanitarian Ethics,* 116.

16. These local aid workers were not hired by the ICRC. The Red Cross was not active outside refugee camps in the Somali Region during the period of this research, and I did not speak to Red Cross employees in Ethiopia.

17. For more research on this, see: Abby Stoddard, Adele Harmer, and Monica Czwarno, "Aid Worker Security: Figures at a Glance," Humanitarian Outcomes, August 2018, https://www.humanitarianoutcomes.org/publications/aid-worker-security-figures-glance-2018; Silke Roth, "Dealing with Danger—Risk and Security in the Everyday Lives of Aid Workers," in *Inside the Everyday Lives of Development Workers: The Challenges and Futures of Aidland,* ed. Anne-Meike Fechter and Heather Hindman (Sterling, VA: Kumarian Press, 2011); Larissa Fast, "Characteristics, Context and Risk: NGO Insecurity in Conflict Zones," *Disasters* 31, no. 2 (2007): 130–54; Larissa Fast, "Mind the Gap: Documenting and Explaining Violence against Aid Workers," *European Journal of International Relations* 16, no. 3 (2010): 365–89; Koenraad Van Brabant, "Mainstreaming the Organisational Management of Safety and Security: A Review of Aid Agency Practices and a Guide for Management," Humanitarian Policy Group, Report 9, Overseas

Development Institute, March 2001, https://www.odi.org/sites/odi.org.uk/files/odi-assets/publications-opinion-files/297.pdf.

18. Shown elsewhere in Salih Can Aciksoz, "Medical Humanitarianism under Atmospheric Violence: Health Professionals in the 2013 Gezi Protests in Turkey," *Culture, Medicine, and Psychiatry* 40, no. 2 (2016): 198–222; Hamdy and Bayoumi, "Egypt's Popular Uprising and the Stakes of Medical Neutrality"; Fritz Allhoff, ed., *Physicians at War: The Dual-Loyalties Challenge* (Dordrecht: Springer, 2008), 3–11, https://doi.org/10.1007/978-1-4020-6912-3.

19. Benton and Atshan, "'Even War Has Rules'"; Duffield, *Global Governance*.

20. Fassin, *Humanitarian Reason*, 5.

21. Dunant, *A Memory of Solferino*.

22. Mauss, *The Gift*, 3.

23. Alexander de Waal, *Evil Days: Thirty Years of War and Famine in Ethiopia*, Africa Watch Report (New York: Human Rights Watch, 1991), https://www.hrw.org/sites/default/files/reports/Ethiopia919.pdf.

24. Thomas Knecht, "A Pragmatic Response to an Unexpected Constraint: Problem Representation in a Complex Humanitarian Emergency," *Foreign Policy Analysis* 5, no. 2 (2009): 166.

25. M. Peter McPherson, "War Will Not Leave the Hungry Alone," *Washington Post*, March 5, 1985, A15; Alexander Poster, "The Gentle War: Famine Relief, Politics, and Privatization in Ethiopia, 1983–1986," *Diplomatic History* 36, no. 2 (2012): 399–425; Knecht, "A Pragmatic Response," 151.

26. Tanja R. Müller, "'The Ethiopian Famine' Revisited: Band Aid and the Antipolitics of Celebrity Humanitarian Action," *Disasters* 37, no. 1 (2013): 61–79; Poster, "The Gentle War."

27. McPherson, "War Will Not Leave the Hungry Alone."

28. Knecht, "A Pragmatic Response."

29. United States, Congress, Senate, Committee on Finance, *Nomination of M. Peter McPherson: Hearings before the Committee on Finance, United States Senate, One Hundredth Congress, First Session on Nomination of M. Peter McPherson to be Deputy Secretary of the Treasury, May 20, 1987* (Washington, DC: US Government Printing Office, 1987), 102–3.

30. See, for example, Lila Abu-Lughod, "Do Muslim Women Really Need Saving? Anthropological Reflections on Cultural Relativism and Its Others," *American Anthropologist* 104, no. 3 (2002): 783–90; Craig Calhoun, "The Idea of Emergency: Humanitarian Action and Global (Dis)order," in *Contemporary States of Emergency: The Politics of Military and Humanitarian Interventions*, ed. Didier Fassin and Mariella Pandolfi (Brooklyn, NY: Zone Books, 2010), 29–30; Ticktin, "A World without Innocence."

31. See Ferguson, *The Anti-Politics Machine*. However, the goal of the anti-political humanitarian assistance I describe here, unlike in Ferguson's experience of development projects in Lesotho, did not include the objectives of imposing a security or surveillance state in beneficiary communities. Instead, the anti-politics machine in Ethiopia enabled the US to deny political intentions for its support to Ethiopia—a move presumably highlighting the morality of American democracy over Ethiopia's Soviet-style communist dictatorship.

32. Here I am rephrasing the now-famous argument, that, "war is a mere continuation of policy by other means," found in Carl von Clausewitz, *On War*, trans. Colonel J.J. Graham (London: K. Paul, Trench, Trübner, 1909), Book 1, chapter 1, section 24.

33. Tobias Hagmann and Mohamud Hussein Khalif, "State and Politics in Ethiopia's Somali Region since 1991," *Bildhaan: An International Journal of Somali Studies* 6, no. 1 (2008): 34.

34. See also Lauren Carruth, "Kinship, Nomadism, and Humanitarian Aid among Somalis in Ethiopia," *Disasters* 42, no. 1 (2018): 149–68, https://doi.org/10.1111/disa.12236.

35. For additional analyses of conflict and clan in the Somali Region of Ethiopia, see: Andy Catley and Alula Iyasu, "Moving Up or Moving Out? A Rapid Livelihoods and Conflict Analysis in Mieso-Mulu Woreda, Shinile Zone, Somali Region, Ethiopia," Feinstein International Center, Tufts University, April 2010, http://technicalconsortium.org/wp-content/uploads/2014/05/Moving_up_or_moving_out.pdf; Tobias Hagmann, "Beyond Clannishness and Colonialism: Understanding Political Disorder in Ethiopia's Somali Region, 1991–2004," *Journal of Modern African Studies* 43, no. 4 (2005): 509–36; Sarah Vaughan, "Ethiopia, Somalia, and the Ogaden: Still a Running Sore at the Heart of the Horn of Africa," in *Secessionism in African Politics: Aspiration, Grievance, Performance, Disenchantment*, ed. Lotje de Vries, Pierre Englebert, and Mareike Schomerus (Cham, Switzerland: Palgrave Macmillan, 2019), 91–123.

36. This distinction is reflected in the following situation report: United Nations Office for the Coordination of Humanitarian Affairs (UNOCHA), "Ethiopia: Access Snapshot—Afar Region and Siti Zone, Somali Region," January 31, 2020, https://reliefweb.int/sites/reliefweb.int/files/resources/ocha_200204_access_snapshot_afar_sitti_somali_region.pdf.

6. FROM CRISIS TO LIBERATION

1. Catherine Panter-Brick, "Health, Risk, and Resilience: Interdisciplinary Concepts and Applications," *Annual Review of Anthropology* 43 (2014): 438.

2. Lahra Smith, *Making Citizens in Africa: Ethnicity, Gender, and National Identity in Ethiopia* (Cambridge: Cambridge University Press, 2013).

3. The importance of "rule-benders" and "rule-breakers" for organizational functioning and policy change is discussed much more broadly in Susanna P. Campbell, *Global Governance and Local Peace: Accountability and Performance in International Peacebuilding* (Cambridge: Cambridge University Press, 2018).

4. These judgments were also identified during aid work by Ghanaians by Thomas Yarrow, "Maintaining Independence: The Moral Ambiguities of Personal Relations amongst Ghanaian Development Workers," in *Inside the Everyday Lives of Development Workers: The Challenges and Futures of Aidland*, ed. Anne-Meike Fechter and Heather Hindman (Sterling, VA: Kumarian Press, 2011), 41–58.

5. See Joan C. Tronto, *Moral Boundaries: A Political Argument for an Ethic of Care* (New York: Routledge, 1993), 155; Joan C. Tronto, "Care as a Political Concept," in *Revisioning the Political: Feminist Reconstructions of Traditional Concepts in Western Political Theory*, ed. Nancy J. Hirshmann and Christine Di Stefano (New York: Routledge, 2018): 139–56.

6. Tronto, *Moral Boundaries*, 157.

7. Christina Sharpe, "And to Survive," *Small Axe: A Caribbean Journal of Criticism* 22, no. 3 (57) (2018): 175, https://doi.org/10.1215/07990537-7249304.

8. Sharpe, "And to Survive," 171.

9. Safia Aidid, "Can the Somali Speak?" #CadaanStudies, Africa Is a Country, March 30, 2015, https://africasacountry.com/2015/03/can-the-somali-speak-cadaan studies. Here she echoes Gayatri Chakravorty Spivak, "Can the Subaltern Speak?," in *Marxism and the Interpretation of Culture*, ed. C. Nelson and L. Grossberg (Urbana: University of Illinois Press, 1988), 271–314.

Bibliography

Aalen, Lovise. "Ethnic Federalism in a Dominant Party State: The Ethiopian Experience, 1991–2000." Chr. Michelsen Institute Report 2 (2002). https://www.cmi.no/publications/769-ethnic-federalism-in-a-dominant-party-state.

Abbay, Alemseged. "Diversity and State-Building in Ethiopia." *African Affairs* 103, no. 413 (2004): 593–614.

Abbink, Jon G. "Dervishes, 'Moryaan' and Freedom Fighters: Cycles of Rebellion and the Fragmentation of Somali Society, 1900–2000." In *African Dynamics*, edited by Jon G. Abbink, K. van Walraven, and M. E. de Brujn, 328–65. Leiden: Brill, 2003.

Abbink, Jon G., and Tobias Hagmann. *Reconfiguring Ethiopia: The Politics of Authoritarian Reform*. London: Routledge, 2016.

Abdi, Cawo M. *Elusive Jannah: The Somali Diaspora and a Borderless Muslim Identity*. Minneapolis: University of Minnesota Press, 2015.

Abdullahi, Abdi M. "The Ogaden National Liberation Front (ONLF): The Dilemma of Its Struggle in Ethiopia." *Review of African Political Economy* 34, no. 113 (2007): 556–62.

Abramowitz, Sharon A., and Catherine Panter-Brick, eds. *Medical Humanitarianism: Ethnographies of Practice*. Philadelphia: University of Pennsylvania Press, 2015.

Abu-Lughod, Lila. "Do Muslim Women Really Need Saving? Anthropological Reflections on Cultural Relativism and Its Others." *American Anthropologist* 104, no. 3 (2002): 783–90.

Aciksoz, Salih Can. "Medical Humanitarianism under Atmospheric Violence: Health Professionals in the 2013 Gezi Protests in Turkey." *Culture, Medicine, and Psychiatry* 40, no. 2 (2016): 198–222.

Adams, Vincanne. *Metrics: What Counts in Global Health*. Durham, NC: Duke University Press, 2016.

Adams, Vincanne, Taslim Van Hattum, and Diana English. "Chronic Disaster Syndrome: Displacement, Disaster Capitalism, and the Eviction of the Poor from New Orleans." *American Ethnologist* 36, no. 4 (2009): 615–36.

Aellah, Gemma, and Paul Wenzel Geissler. "Seeking Exposure: Conversions of Scientific Knowledge in an African City." *Journal of Modern African Studies* 54, no. 3 (2016): 389–417.

Afifi, Tamer, Radha Govil, Patrick Sakdapolrak, and Koko Warner. "Climate Change, Vulnerability and Human Mobility: Perspectives of Refugees from the East and Horn of Africa." Report 1. UNU-EHS and UNHCR. June 2012. https://www.unhcr.org/uk/4fe8538d9.pdf.

Agamben, Giorgio. *Homo Sacer: Sovereign Power and Bare Life*. Palo Alto, CA: Stanford University Press, 1998.

Ahmed, Ali Jimale, ed. *The Invention of Somalia*. Lawrenceville, NJ: Red Sea Press, 1995.

Ahmed, Sara. "A Phenomenology of Whiteness." *Feminist Theory* 8, no. 2 (2007): 149–68.

Aidid, Safia. "Can the Somali Speak?" #CadaanStudies. Africa Is a Country. March 30, 2015. https://africasacountry.com/2015/03/can-the-somali-speak-cadaanstudies.

Aidid, Safia. "Pan-Somali Dreams: Ethiopia, Greater Somalia, and the Somali Nationalist Imagination." PhD diss., Harvard University, 2020.

Aizenman, Nurith, and Malaka Gharib. "American with No Medical Training Ran Center for Malnourished Ugandan Kids: 105 Died." National Public Radio. August 9, 2019. https://www.npr.org/sections/goatsandsoda/2019/08/09/749005287/american-with-no-medical-training-ran-center-for-malnourished-ugandan-kids-105-d.

Alber, Erdmute, and Heike Drotbohm, eds. *Anthropological Perspectives on Care: Work, Kinship, and the Life-Course*. New York: Palgrave Macmillan, 2015.

Alexander, Jessica. *Chasing Chaos: My Decade in and out of Humanitarian Aid*. New York: Broadway Books, 2015.

Allen, Jafari Sinclaire, and Ryan Cecil Jobson. "The Decolonizing Generation: (Race and) Theory in Anthropology since the Eighties." *Current Anthropology* 57, no. 2 (2016): 129–48. https://doi.org/10.1086/685502.

Allhoff, Fritz, ed. *Physicians at War: The Dual-Loyalties Challenge*. Dordrecht: Springer, 2008.

Aly, H. "What Future for Private Sector Involvement in Humanitarianism?" IRIN (Integrated Regional Information Networks). August 26, 2013. http://www.irinnews.org/analysis/2013/08/26/what-future-private-sector-involvement-humanitarianism.

Anderson, Mary B. *Do No Harm: How Aid Can Support Peace—or War*. Boulder, CO: Lynne Rienner, 1999.

Anderson, Mary B., Dayna Brown, and Isabella Jean. "Time to Listen: Hearing People on the Receiving End of International Aid." CDA Collaborative Learning Projects. December 2012. http://cdacollaborative.org/publication/time-to-listen-hearing-people-on-the-receiving-end-of-international-aid/.

Ansbro, Éimhín Mary, Michel Biringanine, Grazia Caleo, David Prieto-Merino, Zia Sadique, Pablo Perel, Kiran Jobanputra, and Bayard Roberts. "Management of Diabetes and Associated Costs in a Complex Humanitarian Setting in the Democratic Republic of Congo: A Retrospective Cohort Study." BMJ Open 9, no. 11 (2019): e030176. https://doi.org/10.1136/bmjopen-2019-030176.

Appadurai, Arjun, ed. *The Social Life of Things: Commodities in Cultural Perspective*. Cambridge: Cambridge University Press, 1988.

Arman, Abukar. "Transformation Euphoria in the Horn of Africa." *Africa at LSE* (blog). August 9, 2018. https://blogs.lse.ac.uk/africaatlse/2018/08/09/transformation-euphoria-in-the-horn-of-africa/.

Arriola, Leonardo R. "Protesting and Policing in a Multiethnic Authoritarian State: Evidence from Ethiopia." *Comparative Politics* 45, no. 2 (2013): 147–68.

Asad, Talal. "Where Are the Margins of the State?" In *Anthropology in the Margins of the State*, edited by Veena Das and Deborah Poole, 279–88. Santa Fe, NM: School of American Research Press, 2004.

Asgary, Ramin, and Ronald J. Waldman. "The Elephant in the Room: Toward a More Ethical Approach with Accountability toward Intended Beneficiaries in Humanitarian Aid." *International Health* 9, no. 6 (2017): 343–48.

Assefa, Taye, and Tegegne Gebre-Egziabher, eds. *Decentralization in Ethiopia*. Addis Ababa, Ethiopia: Forum for Social Studies, 2007.

Barchiesi, Franco. *Precarious Liberation: Workers, the State, and Contested Social Citizenship in Postapartheid South Africa*. Albany: State University of New York Press, 2011.

Barnes, Cedric. "U dhashay—Ku dhashay: Genealogical and Territorial Discourse in Somali History." *Social Identities* 12, no. 4 (2006): 487–98.

Barnett, Michael. *Empire of Humanity: A History of Humanitarianism.* Ithaca, NY: Cornell University Press, 2011.

Barnett, Michael, and Thomas G. Weiss. *Humanitarianism Contested: Where Angels Fear to Tread.* London: Routledge, 2013.

Barr, Caelainn. "Abuse and Terror in the Ogaden." August 4, 2011. https://www.the bureauinvestigates.com/stories/2011-08-04/abuse-and-terror-in-the-ogaden.

Beamon, Benita M., and Burcu Balcik. "Performance Measurement in Humanitarian Relief Chains." *International Journal of Public Sector Management* 21, no. 1 (2008): 4–25.

Beerli, Monique J. "Saving the Saviors: Security Practices and Professional Struggles in the Humanitarian Space." *International Political Sociology* 12, no. 1 (2018): 70–87.

Bennett, Christina, Matthew Foley, and Sara Pantuliano. "Time to Let Go: Remaking Humanitarian Action for the Modern Era." Humanitarian Policy Group. Overseas Development Institute. April 2016. https://www.odi.org/publications/10381-time-let-go-remaking-humanitarian-action-modern-era.

Bennett, Mary Morrison, and Stephanie Eberts. "The Experiences of Short-Term Humanitarian Aid Workers in Haiti." *Mental Health, Religion & Culture* 18, no. 5 (2015): 319–29.

Benton, Adia. "Exceptional Suffering? Enumeration and Vernacular Accounting in the HIV-Positive Experience." *Medical Anthropology* 31, no. 4 (2012): 310–28.

Benton, Adia. "Risky Business: Race, Nonequivalence and the Humanitarian Politics of Life." *Visual Anthropology* 29, no. 2 (2016): 187–203.

Benton, Adia, and Sa'ed Atshan. "'Even War Has Rules': On Medical Neutrality and Legitimate Non-Violence." *Culture, Medicine, and Psychiatry* 40 (2016): 151–58.

Berry, Maya J., Claudia Chávez Argüelles, Shanya Cordis, Sarah Ihmoud, and Elizabeth Velásquez Estrada. "Toward a Fugitive Anthropology: Gender, Race, and Violence in the Field." *Cultural Anthropology* 32, no. 4 (2017): 537–65.

Besteman, Catherine. *Making Refuge: Somali Bantu Refugees and Lewiston, Maine.* Durham, NC: Duke University Press, 2016.

Besteman, Catherine. *Unraveling Somalia: Race, Class, and the Legacy of Slavery.* Philadelphia: University of Pennsylvania Press, 2014.

Bi, Qifang, Eva Ferreras, Lorenzo Pezzoli, Dominique Legros, Louise C. Ivers, Kashmira Date, Firdausi Qadri, et al. "Protection against Cholera from Killed Whole-Cell Oral Cholera Vaccines: A Systematic Review and Meta-Analysis." *Lancet Infectious Diseases* 17, no. 10 (2017): 1080–88.

Biehl, João, Byron Good, and Arthur Kleinman, eds. *Subjectivity: Ethnographic Investigations.* Berkeley: University of California Press, 2007.

Biehl, João, and Adriana Petryna. "Critical Global Health." In *When People Come First*, edited by João Biehl and Adriana Petryna, 1–22. Princeton: Princeton University Press, 2013.

Biruk, C. *Cooking Data.* Durham, NC: Duke University Press, 2018.

Bishu, Kinfe G., Carolyn Jenkins, Henock G. Yebyo, Merhawit Atsbha, Tewolde Wubayehu, and Mulugeta Gebregziabher. "Diabetes in Ethiopia: A Systematic Review of Prevalence, Risk Factors, Complications, and Cost." *Obesity Medicine* 15 (September 2019): 100132. https://doi.org/10.1016/j.obmed.2019.100132.

Bjerneld, Magdalena, Gunilla Lindmark, Patricia Diskett, and Martha J. Garrett. "Perceptions of Work in Humanitarian Assistance: Interviews with Returning Swedish Health Professionals." *Disaster Management & Response* 2, no. 4 (2004): 101–8.

Blanchet, Karl, Anita Ramesh, Severine Frison, Emily Warren, Mazeda Hossain, James Smith, Abigail Knight, et al. "Evidence on Public Health Interventions in Humanitarian Crises." *The Lancet* 390, no. 10109 (2017): 2287–96. https://doi.org/10.1016/S0140-6736(16)30768-1.

Boddy, Janice. "Spirit Possession Revisited: Beyond Instrumentality." *Annual Review of Anthropology* 23, no. 1 (1994): 407–34.

Bornstein, Erica. *Disquieting Gifts: Humanitarianism in New Delhi.* Palo Alto, CA: Stanford University Press, 2012.

Bornstein, Erica, and Peter Redfield, eds. *Forces of Compassion: Humanitarianism between Ethics and Politics.* Santa Fe, NM: School for Advanced Research Press, 2011.

Bouchet-Saulnier, Françoise. *The Practical Guide to Humanitarian Law.* Translated by Laura Brav and Clémentine Olivier. Lanham, MD: Rowman and Littlefield, 2007.

Bouka, Yolande. "Collaborative Research as Structural Violence." Political Violence at a Glance. July 12, 2018. https://politicalviolenceataglance.org/2018/07/12/collaborative-research-as-structural-violence/.

Boulle, Philippa, Sylvia Kehlenbrink, James Smith, David Beran, and Kiran Jobanputra. "Challenges Associated with Providing Diabetes Care in Humanitarian Settings." *Lancet Diabetes & Endocrinology* 7, no. 8 (August 2019): 648–56. https://doi.org/10.1016/S2213-8587(19)30083-X.

Brada, Betsey Behr. "The Contingency of Humanitarianism: Moral Authority in an African HIV Clinic." *American Anthropologist* 118, no. 4 (2016): 755–71.

Briggs, Charles L., with Clara Martini-Briggs. *Stories in the Time of Cholera: Racial Profiling during a Medical Nightmare.* Berkeley: University of California Press, 2003.

Butt, Leslie. "The Suffering Stranger: Medical Anthropology and International Morality." *Medical Anthropology* 21, no. 1 (2002): 1–24. https://doi.org/10.1080/01459740210619.

Cain, Kenneth, Heidi Postlewait, and Andrew Thomson. *Emergency Sex (and Other Desperate Measures): True Stories from a War Zone.* London: Ebury, 2006.

Calhoun, Craig. "The Idea of Emergency: Humanitarian Action and Global (Dis) order." In *Contemporary States of Emergency: The Politics of Military and Humanitarian Interventions,* edited by Didier Fassin and Mariella Pandolfi, 29–58. Brooklyn, NY: Zone Books, 2010.

Campbell, Susanna P. *Global Governance and Local Peace: Accountability and Performance in International Peacebuilding.* Cambridge: Cambridge University Press, 2018.

Carruth, Lauren. "The Aftermath of Aid: Medical Insecurity in the Northern Somali Region of Ethiopia." PhD diss., University of Arizona, 2011.

Carruth, Lauren. "Camel Milk, Amoxicillin, and a Prayer: Medical Pluralism and Medical Humanitarian Aid in the Somali Region of Ethiopia." *Social Science & Medicine* 120 (2014): 405–12.

Carruth, Lauren. "The Data Hustle: How Beneficiaries Benefit from Continual Data Collection and Humanitarian Aid Research in the Somali Region of Ethiopia." *Medical Anthropology Quarterly* 32, no. 3 (2018): 340–64. https://doi.org/10.1111/maq.12431.

Carruth, Lauren. "Kinship, Nomadism, and Humanitarian Aid among Somalis in Ethiopia." *Disasters* 42, no. 1 (2018): 149–68. https://doi.org/10.1111/disa.12236.

Carruth, Lauren. "Peace in the Clinic: Rethinking 'Global Health Diplomacy' in the Somali Region of Ethiopia." *Culture, Medicine, and Psychiatry* 40, no. 2 (2016): 181–97.

Carruth, Lauren, Mohamed Jama Ateye, Ahmed Nassir, Farah Mussa Hosh, and Emily Mendenhall. "Diabetes in a Humanitarian Crisis: Atypical Clinical Presentations and Challenges to Clinical- and Community-Based Management among Somalis in Ethiopia." *Global Public Health* 15, no. 6 (2020): 828–39. https://doi.org/10.1080/17441692.2020.1718735.

Carruth, Lauren, and Scott Freeman. "Aid or Exploitation? Food-for-Work, Cash-for-Work, and the Production of 'Beneficiary-Workers' in Ethiopia and Haiti." *World Development* (2020): 105283. https://doi.org/10.1016/j.worlddev.2020.105283.

Carruth, Lauren, and Emily Mendenhall. "'Wasting Away': Diabetes, Food Insecurity, and Medical Insecurity in the Somali Region of Ethiopia." *Social Science & Medicine* 228 (2019): 155–63. https://doi.org/10.1016/j.socscimed.2019.03.026.

Carruth, Lauren, Amira A. Roess, Yitagele Tefere Mekonnen, Simenew Keskes Melaku, Mark Nichter, and Mo Salman. "Zoonotic Tuberculosis in Africa: Challenges and Ways Forward." *The Lancet* 388, no. 10059 (2016): 2460–61. https://doi.org/10.1016/S0140-6736(16)32186-9.

Carruth, Lauren, Amira A. Roess, Yitagele Terefe, Farah Mussa Hosh, and M. D. Salman. "Antimicrobial Resistance and Food Safety in Africa." *Lancet Infectious Diseases* 17 (2017): 575–76. https://doi.org/10.1016/S1473-3099(17)30273-6.

Cassanelli, Lee. *The Shaping of Somali Society: Reconstructing the History of a Pastoral People, 1600–1900*. Philadelphia: University of Pennsylvania Press, 1982.

Catley, Andy, and Alula Iyasu. "Moving Up or Moving Out? A Rapid Livelihoods and Conflict Analysis in Mieso-Mulu Woreda, Shinile Zone, Somali Region, Ethiopia." Feinstein International Center. Tufts University. April 2010. http://technicalconsortium.org/wp-content/uploads/2014/05/Moving_up_or_moving_out.pdf.

Charter4Change. "Localisation of Humanitarian Aid: The Charter." Accessed June 2, 2020. https://charter4change.org/.

Chemali, Zeina, Hannah Smati, Kelsey Johnson, Christina P. C. Borba, and Gregory L. Fricchione. "Reflections from the Lebanese Field: 'First, Heal Thyself.'" *Conflict and Health* 12, no. 8 (2018). https://doi.org/10.1186/s13031-018-0144-2.

Clapham, Christopher. "The Ethiopian Developmental State." *Third World Quarterly* 39, no. 6 (2018): 1151–65. https://doi.org/10.1080/01436597.2017.1328982.

Clarke, P. Knox. *The State of the Humanitarian System 2018*. London: ALNAP, 2018.

Cochrane, Logan, and Davin O'Regan. "Legal Harvest and Illegal Trade: Trends, Challenges, and Options in Khat Production in Ethiopia." *International Journal of Drug Policy* 30 (2016): 27–34. https://doi.org/10.1016/j.drugpo.2016.02.009.

Cole, Teju. "The White-Savior Industrial Complex." *Atlantic*, March 21, 2012. https://www.theatlantic.com/international/archive/2012/03/the-white-savior-industrial-complex/254843/.

Cooke, Bill, and Uma Kothari, eds. *Participation: The New Tyranny?* London: Zed Books, 2001.

Core Humanitarian Standard Alliance, Group URD, and the Sphere Project. "Core Humanitarian Standard on Quality and Accountability." Core Humanitarian Standard. 2014. https://corehumanitarianstandard.org/files/files/Core%20Humanitarian%20Standard%20-%20English.pdf.

Crain, Marion, Winifred Poster, and Miriam Cherry. *Invisible Labor: Hidden Work in the Contemporary World*. Berkeley: University of California Press, 2016.

Daccord, Yves. "From 'Victims' to 'Consumers'? Changing Perceptions of Humanitarian Aid Beneficiaries." Humanitarian Practice Network. Overseas Development Institute. March 2, 2015. http://odihpn.org/blog/from-victims-to-consumers-changing-perceptions-of-humanitarian-aid-beneficiaries/.

Dandoy, Arnaud, and Marc-Antoine Pérouse de Montclos. "Humanitarian Workers in Peril? Deconstructing the Myth of the New and Growing Threat to Humanitarian Workers." *Global Crime* 14, no. 4 (2013): 341–58. https://doi.org/10.1080/17 440572.2013.831345.

Danieli, Yael, ed. *Sharing the Front Line and the Back Hills: International Protectors and Providers; Peacekeepers, Humanitarian Aid Workers and the Media in the Midst of Crisis*. Boca Raton, FL: CRC Press, 2018.

Das, Veena, and Deborah Poole, eds. *Anthropology in the Margins of the State*. Santa Fe, NM: School of American Research Press, 2004.

Das, Veena, and Deborah Poole. "State and Its Margins: Comparative Ethnographies." *Anthropology in the Margins of the State*, edited by Veena Das and Deborah Poole, 1–33. Santa Fe, NM: School of American Research Press, 2004.

Davies, Hannah G., Conor Bowman, and Stephen P. Luby. "Cholera—Management and Prevention." Supplement 1, *Journal of Infection* 74 (2017): S66–73. https://doi.org/10.1016/S0163-4453(17)30194-9.

Debes, Amanda K., Jerome Ateudjieu, Etienne Guenou, Walter Ebile, Isaac Tadzong Sonkoua, Anthony Chebe Njimbia, Peter Steinwald, Malathi Ram, and David A. Sack. "Clinical and Environmental Surveillance for Vibrio cholerae in Resource Constrained Areas: Application during a 1-Year Surveillance in the Far North Region of Cameroon." *American Journal of Tropical Medicine and Hygiene* 94, no. 3 (2016): 537–43.

De Lauri, Antonio. *The Politics of Humanitarianism: Power, Ideology and Aid*. London: I. B. Tauris, 2016. http://hdl.handle.net/11250/2475398.

Devermont, Judd, and Jon Temin. "Africa's Democratic Moment? The Five Leaders Who Could Transform the Region." *Foreign Affairs*, July/August 2019. https://www.foreignaffairs.com/articles/africa/2019-06-11/africas-democratic-moment.

De Waal, Alexander. "Anthropology and the Aid Encounter." In *Exotic No More: Anthropology on the Front Lines*, edited by J. MacClancy, 251–69. Chicago: University of Chicago Press, 2002.

De Waal, Alexander. *Evil Days: Thirty Years of War and Famine in Ethiopia*. New York: Human Rights Watch, 1991.

De Waal, Alexander. *Famine Crimes: Politics and the Disaster Relief Industry in Africa*. Bloomington: Indiana University Press, 1997.

De Waal, Alexander. "The Humanitarians' Tragedy: Escapable and Inescapable Cruelties." *Disasters* 34 (2010): S130–37. https://doi.org/10.1111/j.1467-7717.2010.01149.x.

De Waal, Alexander, Alemayou Seyoum Taffesse, and Lauren Carruth. "Child Survival during the 2002–2003 Drought in Ethiopia." *Global Public Health* 1, no. 2 (2006): 125–32.

Donais, Timothy. *Peacebuilding and Local Ownership: Post-Conflict Consensus-Building*. London: Routledge, 2012.

Donini, Antonio. "The Far Side: The Meta Functions of Humanitarianism in a Globalised World." *Disasters* 34, no. 1 (2010): S220–37.

Donini, Antonio, ed. *The Golden Fleece: Manipulation and Independence in Humanitarian Action*. West Hartford, CT: Kumarian Press, 2012.

Donini, Antonio, Larry Minear, and Peter Walker. "The Future of Humanitarian Action: Mapping the Implications of Iraq and Other Recent Crises." *Disasters* 28, no. 2 (2004): 190–204.

Douglas, Mary. "Foreword: No Free Gifts." In *The Gift: The Form and Reason for Exchange in Archaic Societies*, by Marcel Mauss, vii–xviii. Translated by W. D. Halls. New York: W. W. Norton, 1990.

Douglas, Mary. *Purity and Danger: An Analysis of Concepts of Pollution and Taboo.* London: Routledge, 2003.

Drieskens, Barbara. *Living with Djinns: Understanding and Dealing with the Invisible in Cairo.* London: Saqi Books, 2008.

Drotbohm, Heike, and Erdmute Alber. "Introduction." In *Anthropological Perspectives on Care: Work, Kinship, and the Life-Course,* edited by Erdmute Alber and Heike Drotbohm, 1–20. New York: Palgrave Macmillan, 2015.

Duffield, Mark. "Challenging Environments: Danger, Resilience and the Aid Industry." *Security Dialogue* 43, no. 5 (2012): 475–92.

Duffield, Mark. *Development, Security and Unending War: Governing the World of Peoples.* Cambridge: Polity, 2007.

Duffield, Mark. *Global Governance and the New Wars: The Merging of Development and Security.* London: Zed Books, 2014.

Dunant, J. Henry. *A Memory of Solferino.* Geneva: International Committee of the Red Cross, 1986. https://www.icrc.org/en/doc/assets/files/publications/icrc-002-0361.pdf.

Dunn, Elizabeth Cullen. *No Path Home: Humanitarian Camps and the Grief of Displacement.* Ithaca, NY: Cornell University Press, 2018.

Eckersley, William, Ruth Salmon, and Mulugeta Gebru. "Khat, Driver Impairment and Road Traffic Injuries: A View from Ethiopia." *Bulletin of the World Health Organization* 88 (2010): 235–36.

Edkins, Jenny. *Whose Hunger? Concepts of Famine, Practices of Aid.* Minneapolis: University of Minnesota Press, 2000.

Elliesen, T. "Imported Dependency: Food Aid Weakens Ethiopia's Self Help Capacity." *Development and Cooperation* 1 (2002): 21–23.

Els, Christian, Kholoud Mansour, and Nils Carstensen. "Funding to National and Local Humanitarian Actors in Syria: Between Sub-Contracting and Partnerships." Local to Global Protection Initiative. May 2016. http://www.local2global.info/wp-content/uploads/L2GP_funding_Syria_May_2016.pdf.

Erie, Matthew S. "Sharia, Charity, and Minjian Autonomy in Muslim China: Gift Giving in a Plural World." *American Ethnologist* 43, no. 2 (2016): 311–24.

Eriksson, Cynthia B., Jeff P. Bjorck, Linnea C. Larson, Sherry M. Walling, Gary A. Trice, John Fawcett, Alexis D. Abernethy, and David W. Foy. "Social Support, Organisational Support, and Religious Support in Relation to Burnout in Expatriate Humanitarian Aid Workers." *Mental Health, Religion and Culture* 12, no. 7 (2009): 671–86.

Fadlalla, Amal Hassan. "Modest Women, Deceptive Jinn: Identity, Alterity, and Disease in Eastern Sudan." *Identities: Global Studies in Culture and Power* 12, no. 2 (2005): 143–74.

Fassin, Didier. *Humanitarian Reason: A Moral History of the Present.* Berkeley: University of California Press, 2012.

Fassin, Didier, and Mariella Pandolfi, eds. *Contemporary States of Emergency: The Politics of Military and Humanitarian Interventions.* Brooklyn, NY: Zone Books, 2010.

Fast, Larissa. *Aid in Danger: The Perils and Promise of Humanitarianism.* Philadelphia: University of Pennsylvania Press, 2014.

Fast, Larissa. "Characteristics, Context and Risk: NGO Insecurity in Conflict Zones." *Disasters* 31, no. 2 (2007): 130–54.

Fast, Larissa. "Mind the Gap: Documenting and Explaining Violence against Aid Workers." *European Journal of International Relations* 16, no. 3 (2010): 365–89.

Fechter, Anne-Meike, and Heather Hindman, eds. *Inside the Everyday Lives of Development Workers: The Challenges and Futures of Aidland.* Sterling, VA: Kumarian Press, 2011.

Federal Democratic Republic of Ethiopia. Central Statistical Agency. "Ethiopia: Demographic and Health Survey 2016." Addis Ababa, Ethiopia. 2016. Accessed July 13, 2017. https://dhsprogram.com/publications/publication-FR328-DHS-Final-Reports.cfm.

Federal Democratic Republic of Ethiopia. Central Statistical Agency. "Population Projection of Ethiopia for All Regions at Wereda Level from 2014–2017." Addis Ababa, Ethiopia. August 2013.

Federal Democratic Republic of Ethiopia. Constitution. 1994.

Federal Democratic Republic of Ethiopia. Ministry of Agriculture. "Productive Safety Net Programme Phase IV: Programme Implementation Manual." December 2014. https://srbofed.gov.et/wp-content/uploads/2019/09/PSNP-IV-Programme-Implementation-Manual-Final-14-Dec-14-1.pdf.

Feldman, Ilana. *Life Lived in Relief: Humanitarian Predicaments and Palestinian Refugee Politics.* Berkeley: University of California Press, 2018.

Feldman, Ilana. "The Quaker Way: Ethical Labor and Humanitarian Relief." *American Ethnologist* 34, no. 4 (2007): 689–705. https://doi.org/10.1525/ae.2007.34.4.689.

Ferguson, James. *The Anti-Politics Machine: "Development," Depoliticization, and Bureaucratic Power in Lesotho.* Minneapolis: University of Minnesota Press, 1994.

Ferguson, James. *Give a Man a Fish: Reflections on the New Politics of Distribution.* Durham, NC: Duke University Press, 2015.

Fiseha, Assefa. "Theory versus Practice in the Implementation of Ethiopia's Ethnic Federalism." In *Ethnic Federalism: The Ethiopian Experience in Comparative Perspective,* edited by David Turton, 131–64. Athens, OH: Ohio University Press, 2006.

Forsythe, David P. *The Humanitarians: The International Committee of the Red Cross.* Cambridge: Cambridge University Press, 2005.

Foucault, Michel. *The Order of Things: An Archaeology of the Human Sciences.* London: Routledge, 2002.

Fox, Fiona. "New Humanitarianism: Does It Provide a Moral Banner for the 21st Century?" *Disasters* 25, no. 4 (2001): 275–89.

Fox, Jonathan. "The Uncertain Relationship between Transparency and Accountability." *Development in Practice* 17, nos. 4–5 (2007): 663–71.

Fox, Renée C. *Doctors Without Borders: Humanitarian Quests, Impossible Dreams of Médecins Sans Frontières.* Baltimore: Johns Hopkins University Press, 2014.

Gaventa, John. "Towards Participatory Governance: Assessing the Transformative Possibilities." In *Participation: From Tyranny to Transformation?,* edited by Samuel Hickey and Giles Mohan, 25–41. London: Zed Books, 2004.

Gaventa, John, and Rosemary McGee. "The Impact of Transparency and Accountability Initiatives." *Development Policy Review* 31 (2013): s3–s28. https://doi.org/10.1111/dpr.12017.

Gebre-Egziabher, Tegegne, and Kassahun Berhanu. "A Literature Review of Decentralization in Ethiopia." In *Decentralization in Ethiopia,* edited by Taye Assefa and Tegegne Gebre-Egziabher, 9–68. Addis Ababa, Ethiopia: Forum for Social Studies, 2007.

Gebremariam, Kidanu, Demeke Assefa, and Fitsum Weldegebreal. "Prevalence and Associated Factors of Female Genital Cutting among Young Adult Females in Jigjiga District, Eastern Ethiopia: A Cross-Sectional Mixed Study." *International Journal of Women's Health* 8 (2016): 357–65. https://doi.org/10.2147/IJWH.S111091.

Geissler, Paul Wenzel. "'We Are Not Paid—They Just Give Us': Liberalisation and the Longing for Biopolitical Discipline around an African HIV Prevention Trial." In *Rethinking Governance and Biomedicine in Africa*, edited by Paul Wenzel Geissler, Richard Rottenburg, and Julia Zenker, 197–228. Bielefeld: Transcript Verlag, 2012.

George, Christine M., Mahamud-ur Rashid, David A. Sack, R. Bradley Sack, K.M. Saif-Ur-Rahman, Andrew S. Azman, Shirajum Monira, et al. "Evaluation of Enrichment Method for the Detection of *Vibrio cholerae* O1 Using a Rapid Dipstick Test in Bangladesh." *Tropical Medicine & International Health* 19, no. 3 (2014): 301–7. https://doi.org/10.1111/tmi.12252.

Ghosh, Ishita, and Lester Coutinho. "Normalcy and Crisis in Time of Cholera: An Ethnography of Cholera in Calcutta." *Economic and Political Weekly*, February 26, 2000, 684–96.

Gill, Peter. *Famine and Foreigners: Ethiopia since Live Aid*. Oxford: Oxford University Press, 2010.

Gingerich, Tara R., and Marc J. Owen. "Turning the Humanitarian System on Its Head: Saving Lives and Livelihoods by Strengthening Local Capacity and Shifting Leadership to Local Actors." Oxfam America. July 2015. https://s3.amazonaws.com/oxfam-us/www/static/media/files/rr-turning-humanitarian-system-local-capacity-270715-en.pdf.

Global Humanitarian Assistance Program. "Private Funding: An Emerging Trend in Humanitarian Donorship." UNOCHA. April 12, 2012. http://reliefweb.int/report/world/private-funding-emerging-trend-humanitarian-donorship.

Gordon, Edmund T. "Anthropology and Liberation." In *Decolonizing Anthropology: Moving Further Toward an Anthropology of Liberation*, edited by Faye V. Harrison, 149–67. Arlington: VA: American Anthropological Association, 2011.

Gupta, Akhil, and Aradhana Sharma. "Introduction: Rethinking Theories of the State in an Age of Globalization." In *The Anthropology of the State: A Reader*, edited by Aradhana Sharma and Akhil Gupta, 1-42. Oxford: Blackwell, 2009.

Hacking, Ian. "Making Up People: Clinical Classifications." *London Review of Books* 28, no. 16 (2006): 23–26.

Hagmann, Tobias. "Beyond Clannishness and Colonialism: Understanding Political Disorder in Ethiopia's Somali Region, 1991–2004." *Journal of Modern African Studies* 43, no. 4 (2005): 509–36.

Hagmann, Tobias, and Mohamud Hussein Khalif. "State and Politics in Ethiopia's Somali Region since 1991." *Bildhaan: An International Journal of Somali Studies* 6, no. 1 (2008): 25–49.

Hagmann, Tobias, and Benedikt Korf. "Agamben in the Ogaden: Violence and Sovereignty in the Ethiopian-Somali Frontier." *Political Geography* 31, no. 4 (2012): 205–14.

Hamdy, Sherine F., and Soha Bayoumi. "Egypt's Popular Uprising and the Stakes of Medical Neutrality." *Culture, Medicine, and Psychiatry* 40, no. 2 (2016): 223–41.

Hancock, G. *Lords of Poverty: The Power, Prestige, and Corruption of the International Aid Business*. London: Macmillan, 1989.

HAP International and Oxfam. "The Guide to the HAP Standard: Humanitarian Accountability and Quality Management." 2008. https://reliefweb.int/sites/reliefweb.int/files/resources/hap-guide.pdf.

Hardt, Michael. "Affective Labor." *Boundary* 2, no. 26 (Summer 1999): 89–100.

Hardt, Michael, and Antonio Negri. *Empire*. Cambridge, MA: Harvard University Press, 2000.

Harrison, Faye V. *Decolonizing Anthropology: Moving Further toward an Anthropology for Liberation.* Arlington, VA: American Anthropological Association, 2011.

Harvey, Paul, and Jeremy Lind. "Dependency and Humanitarian Relief: A Critical Analysis." Humanitarian Policy Group. Report 19. Overseas Development Institute. July 2005. https://www.odi.org/sites/odi.org.uk/files/odi-assets/publi cations-opinion-files/277.pdf.

Headey, Derek, Alemayehu Seyoum Taffesse, and Liangzhi You. "Diversification and Development in Pastoralist Ethiopia." *World Development* 56 (2014): 200–213.

Heller, Alison. *Fistula Politics: Birthing Injuries and the Quest for Continence in Niger.* New Brunswick, NJ: Rutgers University Press, 2019.

Hendrie, Barbara. "Knowledge and Power: A Critique of an International Relief Operation." *Disasters* 21, no. 1 (1997): 57–76.

Hickel, Jason. "The True Extent of Global Poverty and Hunger: Questioning the Good News Narrative of the Millennium Development Goals." *Third World Quarterly* 37, no. 5 (2016): 749–67.

Hickey, Samuel, and Giles Mohan, eds. *Participation: From Tyranny to Transformation? Exploring New Approaches to Participation in Development.* London: Zed Books, 2004.

Hickey, Samuel, and Giles Mohan. "Towards Participation as Transformation: Critical Themes and Challenges." In *Participation: From Tyranny to Transformation,* edited by Samuel Hickey and Giles Mohan, 3–24. London: Zed Books, 2004.

Hilhorst, Dorothea. "Being Good at Doing Good? Quality and Accountability of Humanitarian NGOs." *Disasters* 26, no. 3 (2002): 193–212.

Hodgson, Dorothy Louise. *Once Intrepid Warriors: Gender, Ethnicity, and the Cultural Politics of Maasai Development.* Bloomington: Indiana University Press, 2001.

Hodžić, Saida. *The Twilight of Cutting: African Activism and Life after NGOs.* Berkeley: University of California Press, 2017.

Holmes, Seth. *Fresh Fruit, Broken Bodies: Migrant Farmworkers in the United States.* Berkeley: University of California Press, 2013.

Hondagneu-Sotelo, Pierrette. *Doméstica: Immigrant Workers Cleaning and Caring in the Shadows of Affluence.* With a new preface. Berkeley: University of California Press, 2007.

Human Rights Watch. "Collective Punishment—War Crimes and Crimes against Humanity in the Ogaden Area of Ethiopia's Somali Region." June 12, 2008. https://www.refworld.org/docid/4850d01a2.html.

Human Rights Watch. "Development without Freedom: How Aid Underwrites Repression in Ethiopia." October 19, 2010. https://www.hrw.org/report/2010/10/19/ development-without-freedom/how-aid-underwrites-repression-ethiopia.

Human Rights Watch. "'We Are Like the Dead': Torture and Other Human Rights Abuses in Jail Ogaden, Somali Regional State, Ethiopia." July 4, 2018. https://www.hrw.org/report/2018/07/04/we-are-dead/ torture-and-other-human-rights-abuses-jail-ogaden-somali-regional.

Hutchinson, John F. *Champions of Charity: War and the Rise of the Red Cross.* London: Routledge, 2018.

Hutchinson, John F. "Rethinking the Origins of the Red Cross." *Bulletin of the History of Medicine* 63, no. 4 (1989): 557–78.

Ingold, Tim. "Anthropology contra Ethnography." *HAU: Journal of Ethnographic Theory* 7, no. 1 (2017): 21–26.

Inhorn, Marcia C. *Quest for Conception: Gender, Infertility and Egyptian Medical Traditions.* Philadelphia: University of Pennsylvania Press, 1994.

Inter-Agency Standing Committee. "The Grand Bargain—a Shared Commitment to Better Serve People in Need." May 23, 2016. https://interagencystandingcom mittee.org/system/files/grand_bargain_final_22_may_final-2.pdf.

International Committee of the Red Cross (ICRC). "Code of Conduct for Employees of the International Committee of the Red Cross." May 2018. https://www.icrc. org/sites/default/files/wysiwyg/code_of_conduct_may_2018.pdf.

International Committee of the Red Cross (ICRC). "Fundamental Principles of the Red Cross and Red Crescent Movement." April 11, 2016. https://www.icrc.org/ en/document/fundamental-principles-red-cross-and-red-crescent.

International Committee of the Red Cross (ICRC). "War & Law." Accessed June 2, 2020. https://www.icrc.org/en/war-and-law.

International Crisis Group. "Ethiopia: Prospects for Peace in Ogaden." Africa Report no. 207. August 6, 2013. https://d2071andvip0wj.cloudfront.net/ethiopia-pros pects-for-peace-in-ogaden.pdf.

International Organization for Migration (IOM). "Displacement Tracking Matrix (DTM) Somali, Ethiopia." Round 12. July/August 2018. https://displace ment.iom.int/system/tdf/reports/R12%20Somali%20Regional%20Report. pdf?file=1&type=node&id=4459.

International Organization for Migration (IOM). "Humanitarian Needs Overview." February 2019. https://www.humanitarianresponse.info/sites/www.humanitari anresponse.info/files/2019/03/02_HNO_Summary_030619.pdf.

Jachens, Liza, Jonathan Houdmont, and Roslyn Thomas. "Effort-Reward Imbalance and Burnout among Humanitarian Aid Workers." *Disasters* 43, no. 1 (2019): 67–87.

James, Erica Caple. *Democratic Insecurities: Violence, Trauma, and Intervention in Haiti.* Berkeley: University of California Press, 2010.

Jeffrey, James. "Ethiopia Survives Its Great Drought, but a Way of Life May Not." Integrated Regional Information Networks (IRIN). June 13, 2016. http:// www.irinnews.org/feature/2016/06/13/ethiopia-survives-its-great- drought-way-life-may-not.

Jerving, Sara. "Why Governments Tiptoe around the Word 'Cholera.'" Devex. March 21, 2018. https://www.devex.com/news/why-governments-tiptoe- around-the-word-cholera-92348.

Jobanputra, Kiran, Philippa Boulle, Bayard Roberts, and Pablo Perel. "Three Steps to Improve Management of Noncommunicable Diseases in Humanitar ian Crises." PLOS Medicine 13, no. 11 (2016): e1002180. https://dx.doi. org/10.1371%2Fjournal.pmed.1002180.

Johnson, Steven. *The Ghost Map: The Story of London's Most Terrifying Epidemic—and How It Changed Science, Cities, and the Modern World.* New York: Penguin, 2006.

Joshi, Anuradha. "Reading the Local Context: A Causal Chain Approach to Social Accountability." IDS Bulletin 45, no. 5 (2014): 23–35. https://doi. org/10.1111/1759-5436.12101.

Kehlenbrink, Sylvia, James Smith, Éimhín Ansbro, Daniela C. Fuhr, Anson Cheung, Ruwan Ratnayake, Philippa Boulle, Kiran Jobanputra, Pablo Perel, and Bayard Roberts. "The Burden of Diabetes and Use of Diabetes Care in Humanitar ian Crises in Low-Income and Middle-Income Countries." *Lancet Diabetes & Endocrinology* 7, no. 8 (August 2019): 638–47. https://doi.org/10.1016/ S2213-8587(19)30082-8.

Keller, Edmond J., and Lahra Smith. "Obstacles to Implementing Territorial Decen tralization: The First Decade of Ethiopian Federalism." In *Sustainable Peace:*

Power and Democracy after Civil Wars, edited by Philip G. Roeder and Donald S. Rothchild, 265–92. Ithaca, NY: Cornell University Press, 2005.

Kelly, Ann H., and Paul Wenzel Geissler. "The Value of Transnational Medical Research." *Journal of Cultural Economy* 4, no. 1 (2011): 3.

Kennedy, David. *The Dark Sides of Virtue: Reassessing International Humanitarianism.* Princeton: Princeton University Press, 2011.

Kibreab, Gaim. "The Myth of Dependency among Camp Refugees in Somalia, 1979–1989." *Journal of Refugee Studies* 6, no. 4 (1993): 321–49.

Kittay, Eva Feder. *Love's Labor: Essays on Women, Equality and Dependency.* London: Routledge, 2019.

Klein, Naomi. *The Shock Doctrine: The Rise of Disaster Capitalism.* New York: Macmillan, 2007.

Kleinman, Arthur. "Caregiving as Moral Experience." *The Lancet* 380, no. 9853 (2012): 1550–51.

Knecht, Thomas. "A Pragmatic Response to an Unexpected Constraint: Problem Representation in a Complex Humanitarian Emergency." *Foreign Policy Analysis* 5, no. 2 (2009): 135–68.

Konyndyk, Jeremy, and Rose Worden. "People-Driven Response: Power and Participation in Humanitarian Action." Center for Global Development Policy Paper 155. September 2019. https://www.cgdev.org/people-driven-response.

Korf, Benedikt, Tobias Hagmann, and Rony Emmenegger. "Re-Spacing African Drylands: Territorialization, Sedentarization and Indigenous Commodification in the Ethiopian Pastoral Frontier." *Journal of Peasant Studies* 42, no. 5 (2015): 881–901.

Kotiswaran, Prabha. *Dangerous Sex, Invisible Labor: Sex Work and the Law in India.* Princeton: Princeton University Press, 2011.

Krause, Monika. *The Good Project: Humanitarian Relief NGOs and the Fragmentation of Reason.* Chicago: University of Chicago Press, 2014.

Kruk, Margaret E., Lynn P. Freedman, Grace A. Anglin, and Ronald J. Waldman. "Rebuilding Health Systems to Improve Health and Promote Statebuilding in Post-Conflict Countries: A Theoretical Framework and Research Agenda." *Social Science & Medicine* 70, no. 1 (2010): 89–97.

Laitin, David D., and Said S. Samatar. *Somalia: Nation in Search of a State.* Boulder, CO: Westview Press, 1987.

Langwick, Stacey Ann. *Bodies, Politics, and African Healing: The Matter of Maladies in Tanzania.* Bloomington: Indiana University Press, 2011.

Lashitew, Addisu. "Ethiopia Will Explode If It Doesn't Move beyond Ethnic-Based Politics." *Foreign Policy*, November 8, 2019. https://foreignpolicy.com/2019/11/08/ethiopia-will-explode-if-abiy-ahmed-doesnt-move-beyond-ethnic-based-politics/.

Lautze, Sue, Angela Raven-Roberts, and Teshome Erkineh. "Humanitarian Governance in the New Millennium: An Ethiopian Case Study." Humanitarian Policy Group. Overseas Development Institute. February 2009. https://www.odi.org/publications/3190-humanitarian-governance-new-millennium-ethiopian-case-study.

Leaning, Jennifer, S. M. Briggs, and Lincoln C. Chen. *Humanitarian Crises: The Medical and Public Health Response.* Cambridge, MA: Harvard University Press, 1999.

Lefort, René. "Free Market Economy, 'Developmental State' and Party-State Hegemony in Ethiopia: The Case of the 'Model Farmers.'" *Journal of Modern African Studies* 50, no. 4 (2012): 681–706.

Lewis, David, and David Mosse, eds. *Development Brokers and Translators: The Ethnography of Aid and Agencies.* Bloomfield, CT: Kumarian Press, 2006.

Lewis, Ioan Myrddin. *Blood and Bone: The Call of Kinship in Somali Society.* Lawrenceville, NJ: Red Sea Press, 1994.

Lewis, Ioan Myrddin. "Visible and Invisible Differences: The Somali Paradox." *Africa* 74, no. 4 (2004): 489–515.

Lind, Jeremy, and Teriessa Jalleta. "Poverty, Power and Relief Assistance: Meanings and Perceptions of 'Dependency' in Ethiopia." Humanitarian Policy Group. Overseas Development Institute. July 2005. https://www.odi.org/sites/odi.org.uk/files/odi-assets/publications-opinion-files/428.pdf.

Little, Peter D. "Food Aid Dependency in Northeastern Ethiopia: Myth or Reality?" *World Development* 36, no. 5 (2008): 860–74.

Little, Peter D. *Somalia: Economy without State.* Bloomington: Indiana University Press, 2003.

Livingston, Julie. "Productive Misunderstandings and the Dynamism of Plural Medicine in Mid-Century Bechuanaland." *Journal of Southern African Studies* 33, no. 4 (2007): 801–10.

Lopes Cardozo, Barbara, Teresa I. Sivilli, Carol Crawford, Willem F. Scholte, Pilar Petit, Frida Ghitis, Alastair Ager, and Cynthia Eriksson. "Factors Affecting Mental Health of Local Staff Working in the Vanni Region, Sri Lanka." *Psychological Trauma: Theory, Research, Practice, and Policy* 5, no. 6 (2013): 581–90.

Long, Nicholas J., and Henrietta L. Moore. "Introduction." In *Sociality: New Directions,* edited by Nicholas J. Long and Henrietta L. Moore, 1–24. New York: Berghahn Books, 2013.

Luling, Virginia. "Come Back Somalia? Questioning a Collapsed State." *Third World Quarterly* 18, no. 2 (1997): 287–302.

Luling, Virginia. "Genealogy as Theory, Genealogy as Tool: Aspects of Somali 'Clanship.'" *Social Identities* 12, no. 4 (2006): 471–85.

Luling, Virginia. "Somali." In *Muslim Peoples: A World Ethnographic Survey,* edited by Richard Weekes, 364–69. Westport, CT: Greenwood Press, 1978.

Lyons, Scott W. "Joint Declaration of Peace and Friendship between Eritrea and Ethiopia." *International Legal Materials* 58, no. 1 (2019): 237–39.

Lyons, Terrence. "Ethiopian Elections: Past and Future." *International Journal of Ethiopian Studies* 5, no. 1 (2010): 107–21.

Macrae, Joanna. "Humanitarianism: Facing New Challenges." Great Decisions. Overseas Development Institute. 2000. https://www.odi.org/sites/odi.org.uk/files/odi-assets/publications-opinion-files/6319.pdf.

Maes, Kenneth. *The Lives of Community Health Workers: Local Labor and Global Health in Urban Ethiopia.* New York: Routledge, 2016.

Mahmood, Jemilah. "Opinion: Yes, the Humanitarian Sector Really Is Going to Localize." Devex. June 16, 2017. https://www.devex.com/news/opinion-yes-the-humanitarian-sector-really-is-going-to-localize-90487.

Mains, Daniel. "Blackouts and Progress: Privatization, Infrastructure, and a Developmentalist State in Jimma, Ethiopia." *Cultural Anthropology* 27, no. 1 (2012): 3–27.

Malkki, Liisa H. *The Need to Help: The Domestic Arts of International Humanitarianism.* Durham, NC: Duke University Press, 2015.

Malkki, Liisa H. *Purity and Exile: Violence, Memory, and National Cosmology among Hutu Refugees in Tanzania.* Chicago: University of Chicago Press, 1995.

Malkki, Liisa H. "A Tale of Two Affects: Humanitarianism and Professionalism in Red Cross Aid Work." *Radical Egalitarianism: Local Realities, Global Relations,* edited by Felicity Aulino, Miriam Goheen, and Stanley J. Tambiah, 209–19. New York: Fordham University Press, 2013.

Manderson, Lenore, and Narelle Warren. "'Caring for' and 'Caring about': Embedded Interdependence and Quality of Life." In *Reframing Disability and Quality of Life*, edited by Narelle Warren and Lenore Manderson, 179–93. Dordrecht: Springer, 2013.

Mansur, Abdalla Omar. "The Nature of the Somali Clan System." In *The Invention of Somalia*, edited by A. J. Ahmed, 117–34. Trenton, NJ: Red Sea Press, 1995.

Markakis, John. "Ethnic Conflict and the State in the Horn of Africa." In *Ethnicity and Conflict in the Horn of Africa*, edited by Katsuyoshi Fukui and John Markakis, 217–38. London: James Currey, 1994.

Mauss, Marcel. *The Gift: The Form and Reason for Exchange in Archaic Societies*. Translated by W. D. Halls. New York: W. W. Norton, 1990.

McGranahan, Carole. "Explaining Ethnography in the Field." Savage Minds: Notes and Queries in Anthropology, September 25, 2017, https://savageminds. org/2017/09/25/explaining-ethnography-in-the-field-a-conversation-between-pasang-yangjee-sherpa-and-carole-mcgranahan/.

McKay, Ramah. *Medicine in the Meantime: The Work of Care in Mozambique*. Durham, NC: Duke University Press, 2017.

McNeil, Donald G. "Candidate to Lead the W.H.O Accused of Covering Up Epidemics." *New York Times*, May 13, 2017. https://www.nytimes.com/2017/05/13/health/candidate-who-director-general-ethiopia-cholera-outbreaks.html.

McPherson, M. Peter. "War Will Not Leave the Hungry Alone." *Washington Post*, March 5, 1985, A15.

Mendenhall, Emily. *Rethinking Diabetes: Entanglements with Trauma, Poverty, and HIV*. Ithaca, NY: Cornell University Press, 2019.

Mengisteab, Kidane. "New Approaches to State Building in Africa: The Case of Ethiopia's Ethnic-Based Federalism." *African Studies Review* 40, no. 3 (1997): 111–32.

Milián, Iván Navarro, Josep Maria Royo Aspa, Jordi Urgell García, Pamela Urrutia Arestizábal, Ana Villellas Ariño, and María Villellas Ariño. "Alert 2019! Report on Conflicts, Human Rights and Peacebuilding." February 2019. https://reliefweb.int/report/world/alert-2019-report-conflicts-human-rights-and-peacebuilding.

Minn, Pierre. "Toward an Anthropology of Humanitarianism." Journal of Humanitarian Assistance 6 (2007). https://sites.tufts.edu/jha/archives/51.

Mittermaier, Amira. "Beyond Compassion: Islamic Voluntarism in Egypt." *American Ethnologist* 41, no. 3 (2014): 518–31.

Mohan, Giles, and Kristian Stokke. "Participatory Development and Empowerment: The Dangers of Localism." *Third World Quarterly* 21, no. 2 (2000): 247–68.

Mol, Annemarie. *The Logic of Care: Health and the Problem of Patient Choice*. London: Routledge, 2008.

Mol, Annemarie, Ingunn Moser, and Jeannette Pols. "Care: Putting Practice into Theory." In *Care in Practice: On Tinkering in Clinics, Homes and Farms*, edited by Annemarie Mol, Ingunn Moser, and Jeannette Pols, 7–26. Bielefeld: Transcript Verlag, 2010.

Moorehead, Caroline. *Dunant's Dream: War, Switzerland and the History of the Red Cross*. London: Harper Collins, 1998.

Mosse, David. "The Making and Marketing of Participatory Development." In *A Moral Critique of Development*, edited by Philip Quarles van Ufford and Anata Kumar Giri, 57–89. London: Routledge, 2003.

Muehlebach, Andrea. *The Moral Neoliberal: Welfare and Citizenship in Italy*. Chicago: University of Chicago Press, 2012.

Müller, Tanja R. "'The Ethiopian Famine' Revisited: Band Aid and the Antipolitics of Celebrity Humanitarian Action." *Disasters* 37, no. 1 (2013): 61–79.

Musa, Saif Ali, and Abdalla A. R. M. Hamid. "Psychological Problems among Aid Workers Operating in Darfur." *Social Behavior and Personality: An International Journal* 36, no. 3 (2008): 407–16.

Mwambari, David. "Local Positionality in the Production of Knowledge in Northern Uganda." International Journal of Qualitative Methods 18 (2019). https://doi.org/10.1177/1609406919864845.

Mwambari, David, and Arthur Owor. "The 'Black Market' of Knowledge Production." April 2, 2019. https://oxfamblogs.org/fp2p/the-black-market-of-knowledge-production/.

Newbrander, William, Ronald Waldman, and Megan Shepherd-Banigan. "Rebuilding and Strengthening Health Systems and Providing Basic Health Services in Fragile States." *Disasters* 35, no. 4 (2011): 639–60.

Nichter, Mark. *Global Health: Why Cultural Perceptions, Social Representations, and Biopolitics Matter.* Tucson: University of Arizona Press, 2008.

Nichter, Mark. "Idioms of Distress: Alternatives in the Expression of Psychosocial Distress; A Case Study from South India." *Culture, Medicine and Psychiatry* 5, no. 4 (1981): 379–408.

Nichter, Mark. "Idioms of Distress Revisited." *Culture, Medicine, and Psychiatry* 34, no. 2 (2010): 401–16.

Norris, John. *The Disaster Gypsies: Humanitarian Workers in the World's Deadliest Conflicts.* Westport, CT: Praeger Security International, 2007.

Ollman, Bertell. *Dance of the Dialectic.* Urbana: University of Illinois Press, 2003.

Ollman, Bertell and Tony Smith, eds. *Dialectics for the New Century.* New York: Palgrave Macmillan, 2008.

Ong, Jonathan Corpus, and Pamela Combinido. "Local Aid Workers in the Digital Humanitarian Project: Between 'Second Class Citizens' and 'Entrepreneurial Survivors.'" *Critical Asian Studies* 50, no. 1 (2018): 86–102. https://doi.org/10.1080/14672715.2017.1401937.

Organization for Economic Co-operation and Development (OECD). "Aid at a Glance Charts." Accessed June 19, 2020. http://www.oecd.org/countries/ethiopia/aid-at-a-glance.htm#recipients.

Østebø, Marit Tolo, Megan D. Cogburn, and Anjum Shams Mandani. "The Silencing of Political Context in Health Research in Ethiopia: Why It Should Be a Concern." *Health Policy and Planning* 33, no. 2 (2018): 258–70. https://doi.org/10.1093/heapol/czx150.

Overseas Development Institute. Humanitarian Policy Group. "Humanitarian Space: Concept, Definitions and Uses." October 20, 2010. https://www.odi.org/sites/odi.org.uk/files/odi-assets/events-documents/4648.pdf.

Overseas Development Institute. "Localising Aid." Accessed June 2, 2020. https://www.odi.org/projects/2696-localising-aid-budget-support-southern-actors.

Oxfam. "Accountability and Ownership: The Role of Aid in a Post-2015 World." Oxfam Briefing Paper. September 2016. https://s3.amazonaws.com/oxfam-us/www/static/media/files/bp-accountability-and-ownership-11-16.pdf.

Oxfam. "Accountability and Ownership: The Role of Aid in a Post-2015 World." Oxfam Briefing Paper. September 2016. https://www.oxfamamerica.org/static/media/files/bp-accountability-and-ownership-11-16.pdf.

Oxfam. "Local Aid Workers, Heroes of World Humanitarian Day." August 19, 2014. https://politicsofpoverty.oxfamamerica.org/2014/08/local-aid-workers-heroes-world-humanitarian-day/.

Pandian, Anand. *A Possible Anthropology: Methods for Uneasy Times*. Durham, NC: Duke University Press, 2019.

Pankhurst, Richard. "The History of Cholera in Ethiopia." *Medical History* 12, no. 3 (1968): 262–69.

Pankhurst, Sylvia. "His Imperial Majesty's Speech to the Ogaden." *Ethiopia Observer* 1, no. 1 (1956): 5–8.

Panter-Brick, Catherine. "Health, Risk, and Resilience: Interdisciplinary Concepts and Applications." *Annual Review of Anthropology* 43 (2014): 431–48. https://doi.org/10.1146/annurev-anthro-102313-025944.

Paravicini, Giulia. "Ethiopian Who Demanded Justice Now Has Half a Year to Deliver It." Reuters. January 28, 2020. https://www.reuters.com/article/us-ethiopia-justice/ethiopian-who-demanded-justice-now-has-half-a-year-to-deliver-it-idUSKBN1ZR10K.

Petryna, Adriana. *When Experiments Travel: Clinical Trials and the Global Search for Human Subjects*. Princeton: Princeton University Press, 2009.

Pigni, Alessandra. "Building Resilience and Preventing Burnout among Aid Workers in Palestine: A Personal Account of Mindfulness Based Staff Care." *Intervention* 12, no. 2 (2014): 231–39.

Poster, Alexander. "The Gentle War: Famine Relief, Politics, and Privatization in Ethiopia, 1983–1986." *Diplomatic History* 36, no. 2 (2012): 399–425.

Redfield, Peter. "Clinic in Crisis Response: Imagined Immunities." *Culture, Medicine, and Psychiatry* 40, no. 2 (2016): 263–67.

Redfield, Peter. *Life in Crisis: The Ethical Journey of Doctors Without Borders*. Berkeley: University of California Press, 2013.

Redfield, Peter. "The Unbearable Lightness of Ex-Pats: Double Binds of Humanitarian Mobility." *Cultural Anthropology* 27, no. 2 (2012): 358–82.

Redfield, Peter. "Vital Mobility and the Humanitarian Kit." In *Biosecurity Interventions: Global Health & Security in Question*, edited by Andrew Lakoff and Stephen J. Collier, 147–172. New York: Columbia University Press, 2008.

ReliefWeb. "Ethiopia: Drought—2015–2020; Disaster Description." ReliefWeb and UNOCHA. Accessed June 2, 2020. https://reliefweb.int/disaster/dr-2015-000109-eth.

Reuters. "Filth Spreads Yemen's Deadly Cholera Outbreak." July 27, 2017. https://www.reuters.com/article/us-yemen-cholera-sanitation-idUSKBN1AC1W9?il=0.

Ribot, Jesse C. "African Decentralization: Local Actors, Powers and Accountability." UN Research Institute for Social Development. December 2002. http://www.unrisd.org/unrisd/website/document.nsf/(httpPublications)/3345AC67E687575 4C1256D12003E6C95?OpenDocument.

Richards, Simon, and Gezu Bekele. "Conflict in the Somali Region of Ethiopia: Can Education Promote Peace-Building?" Feinstein International Center. Tufts University. March 2011. https://fic.tufts.edu/assets/Conflict-Somali-Ethiopia.pdf.

Rieff, David. *A Bed for the Night: Humanitarianism in Crisis*. New York: Simon and Schuster, 2003.

Robbins, Joel. "Beyond the Suffering Subject: Toward an Anthropology of the Good." *Journal of the Royal Anthropological Institute* 19, no. 3 (2013): 447–62.

Roess, Amira A., et al. "Camels, MERS-CoV, and Other Emerging Infections in East Africa." *Lancet Infectious Diseases* 16, no. 1 (2016): 14–15. https://doi.org/10.1016/S1473-3099(15)00471-5.

Roitman, Janet. *Anti-Crisis*. Durham, NC: Duke University Press, 2013.

Rossi, Benedetta. "Aid Policies and Recipient Strategies in Niger." In *Development Brokers and Translators: The Ethnography of Aid and Agencies*, edited by David Lewis and David Mosse, 27–50. Bloomfield, CT: Kumarian Press, 2006.

Roth, Silke. "Aid Work as Edgework—Voluntary Risk-Taking and Security in Humanitarian Assistance, Development and Human Rights Work." *Journal of Risk Research* 18, no. 2 (2015): 139–55. https://doi.org/10.1080/13669877.2013.875934.

Roth, Silke. "Dealing with Danger—Risk and Security in the Everyday Lives of Aid Workers." In *Inside the Everyday Lives of Development Workers: The Challenges and Futures of Aidland*, edited by Anne-Meike Fechter and Heather Hindman, 151–68. Sterling, VA: Kumarian Press, 2011.

Roth, Silke. *The Paradoxes of Aid Work: Passionate Professionals*. London: Routledge, 2015.

Rozakou, Katerina. "Socialities of Solidarity: Revisiting the Gift Taboo in Times of Crises." *Social Anthropology* 24, no. 2 (2016): 185–99.

Sabates-Wheeler, Rachel, Jeremy Lind, and John Hoddinott. "Implementing Social Protection in Agro-Pastoralist and Pastoralist Areas: How Local Distribution Structures Moderate PSNP Outcomes in Ethiopia." *World Development* 50 (2013): 1–12.

Samatar, Abdi Ismail. *Africa's First Democrats: Somalia's Aden A. Osman and Abdirazak H. Hussen*. Bloomington: Indiana University Press, 2016.

Samatar, Ahmed Ismail. "Beginning Again: From Refugee to Citizen." *Bildhaan: An International Journal of Somali Studies* 4, no. 1 (2008): 5.

Samatar, Abdi Ismail. "Debating Somali Identity in a British Tribunal: The Case of the BBC Somali Service." *Bildhaan: An International Journal of Somali Studies* 10, no. 8 (2011): 36–88.

Samatar, Abdi Ismail. "Ethiopian Ethnic Federalism and Regional Autonomy: The Somali Test." *Bildhaan: An International Journal of Somali Studies* 5 (2005): 44–76.

Samatar, Abdi Ismail. "Ethiopian Federalism: Autonomy versus Control in the Somali Region." *Third World Quarterly* 25, no. 6 (2004): 1131–54. https://doi.org/10.1080/0143659042000256931.

Schuller, Mark, and Julie K. Maldonado. "Disaster Capitalism." *Annals of Anthropological Practice* 40, no. 1 (2016): 61–72.

Scrascia, Maria, Nicola Pugliese, Francesco Maimone, Kadigia A. Mohamud, Imran A. Ali, Patrick A. D. Grimont, and Carlo Pazzani. "Cholera in Ethiopia in the 1990s: Epidemiologic Patterns, Clonal Analysis, and Antimicrobial Resistance." *International Journal of Medical Microbiology* 299, no. 5 (2009): 367–72.

Sengers, Gerda. *Women and Demons: Cult Healing in Islamic Egypt*. Leiden: Brill, 2003.

Shaban, Abdur Rahman Alfa. "Ethiopia's Somali Regional Politics: New Leader, Abdi Illey Charged, Liyu Police." Africa News. August 30, 2018. Accessed September 1, 2019. https://www.africanews.com/2018/08/30/ethiopias-somali-regional-politics-new-leader-abdi-illey-charged-liyu-police/.

Sharma, Aradhana, and Akhil Gupta, eds. *The Anthropology of the State: A Reader*. Oxford: Blackwell, 2006.

Sharp, Kay, and Stephen Devereux. "Destitution in Wollo (Ethiopia): Chronic Poverty as a Crisis of Household and Community Livelihoods." *Journal of Human Development* 5, no. 2 (2004): 227–47.

Sharpe, Christina. "And to Survive." *Small Axe: A Caribbean Journal of Criticism* 22, no. 3 (57) (2018): 171–80. https://doi.org/10.1215/07990537-7249304.

Sheik-Abdi, Abdi. "Somali Nationalism: Its Origins and Future." *Journal of Modern African Studies* 15, no. 4 (1977): 657–65.

Slim, Hugo. "The Continuing Metamorphosis of the Humanitarian Practitioner: Some New Colours for an Endangered Chameleon." *Disasters* 19, no. 2 (1995): 110–26.

Slim, Hugo. *Humanitarian Ethics: A Guide to the Morality of Aid in War and Disaster.* Oxford: Oxford University Press, 2015.

Slim, Hugo. "Relief Agencies and Moral Standing in War: Principles of Humanity, Neutrality, Impartiality and Solidarity." *Development in Practice* 7, no. 4 (1997): 342–52.

Smirl, Lisa. *Spaces of Aid: How Cars, Compounds and Hotels Shape Humanitarianism.* London: Zed Books, 2015.

Smith, Lahra. *Making Citizens in Africa: Ethnicity, Gender, and National Identity in Ethiopia.* Cambridge: Cambridge University Press, 2013.

Smith, Linda Tuhiwai. *Decolonizing Methodologies: Research and Indigenous Peoples.* London: Zed Books, 2013.

Smith-Morris, Carolyn. *Diabetes among the Pima: Stories of Survival.* Tucson: University of Arizona Press, 2008.

Sphere Association. "The Sphere Handbook: Humanitarian Charter and Minimum Standards in Humanitarian Response." 4th ed. Geneva, Switzerland, 2018. https://spherestandards.org/handbook-2018/.

Spivak, Gayatri Chakravorty. "Can the Subaltern Speak?" In *Marxism and the Interpretation of Culture,* edited by C. Nelson and L. Grossberg, 271–314. Urbana: University of Illinois Press, 1988.

Stoddard, Abby, Adele Harmer, and Monica Czwarno. "Aid Worker Security: Figures at a Glance." Humanitarian Outcomes. August 2018. https://www.humanitarianoutcomes.org/publications/aid-worker-security-figures-glance-2018.

Strathern, Marilyn. *Audit Cultures: Anthropological Studies in Accountability, Ethics and the Academy.* London: Routledge, 2003.

Strohmeier, Hannah, and Willem F. Scholte. "Trauma-Related Mental Health Problems among National Humanitarian Staff: A Systematic Review of the Literature." *European Journal of Psychotraumatology* 6, no. 1 (2015): 28541.

Swidler, Ann, and Susan Cotts Watkins. "'Teach a Man to Fish': The Sustainability Doctrine and Its Social Consequences." *World Development* 37, no. 7 (2009): 1182–96. https://doi.org/10.1016/j.worlddev.2008.11.002.

Tadesse, Bamlaku, Fekadu Beyene, Workneh Kassa, and Richard Wentzell. "The Dynamics of (Agro) Pastoral Conflicts in Eastern Ethiopia." *Ethiopian Journal of the Social Sciences and Humanities* 11, no. 1 (2015): 29–60.

Terry, Fiona. *Condemned to Repeat? The Paradox of Humanitarian Action.* Ithaca, NY: Cornell University Press, 2013.

Ticktin, Miriam. *Casualties of Care: Immigration and the Politics of Humanitarianism in France.* Berkeley: University of California Press, 2011.

Ticktin, Miriam. "A World without Innocence." *American Ethnologist* 44, no. 4 (2017): 577–90.

Tronto, Joan C. "Care as a Political Concept." In *Revisioning the Political: Feminist Reconstructions of Traditional Concepts in Western Political Theory,* edited by Nancy J. Hirshmann and Christine Di Stefano, 139–56. New York: Routledge, 2018.

Tronto, Joan C. *Moral Boundaries: A Political Argument for an Ethic of Care.* New York: Routledge, 1993.

Tull, Kerina. "Humanitarian Interventions in Ethiopia Responding to Acute Watery Diarrhoea." K4D Helpdesk Report. Brighton, UK. Institute of Development Studies. January 10, 2018. https://opendocs.ids.ac.uk/opendocs/bitstream/handl e/20.500.12413/13568/14576?sequence=1.

United Nations Children's Fund (UNICEF) Ethiopia. "Ethiopia Humanitarian Situation." UNICEF Ethiopia. Report #12. December 2018. https://reliefweb.int/report/ethiopia/unicef-ethiopia-humanitarian-situation-report-12-january-december-2018#:~:text=In%202018%2C%20UNICEF%20Ethiopia's%20Humanitarian,cent%20of%20those%20in%20need).

United Nations Children's Fund (UNICEF). "Ethiopia: Key Demographic Indicators." Accessed May 31, 2020. https://data.unicef.org/country/eth/.

United Nations Children's Fund (UNICEF). "Situation Analysis of Children and Women: Somali Region." Accessed June 5, 2020. https://www.unicef.org/ethio pia/media/2401/file/Somali%20region%20.pdf.

United Nations Children's Fund (UNICEF). "Thank These Humanitarian Heroes." Accessed June 20, 2019. https://www.unicefusa.org/pledge/thank-these-humanitarian-heroes.

United Nations Children's Fund (UNICEF). "UNICEF/WHO/World Bank Joint Child Malnutrition Estimates." Last updated March 2020. https://data.unicef.org/resources/joint-child-malnutrition-estimates-interactive-dashboard-2020/.

United Nations Office for the Coordination of Humanitarian Affairs (UNOCHA). "Ethiopia: Access Snapshot—Afar Region and Siti Zone, Somali Region." January 31, 2020. https://reliefweb.int/sites/reliefweb.int/files/resources/ocha_200204_access_snapshot_afar_sitti_somali_region.pdf.

United Nations Office for the Coordination of Humanitarian Affairs (UNOCHA). "Ethiopia: Humanitarian Response." Situation Report no. 23. June 2019. https://www.humanitarianresponse.info/en/operations/ethiopia/document/ethiopia-humanitarian-response-situation-report-no-23-june-2019.

United Nations Office for the Coordination of Humanitarian Affairs (UNOCHA). "Ethiopia: Oromia-Somali Conflict-Induced Displacement." Situation Report no. 4. June 2018. https://reliefweb.int/sites/reliefweb.int/files/resources/ethio pia_-_oromia_somali_conflict_induced_displacement_june_2018c.pdf.

United Nations Office for the Coordination of Humanitarian Affairs (UNOCHA). "Resolution 46/182, Which Created the Humanitarian System, Turns Twenty-Five." December 19, 2016. https://www.unocha.org/story/resolution-46182-which-created-humanitarian-system-turns-twenty-five#:~:text=On%2019%20December%201991%2C%20the,when%20they%20need%20it%20most.

United Nations Office for the Coordination of Humanitarian Affairs (UNOCHA). "Safety and Security for National Humanitarian Workers." 2011. https://www.unocha.org/sites/unocha/files/Safety%20and%20Security%20for%20National%20Humanitar ian%20Workers%2C%20PDSB%2C%202011%2C%20English.pdf.

United Nations World Food Programme (UNWFP). "Gender Equality and WFP." January 22, 2019. https://docs.wfp.org/api/documents/5389e10f4fb74c2fab08db 1f725d3965/download/.

United States Agency for International Development (USAID). "Ethiopia—Complex Emergency." Fact Sheet #5. USAID. September 30, 2018. https://www.usaid.gov/sites/default/files/documents/1866/ethiopia_ce_fs05_09-30-2018.pdf.

United States. Central Intelligence Agency. "Africa: Ethiopia." In World Factbook. Central Intelligence Agency. Accessed June 11, 2020. https://www.cia.gov/library/publications/the-world-factbook/geos/print_et.html.

United States. Congress. Senate. Committee on Finance. *Nomination of M. Peter McPherson: Hearings before the Committee on Finance. United States Senate. One Hundredth Congress. First Session on Nomination of M. Peter McPherson to be Deputy Secretary of the Treasury, May 20, 1987.* Washington, DC: US Government Printing Office, 1987.

UN Women. "Preliminary Gender Profile of Ethiopia." November 2014. https://www.usaid.gov/sites/default/files/documents/1860/Preliminary%20Gender%20Profile%20of%20Ethiopia%20Nov%2017%20final.pdf.

Van Brabant, Koenraad. "Mainstreaming the Organisational Management of Safety and Security: A Review of Aid Agency Practices and a Guide for Management." Humanitarian Policy Group. Report 9. Overseas Development Institute. March 2001. https://www.odi.org/sites/odi.org.uk/files/odi-assets/publications-opinion-files/297.pdf.

Vaughan, Sarah. "Ethiopia, Somalia, and the Ogaden: Still a Running Sore at the Heart of the Horn of Africa." In *Secessionism in African Politics: Aspiration, Grievance, Performance, Disenchantment*, edited by Lotje de Vries, Pierre Englebert, and Mareike Schomerus, 91–123. Cham, Switzerland: Palgrave Macmillan, 2019.

Vaux, Tony. *The Selfish Altruist: Relief Work in Famine and War.* London: Routledge, 2001.

Von Clausewitz, Carl. *On War.* Translated by Colonel J. J. Graham. London: K. Paul, Trench, Trübner, 1909.

Waterston, Alisse. "Intimate Ethnography and the Anthropological Imagination: Dialectical Aspects of the Personal and Political in My Father's Wars." *American Ethnologist* 46, no. 1 (2019): 7–19.

Watkins, Ben, and Michael L. Fleisher. "Tracking Pastoralist Migration: Lessons from the Ethiopian Somali National Regional State." *Human Organization* 61, no. 4 (2002): 328–38.

World Health Organization (WHO). "Child Health in the Community: Community IMCI; Briefing Package for Facilitators." Accessed June 13, 2020. https://apps.who.int/iris/handle/10665/43006.

World Health Organization (WHO). "Cholera." Accessed June 9, 2020. https://www.who.int/cholera/en/.

World Health Organization (WHO). "Health Workforce." Accessed June 8, 2020. http://www.who.int/hrh/en/.

World Health Organization (WHO). "Revised Cholera Kits." Accessed June 9, 2020. https://www.who.int/emergencies/emergency-health-kits/revised-cholera-kits.

Yarrow, Thomas. "Maintaining Independence: The Moral Ambiguities of Personal Relations amongst Ghanaian Development Workers." In *Inside the Everyday Lives of Development Workers: The Challenges and Futures of Aidland*, edited by Anne-Meike Fechter and Heather Hindman, 41–58. Sterling, VA: Kumarian Press, 2011.

Yilma, Girum. "Ethiopia: Land of Silence and Starvation." Abbay Media. November 8, 2009. http://amharic.abbaymedia.info/archives/3019.

Zeleke, Meron. "Too Many Winds to Consider: Which Way and When to Sail! Ethiopian Female Transit Migrants in Djibouti and the Dynamics of Their Decision-Making." *African and Black Diaspora: An International Journal* 12, no. 1 (2019): 49–63.

Index

as shaped by politics and society, 52–53
stereotypes concerning, 53–54
Somali Regional Health Bureau, 27, 95, 144,
  159, 173n17
Somalis
  in eastern Ethiopia, 17–22
  racialization of, 91
  stereotypes concerning, 53–54, 56
spirit possession, 64–65, 67, 185nn11-12
Swidler, Ann, 190n22

Tigray People's Liberation Front (TPLF), 42,
  43
Toyota Land Cruiser SUVs, 34–35
Tronto, Joan C., 166
trust, building relationships of, 78

UNICEF, 49, 69–72, 113
United Nations, 110, 115
United States, 151–54
urinary tract infections (UTIs), 132–34
USAID, 152, 153

violence, 1–4, 23–24, 52–53, 154–57, 167.
  See also ethnic violence
voluntarism
  anti-politics of, 148, 150
  in humanitarian aid, 82

water availability, 126–27
water collection, 121
Waterston, Alisse, 179n60
Watkins, Susan Cotts, 190n22
white Toyota Land Cruiser SUVs, 34–35
women
  advancement opportunities for, 116
  as aid workers, 35, 73–74
  mindheeli suffered by, 126, 131–36
  mobile teams' prioritization of, 69–71
World Health Organization (WHO), 139

Yilma, Girum, 137

zakat/zakah (charity), 61–64, 87
Zenawi, Meles, 42, 180n9

CPSIA information can be obtained
at www.ICGtesting.com
Printed in the USA
LVHW091930210721
693326LV00001B/5